Empires of the Normans

Empires of the Normans

Makers of Europe, Conquerors of Asia

LEVI ROACH

JOHN MURRAY

First published in Great Britain in 2022 by John Murray (Publishers)
An Hachette UK company

I

Copyright © Levi Roach 2022

Maps drawn by Rosie Collins

A CIP catalogue record for this title is available from the British Library

Hardback ISBN 978-1-529-39846-5
Trade Paperback ISBN 978-1-529-30029-1
eBook ISBN 978-1-529-30031-4

Typeset in Bembo MT by Hewer Text UK Ltd, Edinburgh
Printed and bound in Great Britain by Clays Ltd, Elcograf S.p.A.

John Murray policy is to use papers that are natural, renewable and recyclable products and
made from wood grown in sustainable forests. The logging and manufacturing processes
are expected to conform to the environmental regulations of the country of origin.

John Murray (Publishers)
Carmelite House
50 Victoria Embankment
London EC4Y 0DZ

www.johnmurraypress.co.uk

For Clara and Lettie

Contents

CONTENTS

Preface

When the seventeen-year-old Frederick II entered Mainz in early December 1212, he was met by cheering crowds. For years, the German throne had been contested by warring factions. Now the succession of young Frederick – 'the boy from Apulia', as he was affectionately known – looked set to settle matters. Frederick was dressed in finery: furs and a heavy cloak to keep out the winter chill, to which he was unaccustomed. He was guided into the city by the local archdeacon and the crowds parted as they went. Their destination was the great cathedral in the heart of the city. Two bishops wearing relics around their necks met Frederick there at the great brass doors. Then the archbishop, Siegfried, joined them, leading the imperial entourage inside.

As the crowd filed in, Frederick laid his arms and cloak down before the altar. Then he prostrated himself demonstratively in the shape of the cross, entreating divine mercy. All the bishops and clerics did likewise, while others sang litanies, invoking the assistance of the saints. Once Frederick had risen, Archbishop Siegfried asked him if he would fulfil the duties incumbent upon him as king (to defend the Church and his people), which Frederick happily affirmed. Hearing this, all those in attendance shouted their approval: 'Amen! Amen! So let it be! So let it be!' After a series of further prayers, the ceremony now reached its high point, as Siegfried consecrated Frederick with holy oil, formally anointing him king. He then entrusted Frederick with the regalia, the symbols of his office: the sword, that Frederick might defend the Church and chasten the unjust; the ring, as a sign of Christian faith; the sceptre and staff, that he might offer just judgement; and the crown, as a signification of the glory and holiness of his office. After more prayers, Siegfried led the newly crowned Frederick from the altar down the choir to the throne that had been erected there. Here Frederick uttered his coronation oath – his solemn promise to offer peace and justice, and show appropriate mercy – before receiving the kiss of peace from the archbishop. Finally, he ascended the throne. Seated in majesty, Frederick watched the ensuing Mass with deep satisfaction. He had entered Mainz a prince, but he left it an anointed monarch. Frederick was now king by the grace of God, ruler of the Germans (and Holy Roman emperor in waiting).

Frederick was the latest monarch of a distinguished line, stretching back to his grandfather, the legendary German emperor Frederick Barbarossa. Yet the impression of continuity is deceptive. For the young Frederick was not really German. In fact, he barely knew the country. He was an Italian Norman (known as 'the boy from Apulia'), who'd not stepped foot north of the Alps before this. And as his reign would show, Frederick owed far more to the Norman south than to his German roots. For in his relations with his son and co-ruler, Henry (VII), Frederick would repeatedly insist on applying more rigorous Sicilian customs north of the Alps.

As a Norman monarch, Frederick was far from alone. England, most of Wales, and large parts of Ireland – not to mention a number of key holdings in France – were under the authority of the infamous 'bad King John', a direct descendant (in the female line) of the great Norman conquistador William I ('the Conqueror'). To John's north, William the Lion, the long-reigning king of Scots, was himself three-quarters Norman, supported by a largely Norman aristocracy. And in the Mediterranean, Frederick controlled Sicily and southern Italy, while almost half the Holy Land was in the hands of Bohemond IV of Antioch, the great-great-grandson of the notorious Italo-Norman sell-sword Bohemond of Taranto.

With Frederick's coronation, Norman power and influence had reached its apex. In one form or another, the Normans had come to dominate western Europe and the Mediterranean. Their impact can scarcely be exaggerated. To Normandy, they'd brought a new aristocracy and ruling dynasty; to Britain and Ireland, they'd brought castles, chivalric culture, Romanesque architecture and the French language (still spoken by aristocrats in Frederick's day); to southern Italy, they'd brought ties to Rome and the Catholic church; and to Germany, they'd brought new attitudes to law and order. The Norman achievement was, however, remarkably fragile. For in all these regions, the Normans settled and adapted to local society. The result was a world that was recognisably Norman but where the Normans themselves had become more localised. In the Mediterranean, the Normans had long since come to identify as Sicilians, Apulians and Calabrians; in the British Isles, they'd similarly started to see themselves as English and Scottish (albeit of a Francophone aristocratic variety). They were at once everywhere and nowhere – a people with an exalted past, but little future.

These years of Norman ascendancy first saw the emergence of a common European culture, and the Normans were an essential part of this process.[1] It was thanks to them that the British Isles and southern Italy would form part of western (Catholic) Europe. Nor was their influence limited to areas of direct Norman rule. The Normans were involved at crucial moments during the Christian conquest of Islamic Iberia. They established a short-lived kingdom in North Africa, threatening the Fatimid rulers of Egypt and Almohad lords of Morocco. And they played an essential part in the collapse of Byzantine authority in Asia Minor, events which paved the way to the First Crusade.

For the descendants of a few shiploads of Vikings who settled on the northern reaches of the River Seine c.911, the Normans had come a long way. The following pages are dedicated to understanding how, by a combination of luck, pluck and piety, they achieved this. It's a tale of ambitious adventures and fierce freebooters, of fortunes made and kingdoms lost. We begin with the legendary Rollo, whose piratical raids on the Seine laid the foundations for the future duchy of Normandy. Thereafter, we follow his descendants as they achieve dominance in northern France, fighting off threats from neighbours in Flanders and Anjou. In the following years, we see them launch more daring ventures, first to England, where William the Conqueror seized one of Europe's most valuable crowns; then to southern Italy, where the sons of the otherwise obscure Tancred de Hauteville created an equally exalted kingdom of their own. From these new bases, the Normans extended their influence further still, settling in Scotland and conquering large parts of Wales and Ireland. More spectacular, if short-lived, was their impact on the eastern Mediterranean, where we see them come close to toppling the Byzantine Empire. By the time of Frederick's coronation in December 1212, they'd even supplied the next German king. In an age of overachievers, the Normans repeatedly stood out: their churches were bigger, their leaders bolder, their troops fiercer. This is their story.

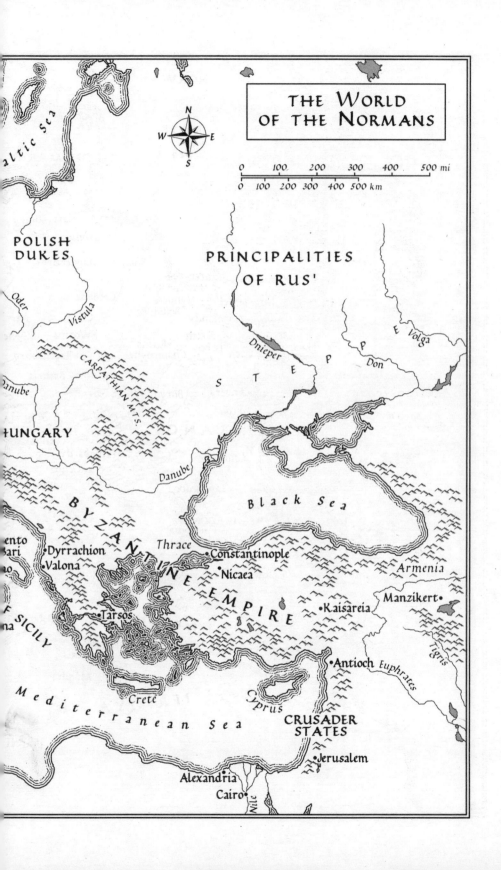

THE WORLD
OF THE NORMANS

N
W   E
S

0   100   200   300   400   500 mi
0   100   200   300   400 500 km

Baltic Sea

POLISH
DUKES

PRINCIPALITIES
OF RUS'

Oder

Vistula

Danube

CARPATHIAN MTS.

HUNGARY

Danube

S   T   E   P   P

Dnieper

Don

Volga

Black Sea

BYZANTINE EMPIRE

Thrace

Constantinople

Nicaea

Armenia

ento
Bari

Dyrrachion

Valona

Kaisareia

Manzikert

F SICILY
na

Tarsos

Antioch Euphrates

Tigris

Mediterranean Sea

Crete

Cyprus

CRUSADER
STATES

Jerusalem

Alexandria

Cairo

Nile

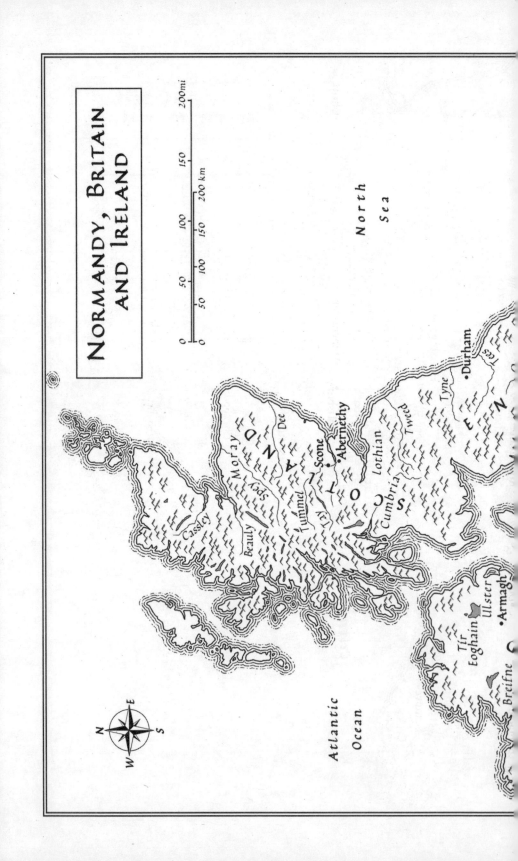

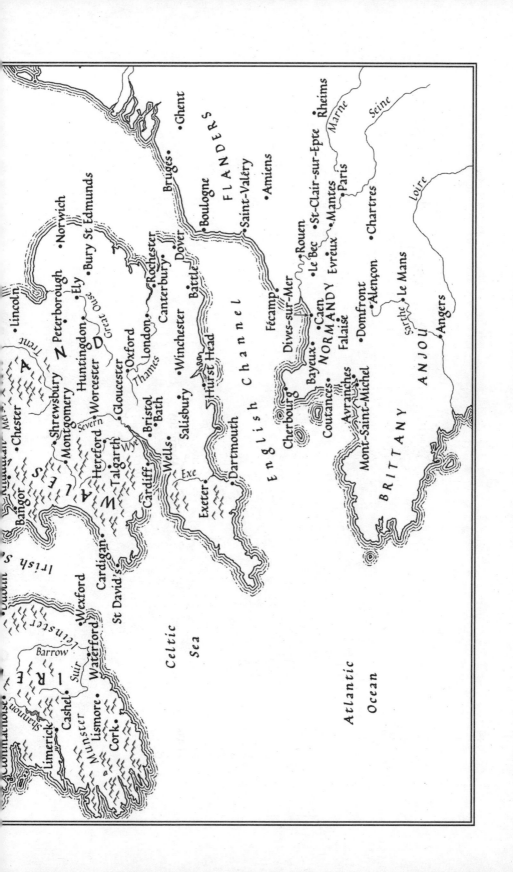

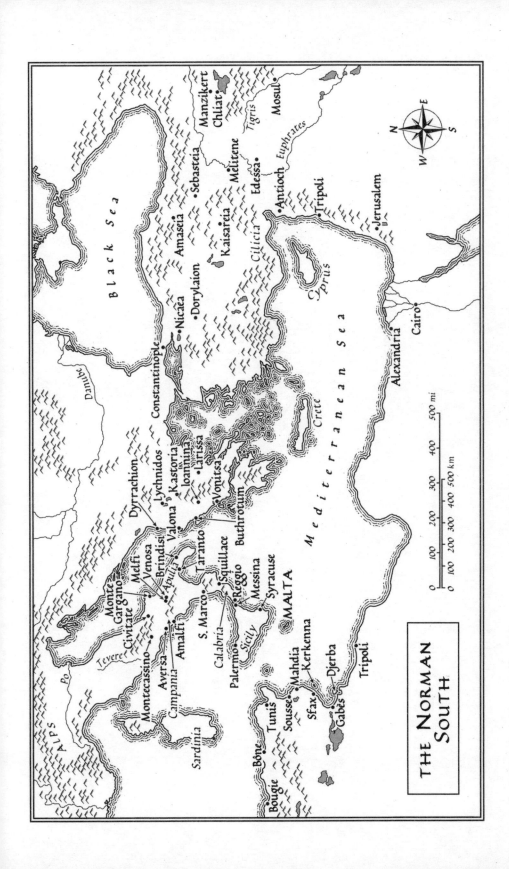

THE NORMAN SOUTH

I

Beginnings: Strange Men from a Strange Land, The Lower Seine, c.911–42

Two armies faced each other across the River Epte in northern France. The atmosphere was tense. On one side, stood the court of the French (or West Frankish) king, Charles the Simple, attended by his leading magnate Robert of Neustria. On the other, was arrayed the host of Rollo, the Viking freebooter who'd been making a nuisance of himself along the Seine in recent years. The ground was, however, set for concord. Shortly before this, Rollo had been defeated by Robert as he attempted to take Chartres, an important cathedral city some 90 km (56 miles) south west of Paris. In the aftermath, Charles had initiated diplomatic contacts. He offered Rollo the hand of his daughter Gisla and coastal territories to the north, if Rollo and his men would pledge future service and adopt the Christian faith. This was a rare opportunity, and the Scandinavian warlord consented readily. All that remained was to ratify the pact – or so it seemed.

We are told that as the forces converged on St-Clair-sur-Epte, Rollo sent the archbishop of Rouen with a message to the French king. The archbishop instructed Charles that Rollo and his men would no longer accept just the lands originally allocated to them (those between the Andelle and the sea); now they demanded the entire territory between the Epte and the coast – a strip some 50 km (31 miles) wider. What from anyone else would have been sheer effrontery, however, was begrudgingly countenanced when it came from the mighty Rollo. Robert of Neustria, who stood prepared to act as the Viking leader's godfather, advised Charles that he would not win the service of such a great warrior without concessions. And so it was that the king slowly relented. He first tried to offer Rollo Flanders and Brittany instead; but Rollo stood firm. In the end, Charles caved in – Rollo would indeed receive all the lands between the Epte and the sea.

Finally, Rollo was ready to submit. He publicly placed his hands within those of the king, in the ritual act of commendation (or homage, as it would later be known). None of Rollo's forebears had been willing to submit to another in this fashion; but then, none of them had won such rich rewards. Still, Rollo did not lose his sense of pride. He refused to kiss the foot of King Charles in gratitude, as was customary. In his place, one of Rollo's men was sent to do so. Yet even he was only willing to go so far. Instead of bending down to kiss the king's foot, as was expected, the bold Viking pulled Charles' leg unceremoniously up to his own head, sending Charles sprawling on the ground. The superiority of Rollo and his men over their French counterparts could scarcely have been clearer.

Or so Dudo of Saint-Quentin, our main narrator of the early Norman settlement, would have us believe.[1] The problem is, Dudo was writing over ninety years after the events (he completed his *History* in the mid-1010s), and it's often impossible to tell where reality ends and Dudo's fertile imagination begins. To take but two examples, Dudo names the archbishop of Rouen as Franco, whereas at the time of Rollo's settlement the archbishop was not Franco but a man called Guy; while Gisla – if she ever existed – would've been no more than three or four years old. It's not even certain that the agreement was made at St-Clair-sur-Epte. The Epte was the later frontier between Normandy and France, to which Norman ducal authority probably first stretched in the 930s. And St-Clair witnessed an important meeting between Rollo's grandson and the French king in 942. Dudo may simply have modelled his account on this.[2]

Unfortunately for us, Dudo's almost all we have. It's clear that some sort of deal was struck with the Vikings around this time. But more than that is hard to say. The lack of contemporary interest in the early Viking settlement is understandable. Despite Dudo's claims, the pact of St-Clair was nothing special. The Vikings (or Northmen) had burst on the scene in the late eighth century, when they initiated a series of Blitzkrieg raids on western Europe's exposed coastlines. What first inspired them to seek their fortunes across the seas remains a matter of debate, but there were clearly a number of incentives. New kingdoms were being created within Scandinavia, which created a pool of discontented petty chiefs (and their men) who'd lost out in the process. Growing maritime capabilities also made foreign ventures easier than ever. Added to which, there was political instability in many parts of Europe (particularly the British Isles). Raids of ever-increasing intensity began in the second half of the eighth century (perhaps as early as the 760s or 770s), eventually culminating in the conquest of large swathes of continental Europe and the British Isles.[3]

Under these circumstances, it's hardly surprising that western European rulers began to recruit Vikings into their own armies. This not only removed a prospective threat, but often provided the best line of defence; it was a matter of setting a thief to catch a thief. Yet the Northmen were not only out to make a quick buck, and it soon became common to offer land in exchange for more extended service. A particularly popular tactic was to settle Viking groups in coastal districts, leaving them to defend these against their own country-men.[4] Parts of Flanders were repeatedly bestowed in this fashion; and this tradition may well have informed Charles' attempts to fob Rollo off with the region.

Rollo himself may have hailed from Norway and began his career as part of the 'Great Viking Army', which conquered large parts of England in the 860s and 870s. He was probably not present for the earliest phases of these conquests. But he'd clearly joined the force by the time it relocated from England to northern France in the early 880s and was present in 885 and 886, when it famously besieged Paris. While the future French capital held firm, elements of the army went on to overrun much of Brittany and the northern Seine. And Rollo was one of the leaders to settle on the Seine.

Without more detailed sources, it's hard to know the precise nature of Rollo's activities in these years. Archaeologists are sometimes tempted to associate early evidence for Scandinavian settlement in what was to become Normandy with Dudo's tall tales of Rollo's exploits in the 890s, painting a detailed picture of the early growth of the new Viking power. But caution is called for where Dudo's vivid (but clearly fantastic) narrative is concerned.[5] It's likely that Rollo and his army were active – and perhaps even settled – on the lower Seine before their pact with Charles c.911. Then at some point these inroads were formalised by an agreement with King Charles (perhaps at St-Clair). Our earliest secure evidence of this comes not from Dudo, but from charters (that is, legal documents, granting land or rights) issued in the name of King Charles.[6] The first of these, from 905, reveals that at this point the core areas of what was to become Normandy were still in royal hands, since Charles then granted eleven serfs at Pîtres (just south of Rouen) to his chancellor, a man called Ernustus. There are, however, signs that the region was already under pressure. In the following year, another charter records that the monks of Saint-Marcoulf in the west of later Normandy had moved the relics of their patron saint Marculf to Corbény (just north of Rheims), on account of attacks by the pagans (i.e. Vikings). Evidently the Northmen were making their presence felt, and it is likely that Rollo and his associates were among them. The situation was far from catastrophic, however, as the charter also alludes to the possibility of Marculf's return.

The most important document is a charter of March 918 in favour of the Parisian monastery of Saint-Germain-des-Prés, which mentions Rollo's pact with King Charles. This grants Saint-Germain the lands of the smaller religious community of La Croix-Saint-Ouen, located on the Eure in modern La Croix-Saint-Leufroy, just 43 km (27 miles) south of Rouen. The reason was that La Croix, like Saint-Marcoulf, had suffered at the hands of its Viking neighbours (the charter speaks dramatically of the 'ferocity of the pagans') to such an extent that its position was no longer tenable. Its estates were therefore now being assigned to the abbey of Saint-Germain, which lay well out of harm's way in Paris. Yet an important reservation is made. King Charles does not grant all of La Croix's lands to the Parisian monastery, but only those which are not in 'that part of the abbey's holdings we granted to the Northmen of the Seine, namely Rollo and his followers, for the protection of the realm.' Evidently the Vikings were now an established presence on the lower Seine – and the royal writ did not run within their domains.

By early 918, a significant portion of what was to become Normandy had thus been ceded to Rollo and his men. Though Dudo presents the king and his leading magnate, Robert of Neustria, working in seamless harmony here, the reality was almost certainly more complicated. Dudo wrote at a time when Robert's descendants had achieved royal status with the support of Rollo's heirs, who repeatedly backed them in factional disputes of the intervening years. It was convenient for Dudo to pretend that the families had been allies from the start. In fact, the settlement of Rollo was, at the time, to the detriment of Duke Robert. For over half a century, Robert and his family had dominated the Neustrian march, a large region of north-western France. Rollo's territories were carved directly out of this, and it's hard to believe that the duke was happy about it – let alone that it was he who persuaded the king to grant the land (as Dudo would have us believe). The La Croix charter confirms this. The abbeys of La Croix and Saint-Germain were both under Robert's control; and the entire transaction is a piece of damage limitation for the duke, granting the holdings of one exposed abbey to another more secure one.

Politically, Charles' pact with Rollo was a success. Rollo's Northmen not only proved an effective deterrent to other Viking groups, they were also staunch allies in the internecine politics of tenth-century France. The biggest threat to Charles lay in Duke Robert, whose elder brother had briefly been king in the 890s. This is why Charles settled Rollo and his men on Robert's lands, and they continued to assist Charles in future years. A crucial moment came in late 922 and early 923, when Robert rebelled, claiming the crown for himself. And though Robert died in battle at Soissons in 923, his side prevailed, eventually capturing Charles. As a result, Robert's son-in-law, Duke Raoul of Burgundy, inherited the French throne. It was at this point that Charles called on his Viking allies. Rollo happily took up arms in the name of the deposed monarch. But Charles' strategy backfired. For Rollo was unable to free him, and his intervention further soured the king's relations with his French subjects. Pacts with pagan Vikings were unpopular at the best of times, and memories of the damage done by Rollo and his men remained fresh.

Yet if Charles reaped little immediate benefit, Rollo was able to profit from the resulting turmoil. Our main source here are the *Annals* of Flodoard, a contemporary record from nearby Rheims. These speak of Rollo as 'prince of the Northmen' (*princeps Nordmannorum*), alluding to the earlier pact he'd forged with Charles – a pact which the king's opponents claimed (rather tendentiously) Rollo had broken by rallying to Charles' aid, since this was done against the wishes of the new king Raoul. This is a clear reference to Rollo's original settlement of *c*.911, mentioned both in the charter of 918 and in Dudo's account. It was, however, more than mere loyalty which stirred Rollo and his men. For Flodoard also states that Charles promised Rollo 'a breath of land' in this connection, a turn of phrase which probably refers to an extension of the original settlement. Certainly when Raoul later made peace with Rollo in 924, he had to buy him off with Maine and the Bessin to the west.[7]

Subsequent years saw further expansion of the new Viking polity on the Seine. Rollo was defeated by Raoul's associates in 925, but in 933 his son William 'Longsword' was in a position to exact further concessions. In exchange for William's submission, Raoul now ceded the Norman duke eastern Brittany (apparently the Cotentin and Avranchin). Slowly but surely, the territory held by the Seine river Northmen was starting to take on the dimensions of the future duchy of Normandy. Slowly but surely, the pagan Northmen were becoming Christian Normans. It would, however, take another half-century of toil and sweat before the process was complete.

If Flodoard's reports and Charles' charters confirm the essentials of Dudo's account, they also highlight its problems. According to Dudo, the duchy of Normandy emerged Athena-like, fully formed from the heads of Rollo and Charles. Yet the initial settlement was much smaller than Dudo would have us believe, only reaching its full dimensions in the 930s at the earliest. In his *History of the Church of Rheims*, Flodoard (a contemporary observer with little reason to mislead here) reports that the initial concession concerned just Rouen and the *pagi* – *pagus* being a local French administrative district – on the northern coast and surrounding the city (Talou, Caux, Roumois, and parts of the Vexin and Evrencin); and this fits well with other evidence suggesting that the duchy grew slowly outward from Rouen and its environs.[8]

Such sources may shine a light on subjects neglected by Dudo, but they do little to reveal the gritty reality of early settlement. Here is where the study of place-names (toponymy) comes in handy. People tend to refer to new settlements and landscape features in their native tongue; and charting the presence of Scandinavian name-forms is a useful means of gauging the nature of early Norse presence. A significant number of place-names of Scandinavian derivation can be identified in what would become Normandy, in sharp contrast with the other regions of northern France. And these are concentrated along the coast, in precisely those regions between Seine and Bresle which according to Flodoard comprised Rollo's initial settlement. Most of the names in question involve a Norse personal name and a French suffix (e.g. Toqueville, 'Toki's *ville*'), or the addition of a Scandinavian suffix such as -tot ('property') to a French or Scandinavian name (e.g. Robertot, Hatteintot). Such mixed forms suggest significant interaction between French and Norse speakers from an early date. Place-names ending in -tuit or -thuit – from the Old Norse for a clearing (*þveit*) – indicate that at least some of the settlers were (or became) farmers, carving out fresh lands for themselves. A few place-names may even be Anglo-Scandinavian, i.e. coined by Vikings who'd previously lived in England. And the presence of Celtic personal names may likewise point to elements drawn from other parts of the British Isles (perhaps Man or the Scottish isles). This linguistic influence extends to the Norman dialect of French, which preserves a number of Old Norse loan-words, particularly for maritime pursuits.

What this amounts to is evidence of a considerable Norse-speaking presence from an early date and much bilingualism, with French soon becoming the dominant tongue (with a few fossilised Norse name forms and technical terms living on).[9] Clearly there was early contact between French and Norse speakers. But despite the relatively high number of Scandinavian place-names – comparable to what we see in parts of northern and eastern England – loan-words in the local Norman dialect of French remain much rarer than in English. Here we must bear in mind that the Old English language was much closer to the Norse of the settlers, a situation which would have encouraged linguistic interaction.[10] By contrast, Old French and Old Norse were mutually incomprehensible, so contact was always likely to remain limited to the borrowing of technical terms and settlement names.

If place-names are no secure guide to the number of settlers, they do put paid to the notion that Scandinavian influence was either superficial or fleeting. New settlement names rarely emerge without significant numbers of native speakers. And the nature and spread of these names indicates that the settlers included farmers and artisans, alongside warriors and aristocrats. That said, it's unlikely that Old Norse speakers were a majority except in small enclaves. And alongside signs of change must be weighed the significant evidence for administrative continuity. Systems of Frankish government survived largely intact in Normandy, with Rollo and his heirs playing much the same role as counts and dukes in neighbouring regions. There are signs of slightly greater disruption in Church structures, as we might expect from an influx of pagan pirates. But even here there are indications of continuity and vitality. A particularly important role was played by the archbishop of Rouen. Dudo gives Franco a central role in the original settlement. And while he clearly got confused about the archbishop's name, it is significant that the territory of what became Normandy maps almost directly on to the church province of Rouen. Contemporaries were well aware of this fact, and in the mid-990s Richer of Rheims equates the (ecclesiastical) province of Rouen with the region of Viking settlement.[11]

Sadly, little is known of the mechanics of settlement and acculturation. Conversion to the Christian faith would certainly have been an important part of the process. Dudo has Rollo baptised at St-Clair-sur-Epte, with Robert of Neustria standing sponsor. The terms of this account clearly evoke the earlier conversion of the Roman emperor Constantine the Great (d. 337). Yet while we may doubt Dudo on the detail, there is every reason to believe that conversion would have been part the deal. Baptism had long been a requirement for entry into royal service in France; and Flodoard similarly reports that Rollo and his men had been given lands in order 'that they should cultivate the [Christian] faith and keep the peace.'[12]

Baptism alone, however, is no guarantee of Christian conduct. We must imagine that the full process of adopting Christian mores took at least a generation or two. Where local bishops remained in place, they played an essential part in fostering the new faith. Two key players here were Guy of Rouen (archbishop of Rouen at the time of Rollo's settlement) and Heriveus (or Hervey) of Rheims. Flodoard reports that the latter had 'worked hard for the softening and conversion of the Northmen, until finally they began to accept the faith, after the battle which Count Robert [of Neustria] fought against them at Chartres.'[13] This is clearly a reference to the circumstances surrounding the original settlement. And Flodoard owes his knowledge of these details to a collection of twenty-three authoritative statements (Latin: *capitula*) on the subject of conversion and the faith, culled from the writings of the Church Fathers. These had been produced by Heriveus in response to a request from Archbishop Guy, who was evidently at the forefront of these efforts. Together, they constitute a missionary handbook of sorts. One of Heriveus' main concerns is those who have been baptised, yet revert to their pagan ways. Apostasy (lapsing from the faith) was a common problem within the missionary field.[14]

Still, all indications are that most of those who settled with Rollo took up the Christian faith swiftly enough. There are no signs of distinctively pagan Scandinavian burials in Normandy, as we see in other parts of Europe in these years. There are also no examples of sculpture or metal-working invoking Norse deities, as was common in large swathes of northern and eastern England. When it came to winning hearts and minds, social integration between the incomers and the local Christian Franks/French must have been as important as the institutional Church. Dudo's imaginative account may be of more assistance here. According to this, during his early attacks Rollo had carried off a local girl called Poppa, whom he then took in marriage. She later gave birth to William, Rollo's eventual successor. The report smacks of legend; and, like Rollo's later match to Gisla, there is good reason to doubt its historical accuracy. It is, nevertheless, entirely conceivable that Rollo's first spouse was French, since William is a good French name. Certainly Rollo would not have been alone in taking a native wife. While some of the incomers may have brought spouses and children with them, men would have outnumbered women and the result must have been a significant element of intermarriage. Since mothers play an especially important role in language acquisition, this would have been a powerful motor for integration, ensuring that the second generation of Seine valley Northmen were largely Francophone.[15] Rollo had perhaps been little more than a pagan pirate, but his son William bore all the trappings of a French nobleman: he was pious, Christian and, most importantly, French-speaking.

The degree to which Rollo's children had integrated into French society is revealed by their marriages. His son William married Liutgard (or Leyarda), the daughter of Heribert II of Vermandois, the most powerful magnate in northern France in the 920s (and William's immediate neighbour to the east), while his daughter Gerloc married William 'Towhead' (III) of Poitou and Aquitaine, the leading figure in the south west, taking on the suitably French name Adela. Their thoroughly French religious and cultural outlook is attested by the poetic dirge (*Planctus*) composed upon William's death, apparently at Adela's behest. This is written in Latin verse and addresses them in the same terms as any other members of the local French aristocracy.[16]

This is not to say that Rollo's men entirely forgot their origins. As Dudo's account and its continuations by William of Jumièges and others in the later eleventh and twelfth centuries reveal, those who became the Normans remained proud of their pagan pedigree for centuries, even if this was rehearsed in French or Latin prose and verse. Nor were contacts with Scandinavia severed, as we can see from subsequent waves of settlement. The catalyst for these was the first major crisis of ducal power, occasioned by the death of William in 942. William did not have any sons by Liutgard. And Richard, his son from an earlier union with a Breton noblewoman, was no more than ten at the time.

In the following years, there are signs that the duchy was unravelling. New Viking bands arrived, drawn in by prospects of pillage and settlement. And new figures established themselves within William's territory, most notably the warlord Harald in and around Bayeux. The divisions that arose were partly religious in nature. Some of the Northmen had recently abandoned the Christian faith (just as Heriveus had feared would happen), calling in associates from abroad, while others remained committed to the ducal court and integration within Frankish society.

Earlier Viking settlements in Brittany and the Loire had been snuffed out after a generation or two; history now looked set to repeat itself on the Seine. This political instability also served to draw in the neighbouring French rulers. Both King Louis IV, the son of Charles the Simple, and Duke Hugh 'the Great', the son of Robert of Neustria, sought to take advantage of Richard's weakness. Robert secured much of the western territory acquired by Rollo and William, only breaking off a promising siege of Bayeux on royal orders. Louis, for his part, was able to assert royal control in the east all the way to Rouen, the main centre of Richard's power and authority.

Only a small portion of the local Northmen still answered to Richard, who was himself too young to play an active part in developments. Yet just when all seemed lost, a typically Norman combination of serendipity and derring-do saved Richard and his men. Relations between Louis and Hugh had long been tense. And soon after the king insisted that Hugh break off his siege of Bayeux, relations between the two broke down irreparably, allowing Richard and his advisers to form an alliance with the aggrieved duke. They also established friendly relations with Harald of Bayeux. The latter move proved crucial, for Louis himself was captured by Harald's men in the course of conflicts in 945, effectively ending the king's plans for northward expansion. Louis was released into the hands of Duke Hugh, who now became the power behind the French throne. With the immediate threat over, Richard and his advisers were able to focus on reconstructing ducal power and authority.[17] It had been a close-run thing, but Rollo's descendants had succeeded where other Vikings had failed. How would they now wield their new-found power and influence?

2

Consolidating a Colony:
Rollo's Heirs, Normandy, 942–1026

When, in December 942, Duke William went to meet Count Arnulf of Flanders on Picquigny, an island in the Somme, he had no reason to suspect foul play. William and Arnulf had been at loggerheads for some time. As the ship-savvy Normans established themselves, they presented a challenge to the counts of Flanders, who'd traditionally controlled the lucrative trade along the northern French coast. And as Rollo and William began expanding their domains, so Count Arnulf of Flanders had been busy extending his influence south and west. Soon, conflict had broken out between the two. But for all their rivalry, William and Arnulf were leading members of the northern French aristocracy – and expected to behave as such. This meant treating one another with respect and honouring the terms of parley.

So it was that William came to meet with Arnulf. No effort had been spared to make the meeting a success. Both sides had already committed to the peace process and agreed to meet on Picquigny in Picardy, roughly halfway between their respective spheres of influence. Islands were favoured sites for such summits. They were neutral territory, from which either party might retreat at the first sign of foul play. Yet even the best laid plans can come a cropper, as William now learned. For while he and Arnulf were indeed able to agree terms (or so he thought), as soon as William departed he was called back to the shore by one of Arnulf's men. When he returned, Arnulf's companions picked up weapons which they had stowed for this purpose, dispatching the Norman duke. The twelve men who'd accompanied William could only look on helplessly from their own vessels on the Somme.[1]

The next decade almost saw the extinction of the Norman settlement, as power fragmented and rival Scandinavian groups set themselves up within the region. This period was of crucial importance for the development of Normandy (as the duchy would soon be known). For it was out of the crucible of disaster and defeat that a unified polity was forged – one both larger and more centralised than that of Rollo and William. One of the main challenges facing William's son and heir, Richard, was how to integrate the new Viking groups who'd flocked to the duchy in his early years. Unlike the armies of Hugh or Louis, such men could not be driven out; rather, Richard would have to win their loyalty. His approach, which becomes increasingly clear from the 960s, was to stress his own Scandinavian heritage, taking pride in the Northman (or rather Norman, as we now know it) heritage they shared.[2] This seems to have been successful, and Richard's own longevity proved to be another major boon. After the initial upheaval of the 940s, his half-century on the ducal throne provided ample opportunity for this Northman/Norman identity to take root. By Richard's final decades, Normandy was a well-established territorial principality on a par with Flanders or Aquitaine. Rollo and William may have conquered Normandy, but it was Richard I who secured its future.

There was certainly much to be done. Ducal authority had always been centred on Rouen and the lower Seine. In the aftermath of the 940s, Richard was left with the unenviable task of reasserting and reconstructing – in practice, often asserting and constructing for the first time – his power and influence elsewhere. An important initial move was achieving a *modus vivendi* with Harald of Bayeux. This meant abrogating direct control of the western parts of the duchy, in exchange for acknowledgement of his overlordship. This then initiated a slow but steady process of integration, first clearly visible in Richard's later years, not least in the pages of Dudo's celebrated *History*.[3] Richard's efforts were assisted by a set of strategic dynastic marriages. The first was to Emma, the daughter of Duke Hugh the Great. Hugh had been the leading power in northern France following the death of Heribert of the Vermandois, and his sphere of influence bordered directly onto Richard's to the south and west. Hugh also had longstanding interests in the Bessin, where his ancestors had long exerted authority, and had helped Richard against Louis after the siege of Bayeux in the mid-940s; the marriage now formalised this alliance. The match itself was probably brokered soon after

Richard's success against Louis, but only came to fruition in 960. By this point, Hugh himself was dead. But such was the power and influence of Hugh's family that the marriage remained a highly desirable one. When Emma died without children in 968, Richard went on to wed Gunnor, the daughter of a local potentate in the Cotentin. This move helped further to secure Richard's position in the western reaches of the duchy, where his authority was weakest.

A sign of Normandy's growing maturity is the sudden flowering of literature and historical writing in and around the ducal court. Pride of place naturally belongs to Dudo of Saint-Quentin. Dudo hailed from the neighbouring Vermandois (later Picardy) and had first come into contact with the Norman court when sent to Rouen as part of an embassy by Count Albert I, the son and successor of Heribert II. By virtue of his position as count, Albert – like his father – controlled the religious communities within his domains, including Dudo's community of Saint-Quentin. Dudo himself seems to have received much of his education here, perhaps with stints for further studies at Liège, Laon or Rheims. Whatever his precise background, by 987 Dudo was a leading canon of Saint-Quentin – a figure worthy of entrusting with a delicate diplomatic mission.[4]

This was a turbulent time in France. The traditional Carolingian dynasty had died out in 987 and was replaced by that of Hugh Capet, the son and successor of Hugh the Great (and thus grandson of Robert of Neustria). Hugh's family were old rivals of the Carolingians, and his accession was not welcomed by all. Among the dissenters were the counts of Vermandois. It was in this connection that Dudo was sent to Richard. The duke had been a close associate of Hugh the Great and now backed his son; Albert hoped that Richard would be an intermediary with the new monarch. Dudo's mission seems to have been a success and he soon became a fast friend of Duke Richard. In the coming years, Dudo enjoyed regular sojourns at the Norman ducal court. And two years before Richard's death, Dudo received a commission to write a history of the duchy. In the following years, Dudo spent much of his time at Rouen. He became a ducal chaplain under Richard's son, Duke Richard II, in which guise he produced charters in the duke's name. Two of these survive in their original format, preserving Dudo's own hand.[5] He was also busy gathering information for his magnum opus, on which he worked in fits and starts: the 'History (or Deeds) of the Normans', which he'd promised Richard I. This work was finally finished c.1015, though large elements had been written earlier.

We've already met Dudo as the notoriously unreliable narrator of Normandy's origins. But what makes Dudo a bad source for the early 900s is precisely what makes him a good source for the 990s and early 1000s. For Dudo's vision of the Norman past is fundamentally anachronistic. He projects the situation of his own day backwards, viewing the duchy's origins in terms of its later constitution.[6] Such creative anachronism is already advertised by Dudo's choice of title. He writes a *History of* the Normans (Latin: *Historia Normannorum*; roman for emphasis). Yet in 911, there were no Normans. There were Vikings based on the lower Seine. But these were no different from the many other groups of Scandinavian marauders in France (not least in the Loire valley), all of whom contemporaries called *Nor(d)manni*, i.e. 'Northmen'. By Dudo's day, however, this Latin term (and its French equivalent) had come to mean something very different. In Normandy, it was now a proper noun referring to the inhabitants of the duchy; from the pagan Northmen had been made the Christian Normans. This connection is preserved in modern French and German, in which 'Normans' and 'Northmen' are the same word (French: *Normands*; German: *Normannen*).

The very fact that Dudo could conceive of history in these terms reveals how far Rollo's descendants had come. Out of the disparate Viking groups that had first settled the region had emerged a single, Christian (Francophone) people: the Normans. This is not the only manner in which Dudo places the cart before the horse. Just as his Normans exist *avant la lettre* in his history, so too does their principality. In Dudo's account, Normandy is not slowly assembled over the course of eighty years, but granted to Rollo outright. The same is true of the titles Dudo accords Rollo and William. Out of convenience, I've spoken so far of all the early Norman rulers as dukes. But the earliest Norman leaders were actually known as 'princes' or (more often) 'counts'. Richard I is the first to be styled 'duke' (as far as we can tell), and Richard II is the first to bear the title routinely – details which Dudo, as a charter scribe, would have known first hand.[7] Yet in Dudo's account, the Norman rulers are all dukes from Rollo on.

Dudo's *History* thus gives voice to a developing sense of Norman identity. It speaks of the newfound confidence within the corridors of power in Rouen, and there is a good chance that it was intended for recitation at the ducal court.[8] Dudo is not, however, our only evidence for these shifts. Ducal charters similarly reveal a growing sense of collective Norman identity, with Richard I and II regularly styled 'duke/count of the Normans' (*dux/comes Normannorum*). Even more striking are the signs that the duchy was starting to be considered a territorial unit. The Latin term for Normandy, *Normanni(c)a*, is first found in ducal charters of 1014 and 1015, just as Dudo was putting the finishing touches to his *History*. One of these documents survives in its original format, written (perhaps not coincidentally) by Dudo himself![9]

Relations between Normandy and its neighbours also reflect these shifts. William's reign had seen the ducal family integrated into the upper echelons of northern French aristocratic society; his son and grandsons now became players on a truly European stage. Richard I's first wife, Emma, had she lived, would have seen her brother crowned the French king. And in Richard's later years, his daughter Matilda was betrothed to Count Odo II of Blois, another major player in French politics. The biggest coup came, however, with the match of Richard's daughter – the sister of Duke Richard II – to the English king, Æthelred, in 1002. The immediate grounds for the marriage were tensions between the two realms, first over the treatment of political exiles and then over Richard II's harbouring of Viking raiders.[10] In 1000, a particularly large Viking force sought shelter in 'Richard's kingdom' (i.e. Normandy) and William of Jumièges reports an English raid on the Cotentin, which may have been a reprisal.[11] Yet out of such conflict soon came compromise. Æthelred needed all the friends he could get – particularly those, like Richard II, with ports and ships. So it was that a marriage alliance was forged. We don't know for certain who proposed the match, but one suspects it was the English king. For some time, Richard's family had been rubbing shoulders with royalty; now they joined its ranks.

∼

Just how Scandinavian the Norman duchy remained is a moot point. The first half of the tenth century had seen substantial Viking settlement, reinforced by new arrivals in the 940s. Norse speakers must, however, now have been a minority in all but pockets. Dudo famously reports that Richard I was sent to Bayeux in his youth, so that he could cultivate a knowledge of the Danish tongue. And though this does not necessarily mean that the language had died out elsewhere, it does suggest that French was the language of the ducal court.[12] That the western parts of the duchy remained more Norse is also indicated by Richard's marriage to Gunnor, the daughter of a local nobleman – a marriage designed to secure the loyalty of the region. As her name suggests, Gunnor was of Scandinavian descent and in all probability a native Norse speaker. Place-names likewise point to continued use of the language into the eleventh century, with a strong presence in the Cotentin.

Similarly significant are the signs of continuing contact with the Normans' Scandinavian homelands. Richard I employed Scandinavian mercenaries when reconstructing his polity in the 960s, and as late as 1013/14 Richard II can be seen calling upon Viking allies during conflicts with his neighbours. (This was, however, the last time a Norman duke would do this.) So if in many respects the Normans had 'gone native', they remained distinct from their French neighbours. Dudo's celebrated narrative attests as much. Though written in the Latin characteristic of French learned culture, Dudo's account strongly emphasises the Scandinavian origins of his protagonists. The Normans may have been culturally French, but they continued to celebrate their Scandinavian roots. This sense of distinctiveness wasn't restricted to the circles around the ducal court. Writing in Rheims in the mid-990s, the French historian Richer refers to Richard I as 'duke of the pirates' (*dux piratae*), a clever play on his real title 'duke of the Normans (i.e. Northmen)' (*dux Normannorum*). In Richer's eyes – and probably those of many at the ducal court – Norman and Northman still amounted to one and the same.[13] The Normans thus became the Australians of the medieval world, taking pride in their criminous pedigree.

Dudo was an essential part of this transition. His history offers the Normans a means of glorying in their past paganism, while still flaunting their Christian credentials. In his narrative, the Norman settlement and conversion were all part of a divine plan. The real hero of the story was not Rollo but Richard I, Dudo's patron; and all signs are that Richard II and his court continued to promote a distinctive brand of Christian Norman identity.[14] The eleventh-century Norman duchy thus makes a Janus-like impression. It owed its existence to Scandinavian settlement and took great pride in this. Yet its evolution and vitality are only understandable within the context of the northern French political culture of the time. The more Dudo insists on the distinctiveness of the Normans, the more it seems like special pleading. The Normans *were* different from their neighbours, but by degree, not nature.

3

Queen Emma, Jewel of the
Normans: England, 1002–42

When Emma set foot in England in early 1002, she must have been daunted by the prospect awaiting her. She was to wed Æthelred, the powerful (yet mercurial) king of the English – a man she'd never met, who spoke a language she didn't understand. Emma had been brought up in expectation of a dynastic marriage of some sort, but nothing could have quite prepared her for this. As a daughter of Duke Richard I, she would have anticipated wedding a northern French magnate – a count of Flanders or Anjou perhaps. The match with Æthelred was considerably more exalted but also considerably riskier. In England, Emma had few supporters and even fewer friends.

The grounds for the union are to be sought in the political difficulties of Æthelred's reign, which had seen the Vikings return to England's shores in force. The aim of such an alliance was to close the Norman ports to Viking raiders, who had found shelter there in 1000. In this respect, the union was also a new departure for the West Saxon royal family that ruled England. Its members had long married their daughters and sisters off to continental rulers, but had rarely (if ever) taken foreign brides in return. The only exception was Æthelwulf, Æthelred's great-great-great-grandfather, a precedent long since forgotten.

The office of queen was itself a new creation. For reasons which remain obscure, West Saxon royal consorts had traditionally been styled 'wife of the king' or 'mother of the king', titles which underlined their dependence on (and subservience to) their menfolk. This only started to change in the 960s with Æthelred's mother, Ælfthryth. She is the first royal spouse to be styled 'queen'. She is also the first royal consort of the dynasty to be formally crowned and consecrated into her office, and she appears prominently in dispute records, petitioning the king and supporting lawsuits.[1]

At the time of his union with Emma, Æthelred was in his early to mid-thirties and had at least six sons and three daughters from a previous marriage. But if Emma was not Æthelred's first wife, she does seem to have been his first queen. For Æthelred's first consort is almost invisible in the sources: she is never mentioned by name and we only know that she was (probably) called Ælfgifu thanks to much later accounts. Some of this silence may be put down to the traditional misogyny of medieval chroniclers, but by no means all of it. Ælfthryth had attracted comment in a range of sources in the 960s and 970s, as would Emma.[2] In fact, Ælfthryth may have been part of the problem. There could only be one true queen at a medieval court. And as long as Ælfthryth – who only died in late 1001 – remained present as queen mother, there was little room for a second leading woman.

When Emma arrived in England in 1002, shortly after Ælfthryth's death, the scene was thus set for the emergence of a new familial matriarch. Like many a medieval bride, Emma was young – no more than twenty and perhaps only in her mid-teens.[3] Like her father and brother, Emma was culturally (and linguistically) French. She may have been conversant in Old Norse, which was probably her mother Gunnor's native tongue, but she would have known little (if any) Old English, the vernacular of her new realm. Emma's response to these cultural and linguistic hurdles was to adapt to her new circumstances. She adopted (or was given) a suitably English name, Ælfgifu, and started making alliances with local noblemen. The fact that her new name (meaning 'elf-gift') had been the name of Æthelred's first wife may raise the odd eyebrow. But where a modern pyschologist would have had a field day, the historian must satisfy herself with observing that this was the most popular female aristocratic name of the era.

In Emma's first year on the throne, she can already be observed witnessing Æthelred's charters (in her new name) – an honour notably denied to her predecessor. And the next year, we see further signs of political activity. In 1003, the *Anglo-Saxon Chronicle* – our most detailed narrative of the period – reports that Exeter was sacked by the Vikings, on account of the Norman (or 'French') follower Emma had appointed to the city. This is veiled criticism of the new queen and her entourage, and the man in question is called a 'churl' (i.e.

peasant) – a term of abuse within aristocratic circles.[4] Still, criticism implies power, a power which would grow in later years.

That all did not welcome Emma should hardly come as a surprise. Medieval courts were cosmopolitan and polyglot places, but they were also riven by faction and intrigue. This was certainly true of Æthelred's. Since 991, the English realm had been subjected to repeated Viking attacks of increasing size and severity. By 1002, the strain was starting to take its toll. A first sign of Æthelred's growing desperation is the infamous 'Massacre of St Brice's Day' of this year, one of the first major political events Emma would have witnessed there. According to the *Chronicle*, the king ordered 'all the Danish men who were in England to be slain' on the feast day of the French saint Brice (13 November), orders given in response to rumours of a plot. This was less an act of ethnic cleansing in the modern sense than a strike against the king's own Viking mercenaries, who'd proven notably unreliable in recent years. But it was hardly the move of a monarch in charge of his own destiny.[5]

The Vikings were, however, only half the problem. For as pressure mounted, Æthelred's regime began to unravel from within. One of the complicating factors here was Emma herself. As her star rose, that of Æthelred's elder sons from his first marriage fell. And once Emma had given birth to her own first son, Edward, at some point before 1005, there were competing lines for the throne. These divided the court, as different factions vied to back different candidates. Emma would have to keep her wits about her, if she were to survive.

But Emma did more than survive – she flourished. Despite, or perhaps rather on account of, these factional divides, she soon established herself as a regular presence by Æthelred's side. Emma may have been among those who counselled the St Brice's Day Massacre, not as a snub to her former countrymen but rather as a necessary (if extreme) measure to master the Viking threat. She was almost certainly one of those who advised Æthelred to part ways with his established counsellors a few years later in the event modern historians have dubbed the 'palace revolution' of 1005 and 1006. Emma's position was further strengthened by the birth of a second son, Alfred, around this time (*c*.1008). And at some point she also gave birth to a daughter, Godgifu (meaning 'gift-of-God'). A key moment came in the winter of 1013/14. Realising the English throne was ripe for the picking, the Danish king Swein Forkbeard had led a massive invasion that summer. By December, Æthelred's position had become untenable; and so he, Emma and their children fled into exile at the court of his brother-in-law in Normandy.[6] The Norman alliance may not have been able to prevent Swein's conquest, but at least it offered a safe haven from which to plot Æthelred's return.

Soon enough, luck landed Æthelred and Emma back in England. On the feast of the Purification of Mary (Candlemas, 2 February) 1014, Swein was struck down by illness – by Saint Edmund, according to later English legend – and Æthelred was able to exploit the resulting uncertainty and re-establish himself on the throne. He returned to England and ejected Swein's teenage son Cnut, whom the Danish army had sought to elect king in his father's stead. Respite, however, proved brief. Cnut returned at the head of a large army the following year (1015). And Æthelred, who'd been ailing for some time, died in the spring of 1016 (on 23 April), with Cnut's forces still on the prowl.

This placed Emma in a difficult situation. With Æthelred dead, her position in England was at risk. Emma's primary interest lay in the eventual succession of her sons, Edward and Alfred. Yet here Æthelred's elder children posed as much of a threat as the would-be conqueror Cnut. Initially, the eldest of these, Edmund Ironside, led a spirited resistance. But Emma's emotions must have been mixed; and in the event, Edmund would die on 30 November 1016, probably of wounds incurred in battle with Cnut. The way was now paved for the accession of the Danish conqueror – the first of a long line of foreign monarchs on the English throne.

Given these uncertainties, Emma's children sensibly sought refuge at the court of their uncle, Richard II of Normandy. The queen herself seems to have remained behind in London, perhaps against her desires. Edmund had every reason to keep a close eye on his stepmother, who'd been part of a rival faction at court, one angling for the succession of her own sons with Æthelred. And Cnut had even less reason to let her go. For if Emma were to leave and wed again, her new husband would have his own claim to the throne as her spouse (the husband of the rightful queen). Perhaps more worryingly, she might seek to back her exiled sons, Cnut's main rivals. It was for this reason that Cnut now sought Emma's hand in marriage. Accounts vary as to the details –

some claim Cnut wooed Emma, others that she was pressured into the match – but all agree that she eventually consented.[7] For Cnut, this was an important victory. He could win England by conquest, but he could not rule by force alone. Marrying the previous king's wife allowed Cnut to present himself as an heir (of sorts) to Æthelred. The union thus took the edge off hardnosed *Realpolitik*. Most importantly, by bringing Emma on side, Cnut had neutralised the threat presented by her sons, the eldest of whom, Edward, was now nearing maturity and had little reason to be grateful to his new stepfather.

If Cnut had much to gain from the match, Emma had just as much to lose. Her future in England now depended on rapprochement with the new regime. But marriage to Cnut, particularly if it produced heirs, risked barring her own sons from the succession (as indeed was Cnut's intention). Faced with an impossible choice – and probably a degree of coercion – Emma plumped for Cnut and career over sons and exile. The decision cannot have been easy, and Edward and Alfred never forgave her. The resulting strains would define English politics for much of the next half century.

That Emma took no pride in her actions is revealed by the account of the period she later commissioned. This propagandist work, appropriately entitled 'In Praise of Queen Emma' (Latin: *Encomium Emmae reginae*), was written by a Flemish cleric in the early 1040s. Significantly, the author avoids all mention of Emma's first marriage to Æthelred, despite the narrative contortions this entails. The existence of Edward and Alfred could not be ignored so easily, but the nature of their birth and parentage is passed over in judicious silence. Evidently, some things were best left unsaid.

However, if Emma had been a force in Æthelred's later years, under Cnut she came into her own. Precisely because the union was so central to the legitimation of Cnut's regime, Emma was placed in a position of unusual power and dignity. She attests his charters more often and more prominently than she had Æthelred's (and she'd been no shrinking violet then). And there are signs that she was entrusted with important political duties. Many documents are addressed to Cnut and Emma jointly; and the pair can be seen undertaking acts of cultural and religious patronage in tandem.[8] Perhaps the most enduring monument to their cooperation is the striking image at the front of the *Liber Vitae* ('Book of Life') of the New Minster in Winchester. This is a record of those for whom the monks of the New Minster prayed. It was produced at the monastery in Cnut's reign and the opening illustration depicts Emma (here given her English designation, Ælfgifu) and Cnut jointly presenting a cross to the abbey. Not only are the two figures of equal size and prominence, but Emma is placed on the right-hand side of the composition (i.e. the left as you look at it). It was a well-established convention that the most important individual was placed on the right (or in the centre) of an illumination; and Emma is thus given pride of place over Cnut.[9] Here she more than warrants her later epithet, 'jewel of the Normans'.[10]

Emma's integration into the new Anglo-Danish regime may have been eased by her own Scandinavian origins and (possible) acquaintance with Old Norse. Certainly it was further encouraged by the birth of two children with Cnut, Harthacnut and Gunnhild. For his part, Cnut had to strike a careful balance between rewarding his Scandinavian followers and winning over the native English aristocracy (or at least elements thereof).[11] On the one hand, he promoted loyal followers to key earldoms across England. On the other, he sought to reach out to elements of the established local elite. It was here that Emma proved invaluable. Marriage with her provided an important link to the previous regime.

This was but one of a number of olive branches Cnut offered the English. Another was the foundation of a religious house at Ashingdon (*Assandun*), the site of Cnut's definitive victory over Edmund Ironside. As significant was a gathering at Oxford in 1018, at which Cnut pledged to uphold the 'laws of Edgar'. Edgar was Æthelred's father and was synonymous with law and justice in England. Cnut's willingness to work with the grain of local politics is further illustrated by the fact that the decrees issued at Oxford were composed by Archbishop Wulfstan of York (d. *c.*1023). Wulfstan had been a leading adviser in Æthelred's later years, entrusted with all major acts of law-making; now he did the same for Cnut.[12] The specific decision to embrace the 'laws of Edgar' is also noteworthy. This not only aligned Cnut with earlier English law and government; it also specifically identified him with the father of the ruler he'd replaced. The message is clear: Edgar is a source of legitimacy, not his son – nor, by implication, the latter's heirs.

Wulfstan and Emma also brought practical know-how to the new Danish regime. Cnut continued to have interests in the wider North Sea world and needed trusted place-holders to rule England during his repeated absences. In the winter of 1019/20 he was already in Denmark, securing succession to his brother there. And he was away again in 1023, 1025 to 1026, 1027 and 1028 to 1029, seizing control of Norway and parts of Sweden. Cnut's son with Emma, Harthacnut, had a part to play here, and he was sent to Denmark to be Cnut's regent, perhaps soon after his first public appearance in England in 1023. There Harthacnut was to represent his father and learn the art of statecraft.

If Emma was more prominent under Cnut than she had been under Æthelred, she soon found herself confronted with similar problems. For like Æthelred, Cnut came into the marriage with baggage. He had two older sons, Swein and Harold (named after their grandfather and great-grandfather), both born to Ælfgifu of Northampton. Sources close to Emma paint Ælfgifu as a lowly concubine and Swein and Harold as bastards – indeed, the *Encomium* even claims that the latter's birth had been faked and he was not Cnut's true offspring – but they clearly protest too much. Ælfgifu was actually a leading noblewoman from the Midlands, whose father and brothers had fallen foul of Æthelred's regime. There is every reason to believe that the union was a *bona fide* marriage, struck in 1013 or 1014 in order to secure the support of a powerful region. (Though the Church frowned on divorce and remarriage, it would be another two centuries before it was in a position to dictate terms to monarchs and aristocrats.)[13]

Emma was right to feel threatened by Swein and Harold, and the Encomiast (as her pet historian is known) claims that a condition of her marriage to Cnut was that any son of theirs would be preferred for the succession. Such a deal is certainly conceivable. But as the Encomiast is Emma's mouthpiece, we must treat his statements with care. He writes *after* Harthacnut had finally succeeded to the English throne in 1040 for an audience at his court. It was in his interest to paint Harthacnut as Cnut's natural heir – and Swein and Harold as usurping upstarts.

What is certain is that Emma worked tirelessly to secure Harthacnut's interests – if need be, at the expense of his half-siblings. She may well have been the one who pushed for Swein to be placed in charge of Norway in the early 1030s (under Ælfgifu of Northampton's tutelage), an act which conveniently removed two rivals from court. And when Cnut died of unknown causes at Shaftesbury in 1035, Emma was quick to agitate for Harthacnut's succession against the claims of his elder half-brother Harold. Emma was joined here by the powerful earl of Wessex, Godwin, who owed his meteoric rise to Cnut's patronage. Godwin's main competitor for power and influence, however, Earl Leofric of Mercia, backed Harold (known to posterity as Harold 'Harefoot').[14] Harold had two main advantages: he was older than Harthacnut and, most crucially, he was at hand in England, when Cnut unexpectedly died.

The situation was further complicated by Harthacnut's slow reaction. Harthacnut had ruled Denmark on Cnut's behalf for over a decade. But here as in England, Cnut's death raised questions about the succession. In particular, Magnus Olafsson, who had recently secured the Norwegian throne, was angling to reconfigure Cnut's North Sea empire from this northern base (as he would briefly do in the 1040s).[15] Under these circumstances, Harthacnut could ill afford a speculative trip to England, a land he knew little of. Despite his absence, Harthacnut's claims were taken seriously. It was initially decided to divide the realm between Harold, who would take north of the Thames (Leofric's sphere of influence), and Harthacnut, who would rule to the south (Godwin's earldom). But as it became clear that the latter could not prize himself away from Denmark, his supporters started to get jittery. Emma now reached out to her sons with Æthelred – Edward and Alfred – who remained in exile in Normandy. Relations between them must have been frosty, but the prospect of a crown is enough to warm even the coldest heart. Soon, both Edward and Alfred were on their way to England, the former sailing to Southampton and the latter making his way north via Flanders to Kent.

Godwin, however, had other plans. He had little to gain from the return of the West Saxon line. If he could not see Harthacnut on the throne, Godwin would back any son of Cnut over one of Æthelred. As earl of Wessex – a region which now encompassed all of southern England – Godwin was uniquely well-placed to rebuff the English princes. Edward faced armed resistance as soon as he landed and was forced to retreat to Normandy. Alfred, on the other hand, was welcomed by the earl, before Godwin killed and scalped or enslaved his companions, then packed him off into the monastery of Ely (apparently at Harold's behest). There Alfred was blinded, dying shortly thereafter of the wounds. The earl had timed his defection to perfection. He may have been an enemy of Harold up until then, but one good turn deserved another – and few turns are better appreciated than removing a would-be rival.

The Encomiast is keen to absolve Emma of any involvement in these events. He claims, rather implausibly, that the entire affair was an elaborate trap sprung by Harold. It was Harold who sent a letter in Emma's name to Edward and Alfred, designed to lure them to England; and it was at his orders that Godwin then violently opposed them. The story is about as credible as a Cold War-era *Pravda* article. But it says much about the shadow cast by these events. Emma desperately wanted to wash her hands of any involvement.[16] Sources close to Godwin, including the later *Life* of Edward and one of the versions of the *Anglo-Saxon Chronicle*, similarly seek to downplay the earl's part, trying to pin as much of the blame as possible on Harold.

Whatever the rights and wrongs of these events, the succession was now settled. Harold would be king. For his good services, Godwin would remain the dominant earl. Emma was the only one to lose out. Not only had Harthacnut been blocked from the succession; she'd lost one of her other sons (Alfred) and damaged relations irreparably with the other (Edward). No longer able to sustain her position, she now fled into exile in Flanders.

Just across the Channel from Kent, Flanders had long enjoyed close social, political and economic ties with England.[17] It was, nevertheless, a most strange place of exile for Emma. The obvious option would have been to return, as she had in 1013, to her native Normandy, where Emma's relatives continued to hold the ducal throne. The reason for her reticence must have been the presence of her son Edward there. Edward had long been welcomed at the ducal court, where he was treated as a king in exile – an alternative to the Anglo-Danish line Emma had embraced. After the tumultuous events of the previous year, Edward must have returned with tales of Emma's perfidy. No succour was now to be found for her there. In Flanders, by contrast, Emma was welcomed warmly. The region lay directly on the sea routes between Harold's England and Harthacnut's Denmark. From here, Emma could plan her return.

She did not have to wait long. In late 1039, Harthacnut was finally in a position to make his move. He sailed to the Flemish port of Bruges to join Emma. They hoped to strike at Harold's regime in the New Year.[18] In the end, force was unnecessary. In mid-March 1040, Harold died and the leading English magnates sent for Harthacnut, offering him the crown. He readily accepted. With Harthacnut came his mother, who once more established herself as the power behind the English throne. Yet Emma's moment of greatest triumph soon became a mounting crisis. For Harthacnut insisted on antagonising the local Anglo-Danish elite, demanding exorbitant taxes and publicly desecrating the body of his predecessor Harold. To make matters worse, there may already have been signs of the unknown affliction which would carry Harthacnut off two years later.

It was in this awkward situation that Emma reached out once more to Edward. He had visited his mother during her exile in Bruges, but relations remained strained. Then, there'd been little he could (or would) do for her; now, with Harthacnut's regime tottering, she hoped Edward would heed her call and return to his native land. The idea was to install Edward as co-ruler, that he might succeed Harthacnut when the time came. One son of Emma would thus follow the other – and she would continue to pull the strings behind the scenes. It was a bold plan, but a good one. It was in this connection that Emma probably commissioned the *Encomium*, a work designed to smooth ruffled feathers. Symbolic of the desired accord is the striking opening image of this work, in which Emma sits enthroned in majesty with her sons Harthacnut and Edward waiting in the wings – a natural triumvirate if there ever was one! – while the Encomiast presents his work to her.[19]

However, Emma had turned her back on Edward more than once already. Not far beneath the surface lurked the jealousy, anger and resentment generated by years of fierce factional politics. Would he really come to her rescue now?

4

Edward the Confessor: A King Across
the Sea, England, 1041–66

W hen Edward looked down on the port of Fécamp on a cool
spring morning in 1041, he felt sudden doubts. Edward had
every reason for concern. Five years previously, he and his younger
brother Alfred had been lured back to England on promises of restoration, only to find another elected king in their stead. In returning,
he was taking a gamble. Yet if the stakes were high, Edward had little
to lose. He'd been made most welcome during his long exile at the
Norman court. But without lands and a crown, Edward was a shadow
king. In Normandy, he commanded sympathy, not respect.

There were, moreover, grounds for greater optimism now. Alfred
had been blinded for the benefit – and probably at the behest – of
Harold Harefoot. Since then, Harold's younger half-brother,
Harthacnut, had acceded. The latter may have been of the same
Danish line, but he was no friend of Harold's and took a more conciliatory tone towards the native English dynasty. Moreover, Harthacnut
himself was in need of support. He had made enemies soon after his
arrival in England. The restoration of the line of his elder English
half-brother – the only other serious contender for the throne –
promised to calm the waters.

The Channel crossing proved uneventful. Edward's crew sighted
land just off the Isle of Wight, an old Viking haunt, well known to
Norman mariners. From there, they proceeded around the coast,
before landing at Hurst Head (modern Hurst Point) on the south
Hampshire coast. The site had been carefully chosen. Hurst Head lies
at the end of a coastal promontory, overlooking the natural port of
Keyhaven. This was a place from which either party might rapidly
retreat at the first sign of treachery.[1]

In the end, precautions proved unnecessary. Harthacnut's offer had indeed been sincere. An outsider to the political scene in England, the young Dane had faced opposition ever since his arrival the previous spring. Harthacnut's problem was that he was doubly foreign. The son of a Danish conqueror (Cnut) and a Norman queen (Emma), he had little prior acquaintance with the English. Harthacnut's own rashness did little to help the situation. He'd arrived with an army, and his first act as king was to demand a massive tax to pay the men. His second had been to have his half-brother's body disinterred and unceremoniously dumped in a fen (or perhaps the Thames – sources disagree on the details) – an act of conscious desecration. These were not actions of a man likely to make friends or win people over. By May 1041, Harthacnut was facing a serious tax revolt in the West Midlands. The situation was reportedly not helped by his own ill health.[2]

Edward was, therefore, welcomed in style, and formal arrangements for power-sharing were soon put in motion. He swore to uphold the laws of Cnut and his sons, and in exchange was accepted as king. Harthacnut would continue to rule, but Edward would be co-ruler (in name) and take over fully upon Harthacnut's death. All of Edward's life had been building up to this moment. The years of exile – the hope, the pain, the misery – had paid off. He would sit on his father's throne.

~

Edward the Confessor (as he came to be known) is typically remembered as the last king of England's native line, a venerable dynasty stretching back to the West Saxon ruler Ecgberht, the grandfather of Alfred the Great. Yet Edward was more than Anglo-Saxon England's last hurrah; he was also the kingdom's first Norman monarch. Half-Norman through his mother Emma, Edward had spent much of his teens and all of his adult life in Normandy before his accession. And as his reign would show, Edward was in many respects more Norman than he was English.

The importance of Edward's exile cannot be exaggerated. The earliest years of this were spent under the protection of his uncle, Duke Richard II. Richard had welcomed Emma and her children when they were driven from England in 1013/14. When Cnut took the realm in 1016–17, the duke welcomed Edward and Alfred – and their sister Godgifu – on their own. Richard had no particular affinity for Cnut, and providing for his nephews was more than a kind avuncular gesture (though it was this too); it was a means of keeping the duke's northern neighbours on their toes. As long as Edward and Alfred were alive and well, they were a threat to Cnut and his would-be heirs. Moreover, if they were ever able to re-establish themselves, the English princes would owe Richard and his sons a good turn. Ducal support for the two brothers finds its clearest expression in the charters issued by Richard's sons. Here Edward and Alfred periodically appear as witnesses within the ducal entourage. And when they do, Edward is sometimes styled 'king', and once even 'king of the English'. Here Edward is a king in exile, awaiting his rightful return.[3]

By the time this came around, Edward was nearly forty and had outlived three Norman dukes (and two Danish kings of England). The years of waiting weighed heavily. In Edward's eyes, he'd been serially betrayed. By his people, who'd accepted Cnut and his sons in his stead. By Earl Godwin, Cnut's right-hand man, who'd barred his way to the throne and delivered his brother up to death. And above all by his mother, who'd abandoned her children from her first marriage to seek her own fame and fortune. The only people who'd done right by Edward were his uncle and cousins, the Norman dukes. The Norman court was home; the Normans were his friends. When Harthacnut died in late spring 1042 and Edward became sole ruler, he therefore looked across the Channel for succour.

Before Harthacnut's body was even in the ground, Edward had himself elected in London. The following Easter, he was formally crowned and consecrated king at the Old Minster (the cathedral) in Winchester by Eadsige, the archbishop of Canterbury. The locations chosen for these acts are significant. Opposition to Cnut and his sons had centred on London (where Edward's father, Æthelred, lay interred); Winchester, by contrast, had been their base of operations. Edward was thus securing support from a position of strength on the Thames, then presenting it (at greater leisure) to a potentially hostile audience in central Hampshire. That old ills had not been forgotten is revealed by the events of the following autumn. On 16 November, Edward returned to Winchester in haste with an armed following. He caught his mother Emma unawares and proceeded to despoil her of her accumulated wealth, in revenge for her earlier disloyalty.

~

As king, Edward faced many of the same difficulties as Harthacnut. He, too, was new to the political scene in England. And while the vast estates that came with the crown made Edward the kingdom's leading landholder, he would have to work with the grain of local politics – at least initially. This meant dealing with those duplicitous souls who'd placed Cnut and his heirs on the throne, foremost amongst them the influential earl of Wessex, Godwin.[4] Since the early 1030s, Godwin had been the power behind the English throne. He'd twice played kingmaker, abandoning Harthacnut for Harold Harefoot in 1036, when it became clear that the latter would prevail, then welcoming Harthacnut back with open arms after Harold's death in 1040. Unlike Emma, Godwin was not dispensable. A deal would have to be struck. Both men had reason to be wary. Edward blamed Godwin for Alfred's death; he also resented the earl's ties to his mother, whose neglect still rankled. Godwin, for his part, had spent much of the past decade seeking to prevent Edward's accession. Edward and Godwin now needed each other, however. The earl's support was necessary if Edward's regime was to get off the ground, while Godwin's continuing influence would depend on Edward's favour.

As was so often the case in the Middle Ages, compromise was achieved by way of marriage: Edward agreed to take Godwin's daughter, Edith, as his wife. The match was probably planned at the start of Edward's reign, but first celebrated in early 1045, perhaps to allow Edith to reach a greater age. This was a marriage of convenience, but convenient it certainly was. Were Edith to bear a son, this would unite the feuding families: the interests of Godwin and Edward would then lie in the succession of their shared progeny. This produced a considerable weight of expectation. The situation was not helped by the fact that at the time of his coronation (Easter 1043), Edward was quite old by medieval standards – at least thirty-eight, and perhaps forty. Only one king had reached a greater age in living memory, Edward's own father Æthelred; and even he had not made it past fifty.

To make matters worse, Edward was without wife or child. The general expectation was a short reign. The only question was what would happen thereafter. From day one, therefore, the succession was *the* defining issue of Edward's reign. All eyes were on him and Edith – they needed an heir, and fast. The risks accompanying failure were high. Edith might be put aside for a more fertile bride. And Edward's position remained precarious till he had a viable successor.

As long as the prospect of an heir was alive, relations between Edward and Godwin remained cordial (if not warm). The earl threw his weight behind the new king, and was rewarded for his support. In 1043, Godwin's eldest son, Swein – named after Cnut's father – was appointed to an earldom around Hereford in the West Midlands. Shortly thereafter, Godwin's second son, Harold – another Danish name – was rewarded with one in East Anglia. In 1045, Beorn, their Danish cousin, was made earl in the East Midlands. With the exception of the large north-west Midlands earldom of Leofric, the Godwin clan now controlled all of southern and middle England – an unprecedented concentration of power and influence in the hands of one family. But their fate was closely linked to that of Edith, and that still stood in the balance. By the late 1040s, it was becoming clear that the couple were having difficulty conceiving. Much has been speculated as to the causes, but what matters are the consequences. Rifts now started to emerge between Edward and Godwin. The king had never liked his father-in-law; and if he could not have a child with Edith, there was little reason to maintain the charade of cosy camaraderie.

The mask started to slip in earnest in 1049. In this year, Edward exiled Swein, Godwin's eldest, a second time. Swein was the black sheep of the Godwin family. Scarcely had he been made earl of Hereford in 1043, than he'd begun upsetting the balance of power on the Welsh frontier. In 1046, he made matters worse by abducting the abbess of nearby Leominster, apparently in a bid to seize the abbey's lands. For this, Swein was exiled. He returned to make amends in 1049, but only compounded his problems by killing his cousin Beorn en route to court (a quarrel gone wrong, reportedly). Swein was now exiled afresh and Beorn's earldom passed to Ralph of Mantes. The latter was not a member of the Godwin clan – indeed, was not even English. He was the Confessor's nephew, the son of Godgifu. The latter had accompanied Edward and Alfred into exile, marrying the local French count Drogo of the Vexin, a strategic region on the Norman frontier. Ralph probably came to England with Edward in 1041 and his promotion was a reward for loyal service. Still, this was a symbolic gesture, the first time an earldom had been placed in Franco-Norman hands. It was an attempt to cut the Godwins down to size, and the West Saxon earl was wily enough to know it. Ralph was one of a small but significant group of French and Norman magnates who now began to make their influence felt.[5]

Matters finally came to a head over the succession to the archbishop-ric of Canterbury. In late October 1049 the previous incumbent, Eadsige, died. Eadsige belonged to the established Anglo-Danish elite, of which Godwin was a leading exponent. He was, however, unpopu-lar with the local monks at Canterbury cathedral, who resented his efforts to sell off Church lands (not least to his patrons, the Godwins). The Godwins thus had a vested interest in the succession and were quick to agitate for Æthelric, a local monk who just happened to be a relative. Edward, however, was not going to let the chance to make further inroads into the Godwins' stranglehold on power slip, parti-cularly as Canterbury was the most senior ecclesiastical post in England. The king therefore insisted on the appointment of Robert of Jumièges, another of the Norman retainers who'd accompanied him over the sea in 1041. Since 1044, Robert had been bishop of London, a poor but strategically significant see, where Edward's father, Æthelred, lay buried.[6] The scene was set for a showdown.

Godwin may have been a remarkable earl, but he was no match for an anointed monarch – at least in matters ecclesiastical. At a well-attended church council in March 1051, Robert's nomination was duly confirmed. Robert then travelled to Rome, where he received the pallium – a white, cross-shaped vestment, symbolising his archi-episcopal office – from the reform-minded Pope Leo IX. By June, Robert was back in England, with papal backing for his disputed succession. Edward was now set on breaking free from the influence of the Godwins. Here the king's childlessness came in handy – there was nothing to bind him to the earl. Later Norman sources claim that Edward promised the young Norman duke, William (the future Conqueror), the succession to the English throne in this connection.

William was the grandson of Richard II (and thus Edward's first cousin once removed), so it's easy to see why the English king might have done so. It was now clear that Edward would have no children, at least with Edith, and William was one of his closest living relatives. Edward had more than a motive; he had the opportunity. Robert's trip to Rome took the new archbishop through northern France, offering a chance to make contact with William. Most sources mentioning such promises come from Normandy *after* 1066, when there was great need to justify William's (legally dubious) conquest of England. They must, therefore, be treated with utmost caution. Still, the promise is recorded by not only the sycophantic William of Poitiers, but also the more sober William of Jumièges and is mentioned by the later Englishman Eadmer of Canterbury.[7]

Whatever the nature of contacts between Edward and William, they were not in Godwin's interests. And when Archbishop Robert returned to England, he too began to move against the earl. Robert demanded the return of lands to Canterbury, which he claimed – perhaps with some justification – the Godwins had misappropriated in previous years. Tensions finally boiled over in late summer, when Edward's brother-in-law, Eustace of Boulogne – the second husband of Godgifu, following Drogo's death in 1035 – came to visit Edward. The precise purpose of the trip is unclear, but presumably lay in shoring up the Norman party. Certainly Eustace's presence raised alarm among the Godwins. When he landed at Dover, in Godwin's earldom, fighting broke out between the count's men and the local townsfolk. In response, Edward ordered Godwin to punish the unruly burghers. The earl refused, making armed conflict inevitable.

The king now raised an army against the rebellious earl. Edward's nephew Ralph rallied to the cause. So, too, did Leofric of Mercia and Siward of York, the only other earls not of Godwin's kin. Their forces gradually coalesced at Gloucester in the West Midlands. Godwin and his sons also raised an army, converging on Beverston, some 18 miles (29 km) – or about a day's march – south of Edward's army. The result was a phoney war. Neither side was confident enough to engage the other, but neither was willing to back down. In the end, it was decided to relocate to London, where Godwin would face trial. As the armies marched east, however, Godwin's support slowly evaporated. By the time he had reached his Southwark residence, the earl's forces were no match for Edward's.[8] The king had won, at least for now.

Edward was in no mood for compromise. When Godwin inquired about making amends, the king responded that the earl could have peace and pardon when he'd restored Alfred alive and well.[9] The scars of 1036 had yet to heal. Edward did not want conciliation; he wanted the eradication of the Godwins. Realising that the game was up for now, the earl fled to Flanders with three of his sons (Gytha, Swein and Tostig), while the two others (Harold and Leofwine) headed west to Ireland. As this division of forces suggests, the intention was always to return. The choice of destinations is significant in this regard. In Ireland, Harold and Leofwine sought out the court of Diarmait mac Máel na mBó of Leinster, the most powerful ruler on the island, who'd recently gained control of the strategic port of Dublin. In Flanders, Godwin himself was able to secure the support of one of the great northern French sea powers, the counts of Flanders. During this stay (if not before), the earl's son Tostig married Judith, the count's half-sister.

Edward took advantage of Godwin's absence, declaring the earl and his sons outlawed and setting about redistributing their lands and offices. Among those who benefited were Odda of Deerhurst, who was made earl in the West Country, a region hitherto under Godwin's control; Ralph of Mantes, who now received Swein's earldom in the West Midlands; and Ælfgar, the son of Earl Leofric, who was entrusted with Harold's office in East Anglia. The king also packed Edith off to a nunnery – either Wilton or (more likely) Wherwell, both convents with close ties to the royal family.[10] Edward was probably contemplating dissolving the union, a line of action advocated by his new right-hand man, Archbishop Robert. It was common for medieval monarchs to separate from wives who'd failed to bear male offspring (Henry VIII was no innovator here). And Edward's actions look little different from those of his older French counterpart Robert the Pious, who went through three wives in quick succession in his (ultimately successful) quest for an heir. Evidently hopes of a biological successor were not yet dead, and any promises to Duke William must have been provisional.

As it happened, such plans were overtaken by events. In spring 1052, Godwin and his sons did indeed return. Harold and Leofwine harried the south west, while Godwin and the main force landed in the south east. The local people, who'd resisted Eustace a year earlier, now rose again to back their erstwhile earl. By September, the Godwins were in a position to march on London. This time, Leofric and Siward did not rally to the king. They had little to gain from Godwin's return, but were wary of the growing influence of the Norman party. And so in a reversal of the previous year's fortunes, it was Edward who was now forced to eat humble pie. It was agreed that Godwin and his men would receive a full pardon, provided the earl publicly submit to Edward and beg forgiveness. This was a face-saving exercise, and the reality of Godwin's victory was clear for all to see. A number of Norman courtiers were driven from court, while Robert fled for his life and was replaced at Canterbury by Stigand, the bishop of Winchester – a close ally of Godwin. Stigand's appointment flew in the face of canon (i.e. Church) law, but Godwin cared little. For Edward, it was now a question of damage limitation. He had lost the struggle; all he could hope for was to save his dignity.

These were factional squabbles, but they took on distinctly ethnic undertones. Sources close to Godwin emphasise the foreignness of Edward's Normans – invariably called 'Frenchmen' in the English vernacular – playing on popular anti-immigrant sentiment. There is more than a whiff of sophistry here. Godwin was of good English stock – he hailed from Sussex – but his wife was Danish, his sons were half-Danish and many of his closest associates were Scandinavian too. Yet this does not mean that such rhetoric was any less effective, as the response to Godwin's return reveals. The Anglo-Danish elite may have been of recent vintage, but it was better established than the Norman incomers. Here Edward's experiences contrast with those of Cnut. The latter had come to England with an army at his back, able to impose his will; he had little trouble introducing Danish magnates into positions of power and authority. The Confessor had arrived without an army, and had struggled to position his Norman associates. Local aristocrats looked on warily at the growing Norman presence at court. Leofric and Siward were no fans of the Godwins, but they also had little to gain from the promotion of the likes of Robert and Ralph.

It's easy to tell the story of Edward's later years as one of stalemate and then decline. And in a sense, this is fair. After failure in 1052, the king did little more to rock the boat. He took Edith back as his wife (and queen); he restored Godwin and his sons to their posts; and he left Stigand on the archiepiscopal seat in Canterbury. But it would be wrong to write off the aging Edward. He continued to balance interests deftly at court, using the Mercian and Northumbrian earls as counterweights to the Godwins when required.[11] And while Edward may have stopped showing such ostentatious favour to his Norman companions, Ralph and others remained in place, continuing to add a continental flair to English aristocratic life. It may be in these years that a distinctive stone keep – a proto-castle of sorts – was built in Oxford, within Ralph's domains.[12] And within the Church, Francophone influence actually stepped up apace. Norman appointees were now rare, but there was an influx of bishops from the French-speaking regions between the Meuse and Rhine (known as Lotharingia).[13] Likewise, more middling French and Norman magnates continued to play a part locally, both within and beyond Ralph's sphere of influence.[14] Most importantly, Edward continued to seek solutions to the succession problem. Remarriage was now off the table; so too was the nomination of Duke William. Godwin and latterly his sons were clearly angling for the throne, but Edward did his best to block their efforts. The Godwins might remain king-makers, but they would not be kings – at least, not if Edward had anything to say about it.

It was in this context that Edward decided to recall the last remaining branch of his family – his nephew Edward the Exile. The latter was the son of Edmund Ironside, the Confessor's elder half-brother who'd died in late 1016. Lacking his uncle's Norman connections, the younger Edward had been forced into more distant exile following Cnut's conquest, when he was no more than a year old. Edward would eventually make his way to the recently converted Hungarian realm. En route, he passed through the territory of the Kievan Rus'; and either here or at the Hungarian court, he eventually met and married a noblewoman called Agatha. The identification of the latter has been the cause of much head-scratching, but she was evidently of high status, related to both (or either) the German and Hungarian royal houses (and perhaps also to the Rus' tsar). Edward the Exile offered a convenient solution to the king's quandary. He was at least a decade younger than the Confessor, so stood every chance of succeeding naturally. Even better, Edward was married to a woman of high nobility, with whom he had a son – Edgar the Ætheling (ætheling being the Old English for prince).

Recalling the exiled Edward took time. The king initially sent Bishop Ealdred in search of him in 1054, but it would be 1057 before the Exile and his son arrived. Yet if the Confessor thought he'd finally solved the succession problem, he was sorely disappointed. Scarcely had Edward set foot in England than he died – before the king had even met him. At this point, it's traditionally thought that the Confessor accepted the inevitable: that Harold, Godwin's son and successor as earl of Wessex (and dynastic paterfamilias), would be his heir. The main evidence for this, however, comes from the later *Life* of Edward. This is a work commissioned by Edith, Harold's sister. And it speaks with the benefit of hindsight, in full knowledge of Harold's later kingship. Moreover, it does not actually say that Edward designated Harold his heir, but rather that he entrusted him with his realm on his deathbed (terms which may simply suggest the role of caretaker).[15]

Greater weight should be accorded to a contemporary piece of evidence. This is the entry of Edward, Edith and Edgar the Ætheling in the *Liber Vitae* of the New Minster in Winchester. The entry in question has to come from the time between Edgar's arrival in England (1057) and the king's own death (5 January 1066), since the entries are all of living figures, and probably dates to the Confessor's last three years on the throne. What matters is that Edgar's name is included here alongside those of the king and queen, precisely where we might otherwise expect a son. Moreover, Edgar is accorded the Latin title *clito* or 'prince' – a term reserved for throne-worthy royal offspring. In the eyes of some, Edgar had clearly inherited his father's role as heir-apparent.[16]

The Exile's death had been an unfortunate blip, but Edward remained determined to block the path of the Godwins to the throne, if at all possible. It is this, and not any precise promises to Duke William, which paved the way to the dramatic events of 1066. When

Edward died in early January that year, Harold exploited Edgar's youth to his advantage. Convincing the realm's leading magnates – many of whom were his brothers – that a mature hand was required, Harold was able to seize the reins of power for himself. His efforts were helped by the fact that he was on the spot when Edward died in London. Against all convention, Harold was elected and crowned the very next day. (By way of contrast, the Confessor had waited over nine months after Harthacnut's death before his own coronation.) Harold's accession was a swift *coup de main*, rushed through in the hope of silencing dissent.

If lining up Edward the Exile and his son Edgar for the succession had been intended to secure the Confessor's material legacy, the king's later years saw similar efforts to tend to his spiritual well-being. Childless monarchs frequently embarked on major religious projects. With no biological heirs, they naturally looked to the next world – to works which would serve the Church in the here and now, and their souls in the hereafter. In the earlier years of the century, the childless German emperor Henry II had founded an imposing new bishopric at Bamberg; Edward now did something similar at Westminster.[17] This was already a well-established monastery to the west of the main city of London (hence the name, literally 'the religious house to the west'). Edward now had this rebuilt in style. When construction began is unknown, but by the 1050s it was in full swing.

This new abbey was constructed in a new style, that is known as the Romanesque. This is characterised by thick walls and large, rounded arches. In comparison with the later Gothic style we often associate with the Middle Ages, it displays an elegant simplicity. Romanesque architecture had been gaining popularity on the continent for some time, but this was the first such church to be built in the British Isles. Its novelty was not lost on contemporaries and William of Malmesbury approvingly remarks that it was made 'in a new manner of construction'.[18] The inspiration clearly came from Normandy, where Edward had picked up a taste for such architecture, and the resulting edifice reveals strong similarities with the monastery at Jumièges, which was also built in these years. It's no coincidence that Robert, a sometime monk of Jumièges, was bishop of London when plans for the church were first laid.[19]

Westminster was Edward's crowning achievement. Consecrated on 28 December 1065, just before the king's own death, it was by far the largest church in the British Isles – indeed, one of the largest in western Christendom. By now, Edward was at death's door. He began ailing before Christmas 1065 and was not even able to attend the consecration. With his legacy secure, however – or so it must have seemed – Edward could die happily. On 6 January 1066, the day following his death, he was laid to rest with due pomp at his new church.

As his final resting place, Westminster symbolises Edward's rule. It may have been constructed from English materials and by English hands, but in spirit and style it looked to Normandy. In fact, it's striking just how Norman England had become. Almost all the features we traditionally associate with the later Conquest of 1066 – Francophone aristocrats, reforming prelates, stone keeps, Romanesque architecture – can be seen under the Confessor. This should not come as a surprise; he was a Norman, after all, both by birth and by choice. Not an arrow had been loosed, yet the Normanisation of England had begun.

5

William I: A Conquering King, Normandy and England, 1035–66

As the body of William the Conqueror was carried into Caen, the crowds pressed close around. His destination was the abbey church of Saint-Etienne, long William's favoured religious foundation. Yet as the king's remains entered the city, fire broke out, panicking the onlookers and disrupting the procession. This would not be the only mishap to beset this event. Once within the abbey, Mass passed uneventfully enough, followed by an eloquent sermon by Bishop Gilbert of Evreux. But as the time came to inter the body, a local layman jumped up and complained that the land on which the church stood rightly belonged to him, having been seized by the duke a quarter of a century earlier, at the time of the abbey's foundation. Keen to avoid further embarrassment, the officiating clergy swiftly paid the man off. Yet even so, the problems continued. For as they came to lower William's body into the grave, they found that the sarcophagus was too small. The torso of the duke's corpulent corpse now ruptured, letting off a terrible stench.[1]

This was an inglorious end – deservedly so, at least according to some. For William had made a career out of terror. In a violent age, the Conqueror stood out. And even sympathetic writers were troubled by the ill omens which punctuated his funeral. God-fearing men were meant to die peacefully and be buried in pomp. William's demise had been painful and protracted, and his funeral a comedy of errors. The earth was said to open up to welcome the remains of saints; its rejection of William left little doubt that he was a sinner. Even in death, William was a figure of conflict and controversy. The emotions he stirred reflect the scale both of his achievements and of the sacrifices these demanded.

~

William's stern demeanour was a product of his upbringing. After nine decades of peace and prosperity, Normandy had been thrown into disarray in 1035 by the sudden death of William's father Duke Robert I, the second son of Richard II, while on a pilgrimage. The result was a crisis reminiscent of that of the 940s. Centrifugal tendencies developed, with local lords seeking to establish their own independent domains. Jealous neighbours also exploited the uncertainty, carving up parts of Norman territory.

One of the problems was that William was the child of an informal union. Already in his lifetime, he seems to have been known as 'the bastard'; and legends would develop around this, presenting William as the son of an elicit liaison between Duke Robert and the daughter of a simple tanner. We must put these to one side. The Old French *bâtard* did not designate a child born outside wedlock (a bastard in the modern sense), but rather the child of a *mésalliance* (an unequal union, typically between a nobleman and a woman of lower standing). In William's case, it just meant that his mother was the daughter of a tradesman or minor aristocrat (there are grounds to believe that her father was an undertaker).[2] Under normal circumstances, a bastard would not be first in line for inheritance. But such children could – and did – step into the breach.[3] This had happened in the case of Richard I in 942, without any lasting consequences for ducal power and authority; William was set to do the same. The bigger problem was William's age, much as it had been with Richard in 942. For at the time of Robert's death, William was no more than eight and perhaps as young as six. There had already been signs of instability in recent years; the accession of a child served to exacerbate these.

We should not underestimate the effects of acceding at such a tender age. William grew up in a world in which violence and betrayal were endemic. Friends proved fleeting, and even family members could not be counted upon. In the duke's earliest years, others ruled on William's behalf. But *c.*1040 two of these guardians were killed in a first wave of violence. The next two years saw much instability in the duchy, and only in 1042 are there signs that William was starting to emerge from the fray, with the reins of power firmly in his own hands. The Truce of God, a movement designed to limit aristocratic violence by having laymen swear to refrain from violent acts on certain days, was now instituted in the province with ducal support. The Truce was popular in northern France and the Low Countries, and its introduction was clearly a response to recent upheavals. Then c.1043 comes William's first recorded military activity, the capture of Falaise from Thurstan Goz, the viscount of Avranches. Falaise was an important ducal residence – it's where William himself had been born – and its retaking was symbolic of the court's new-found power and authority.[4]

Respite, however, proved brief. Only a few years later, a more serious rebellion was launched by William's cousin Guy of Brionne. Guy may have had designs of his own on the ducal throne, and his rebellion was a response to William's growing assertiveness. Despite some initial success, Guy and his associates were decisively defeated at Val-ès-Dunes outside Caen in 1047. Later Norman sources make much of William's prowess in this connection, but our earliest account assigns most of the credit to the French king Henry I, who rallied to William's aid. William had formally requested Henry's assistance as his feudal lord. And as Henry had little to gain from instability on his northern frontier, he was more than happy to provide it. The following years saw much further cooperation between duke and king.

It's at this point that many of William's closest friends and associates begin to appear in the sources. From the mid-1040s, for example, William fitz Osbern, Roger de Montgomery and Roger de Beaumont start to attest ducal charters, giving a flavour of the kind of political alliances William would cultivate in his mature years. And in 1049, his half-brother Odo was appointed bishop of Bayeux. Odo was the son of the Conqueror's mother Herleva with her second spouse, Herluin de Conteville (a further sign that Herleva was not the lowly tanner's daughter of later legend). Odo was at most in his late teens, and can scarcely have been prepared for the spiritual and pastoral duties of the post. But the move served to strengthen William's hand in the duchy's second city, in a region in which ducal authority had often been weak – and this is what mattered.

William was not the first Norman duke to exploit the Church in this manner. Richard I had appointed his younger son, Robert, to the archbishopric of Rouen in 989; and when Robert died in 1037, William's regents had appointed his uncle Malger (a son of Richard

II) to the post. William was now extending the policy to Bayeux in the western half of the duchy. This was the sort of politically motivated appointment that later reformers would reprove. But no complaints were raised at the time – or if they were, they were ignored. Odo himself went on to cut a distinctly secular figure within the Norman episcopate. He continued with his aristocratic lifestyle and would participate in William's conquest of England, including participating in the Battle of Hastings.

With internal politics settled for the time being, William was in a position to begin looking to relations with his neighbours. In 1049, he took part in Henry I's campaign against Count Geoffrey of Anjou. Two years later, Geoffrey retaliated in kind, securing the castles of Domfront and Alençon, which straddled the frontier and were held by the Bellême family (who had decided to throw their lot in with Geoffrey). William responded to the threat in person, laying siege to both castles. At the latter, the defenders are said to have taunted the duke by beating animal skins over the rampart and shouting 'pelterer' – an allusion to his humble origins. This was the start of the legend that Herleva had been born of a tanner. The original joke, however, was more subtle: as an undertaker (or embalmer), Herleva's father had dealt in (human) skins.[5] The point was not lost on William. And when he took the castle, he exacted a gruesome revenge: the hands and feet of thirty-two of the defenders hacked off in public sight. As soon as they caught wind of this, the defenders of Domfront were quick to submit. It was also in these years that William wed Matilda (c.1050), the daughter of Count Baldwin V of Flanders. This meant that the duke was now related by marriage to the counts of Flanders, the main supporters of the English king's foes, the Godwins.

Relations with England were of particular importance for the future. By the early 1050s, it was clear that Edward the Confessor would not have any children with his wife Edith. In response, Edward began to break with Edith's family, assisted by a number of Normans and Frenchmen who'd probably come over in his entourage in 1041, most notably Robert of Jumièges and Ralph of Mantes. Duke William must have been aware of these developments. Robert almost certainly passed through the duchy en route to and from the papal court in 1051 and may have taken the opportunity to raise the possibility of

William's succession to the English crown. It's in this connection that we should interpret William's visit to England in 1051, as reported in the D version of the *Anglo-Saxon Chronicle*. Some have suspected that the trip was a later invention, but the D text is a contemporary account for these years, and the entry was probably part of a larger (lost) West Midlands chronicle.[6]

If the early 1050s opened new possibilities across the Channel, soon more pressing matters claimed William's attention. By August 1052, King Henry of France had formed an alliance with the same Geoffrey of Anjou he'd fought against with William three years earlier. This was a troubling development, for the Norman duke and Angevin count were old enemies. Sensing weakness, William of Arques, a leading Norman viscount, now took the opportunity to rebel. William of Arques was the duke's uncle, a brother of Archbishop Malger of Rouen. He had been a staunch ally of the Conqueror in his early years, and the rebellion probably reflects frustration at the promotion of new favourites at court (men such as Roger de Montgomery). Whatever the precise grievance, Geoffrey was quick to rally to the viscount's cause. King Henry's motives are harder to divine, but probably relate to William's own growing stature and ambitions on England. As events would reveal, there was little to be gained for the king of France if one of his dukes were to secure the English throne.

In response, Duke William moved swiftly to besiege his uncle's castle at Arques, which had recently been constructed. Once there, he successfully beat off a relief force. The following year, Henry and Geoffrey returned in force, as part of a two-pronged attack. But Norman aristocrats put the second of the invading armies to flight at Mortemer, forcing the invaders to retreat once more.[7]

This was an important victory for Duke William. At Val-ès-Dunes, he'd only overcome the Norman rebels with King Henry's support. Now, seven years later, he'd seen off the combined might of the king of France and count of Anjou. This left William in a strong position to extend his power and influence over his neighbours. One of the first targets was Guy of Ponthieu, whose sphere of influence lay to William's east. Guy had fallen into William's hands during the campaign, and the duke was now able to secure Norman influence over the county of Ponthieu. William of Arques' lands were likewise redistributed amongst ducal supporters, while Archbishop Malger was removed from his post at Rouen and banished to Guernsey.

Three years later (in 1057), Geoffrey and Henry resurrected their alliance. Combining forces, they marched through the Hiémois and into the Bessin in western Normandy, perhaps aided by the local bishop of Sées, Ivo. Thereafter, they followed the Dives to the coast, where they turned east towards Lisieux and the Pays d'Auge. The invasion seems to have been a face-saving exercise. Henry and Geoffrey had been humiliated in 1054; now they sought revenge. Duke William, however, was too wily to take the bait. He shadowed the invading force closely, waiting for the moment to pounce. As Henry and Geoffrey crossed the Dives at Varaville, the opportunity presented itself. Tides rise fast among the marshes of Varaville and this served to distract the king and count as they crossed. Meanwhile, William attacked their stranded rear-guard. Already on the other side of the river, Geoffrey and Henry could only look on helplessly as a significant part of their force was slaughtered.[8]

Victory at Varaville proved decisive. Although the invading force had been smaller than that of 1054 – as Norman sources acknowledge – it was the second time in succession the duke had seen off the combined forces of his most powerful neighbours. The message was clear: Normandy was not for the taking, nor William for the beating. This would be the last hostile invasion of the duchy in his lifetime. In the coming years, William was left to secure his south-western frontier largely unopposed. He arranged for the marriage of the Bellême heiress Mabel – whose lands straddled the disputed regions of Normandy and Maine – to his close ally Roger de Montgomery. In the process, he also secured the support of Ivo of Sées, Mabel's brother. Since 1053, William had been kept occupied by domestic concerns. But now he could dare to dream.

~

With hindsight, the years between 1057 and 1066 look like the calm before the storm. Yet the impression is misleading. We may be ill-informed about William's actions, but all the signs are of feverish preparation. The primary concern was securing William's position to the south and west. In 1063, he arranged for the succession of his eldest son to Maine and the following year (or perhaps 1065) he led an expedition deep into Brittany. It's hard not to see these acts as a prelude to the dramatic events of 1066. The Confessor was now an old man – older than any reigning English king since Ecgberht in the early ninth century. It was just a matter of time before the throne was vacated.

In his mid-thirties and fresh from victories against the king of France and count of Anjou, William was at the height of his powers. In taking Maine and cowing Brittany, he set the scene for an extended absence. It is telling that, at this time, he chose to designate his eldest son, Robert, as his heir. It was customary for Norman dukes to designate their successors during their own lifetime. But this normally took place in their later years, often once they were ailing. An exception was if they had a particularly risky venture planned. William's own father had – fortuitously, as it transpired – designated William to succeed him before departing on pilgrimage to the Holy Land in 1035, from which he was never to return. That William should do the same for Robert in 1062 or 1063 – at a moment of severe illness, it should also be noted – is significant.[9] Risks lay ahead, and William was hedging his bets.

William's interest in the English crown may have been further stimulated by another event: the visit, probably in 1064, of Harold Godwinson to the ducal court. The precise grounds for this remain a mystery. Later Norman sources claim (rather implausibly) that Harold was sent by Edward to confirm earlier promises of William's succession. More likely is Eadmer of Canterbury's explanation of these events. According to him, Harold wanted to secure the release of his younger brother and nephew, who'd been sent to the ducal court as hostages in the early 1050s.[10]

Harold may have also hoped to make a pact of his own with William. In 1064, it was far from clear that the succession would come down to a two-horse race between Harold and William.[11] Harold must have been aware of William's ambitions. But a more immediate threat may have been presented by Harold's own brother, Tostig (the earl of Northumbria). Though Tostig was younger (and poorer) than Harold, he enjoyed the favour of the queen and was married to Judith of Flanders, whose brother Baldwin was regent for the infant King Phillip I of France. It was conceivable that William might choose to back Tostig rather than claiming the throne himself, a move one imagines Matilda would have happily encouraged.

But whatever Harold's plans, they went awry. His ship was blown off course. And upon landing, Harold was captured by Guy of Ponthieu, who only released him at Duke William's behest. This changed the power dynamic between Harold and William. Rather than arriving as an equal, the English earl was in William's debt from the start. In the coming weeks, Harold was taken on campaign to Brittany, probably as a show of strength, before William finally exacted a famous oath from him. Later Norman sources claim that Harold promised to support William's claim to the English throne, as Edward had always wanted. They probably protest too much. But it's clear that some sort of commitment was made, as Eadmer's later account, which is otherwise very sympathetic to the English plight, also mentions this. So too does the Bayeux Tapestry (a work of English craftsmanship, albeit for a Norman lord), which refers allusively to an oath (Latin: *sacramentum*) sworn by Harold in this connection. It may well be that this was an oath of fidelity, perhaps in connection with an act of homage – an interpretation supported by the fact that Harold receives arms from William in the preceding scene of the Tapestry (and also in the account of William of Poitiers), much as a vassal would in exchange for his fealty. If so, this was a sufficiently ambiguous act to allow room for interpretation on both sides, as was doubtless the intention. From William's perspective, Harold had become his man and now owed him absolute loyalty, if need be in support of his claim to the English throne. From Harold's, he'd acknowledged William's dominance without proffering any specific promises of future conduct.[12]

The year 1065 was a better one for Harold. After many years of unrest, the people of York rose up against his brother Tostig in October, providing the pretext for the latter's removal from office. Harold probably had mixed feelings, but he was able to make the most of the fallout, building an alliance with Edwin and Morcar, the sons of Earl Ælfgar of Mercia. Even better, the Confessor was now ailing. Harold was clearly the power behind the throne, deputising for

Edward in connection with the northern uprising. Slowly but surely, the obstacles were being cleared from Harold's path. The consecration of Edward's prize foundation at Westminster was brought forward to 28 December. But even so, the king was too ill to attend; and by 5 January, he was dead.

Harold's chances were very good. His main potential domestic rival had been expelled from the realm, and he'd just successfully deputised for the man he hoped to succeed. Harold was king in all but name. Best of all, Harold was present in London when Edward died. This meant he was able to press his advantage, ensuring that the succession took place on his terms and arranging for himself to be elected and crowned the very next day – perhaps in the same service that saw Edward's burial.[13]

The grounds for this indecent haste lay in the challenges Harold faced. Tostig may have retreated into Flemish exile, but he now angled for restitution (much as his father had in 1052), while Duke William and the Norwegian king Harald 'Hardrada' had their own ambitions regarding the crown. There were also threats closer to home, in the form of Edgar the Ætheling. Edgar may have lacked Harold's wealth and connections, but his dynastic credentials were second to none.

All indications are, therefore, that Harold's accession was rushed through in the hope of creating a *fait accompli*. He could ill afford to spend the next six months wrangling, so struck while the iron was hot. As the realm's leading statesman, Harold was in an excellent position to do this. In the aftermath of Tostig's fall, he'd supported the claims of Morcar to the Northumbrian earldom. Morcar was the younger son of Ælfgar, who'd long headed the anti-Godwin faction at court. By supporting Morcar's claim, Harold made the best of what might otherwise have been an awkward situation, using his brother's exile to secure the support of their traditional rivals. It may be in this connection that Harold married Edith, Ælfgar's sister, who'd previously been married to the Welsh king Gruffudd ap Llywelyn. When Harold came to press his claims in early 1066, there was thus no-one left to oppose him.

By the time of his death, the Confessor may have come to accept the inevitable. Most English sources agree that the king designated Harold his heir (or at least entrusted the realm to him). Had he lived a few years longer, Edward's chances of lining up Edgar as heir wouldn't have been bad. But with the threat of foreign invasion and Edgar only in his early teens (at most), a more experienced set of hands was always going to be preferred.

While Harold's succession may not have been a surprise, because it was a coup – and a brazen one at that – it raised serious questions about the new regime's legitimacy. For William, this provided the excuse he needed. Whatever the nature of Edward's earlier promises, William could now paint himself as the dead king's rightful heir, snubbed by the ambitious earl of Wessex. Winter was no time for campaigning, however, so William put diplomatic wheels in motion. An early move may have been to get in touch with the pope in Rome. William was well aware that a hostile takeover would prove controversial, so sought wherever possible to undermine the legitimacy of Harold's regime (and burnish that of his own). By securing papal support – symbolised by a banner, according to later sources[14] – William might help to lend his planned invasion the air of a holy war. This was a fight against a usurper and oath-breaker, an enemy of God and man.

William's case was helped by the fact that he'd been supportive of papal initiatives in Normandy in recent years. Since the early 1050s, popes had been making ever more strident calls for the reform of the Church, and William now positioned himself as a potential papal ally in England. Stigand's irregular position at the top of the English Church hierarchy was grist to William's mill here. The appointment had been roundly condemned by successive popes. Now William cast himself as a Christian Hercules, ready to cleanse England's Augean stables.

As spring came, preparations ramped up within the duchy. On 18 June, William had the new abbey church of La Trinité in Caen, the prize foundation of his wife Matilda (and sister church of Saint-Etienne), consecrated. The duke and duchess were aware of the dangers of the coming expedition, and this was a further attempt to court God's favour. Divine assistance would be as important as brawn (if not more so), if William were to prevail. In fact, Matilda and William gave their daughter Cecilia over to monastic life on this occasion. As the couple's eldest daughter, Cecilia would normally have been reserved for an advantageous dynastic marriage; William and Matilda were willing to forgo this in honour of La Trinité.[15] For a pious couple, these were not trifling matters.

In the spring and summer, William placed the government of Normandy in Matilda's hands, securing the support of his friends and allies Roger de Beaumont and Roger de Montgomery. He also toured the duchy and its neighbours, securing the frontiers. Particularly crucial was the support of Guy of Ponthieu and Eustace of Boulogne. Neither of these was in the habit of helping the duke. Guy had only recently been subdued by William, in 1052, and Eustace was an old enemy of the counts of Flanders (who were now William's relatives through Matilda), who'd recently backed his stepson Walter's rival claims to the county of Maine against those of the Conqueror's eldest son. Still, opposition had brought neither Guy nor Eustace any bene-fit to date, and the prospects awaiting them in England were too good to ignore. Supporting William was a win-win scenario. If the venture failed, it would serve to weaken a powerful neighbour; if it succeeded, Guy and Eustace would enjoy a share of the spoils.

Indeed, William's perambulation of Normandy and its neighbours was as much a recruiting drive as a defensive measure. The duke had need of a much larger army than usual, and many of his leading barons required persuasion to commit to this. Much of the final army also hailed from beyond the duchy, enticed by money and promises of rich rewards. By the summer, William had secured the support of noblemen from Flanders to Brittany. Just as pressing as the need for men was that for ships to ferry them over the Channel. Here an enigmatic text known as the Ship List bears essential testi-mony. This is a list of the ships owed to Duke William, added into a manuscript in the twelfth century. It suggests that the duke had upwards of 700 vessels (of varying size and quality) at his disposal – a mighty fleet, by the standards of the day.[16] There is every reason to believe the list is a faithful copy of an earlier document drawn up to assist in the muster.

Initially, the army gathered on the Dives, just north of Caen, in late spring 1066. Estimating the size of medieval forces is a hazardous business at the best of times, and here we are largely reliant upon Norman chroniclers of later years. Historians place William's army anywhere between 7,000 and 14,000 men, with the consensus lying nearer the lower end of this spectrum.[17] What's certain is that this was an unusually large force – one fit for a king. What drew so many men to William's banner? In part, it was his track record. The duke had twice seen off the king of France and count of Anjou in recent years; he'd also secured Maine and ravaged Brittany. Here was a man who could achieve anything, or so it seemed. Norman conquests elsewhere also played into William's hands. In the 1030s and 1040s, William's countrymen had been winning extensive territories – and even greater acclaim – in southern Italy. William was well aware of these ventures – indeed, William of Malmesbury reports that the duke was spurred on by a desire to match the exploits of his southern counterpart, Robert Guiscard.[18] From a recruiting standpoint, these conquests showed that William's venture might be risky, but was far from foolhardy. And if the stakes were high, the risks were worth it. England was one of western Europe's wealthiest kingdoms. It boasted an increasingly centralised government, capable of raising massive volumes of taxation.

It was one thing to raise an army; it was quite another to get it safely across the Channel. The summer months generally have the best weather, but William was unfortunate. He seems to have made an initial attempt to cross the Channel from the Dives, probably right after the dedication of La Trinité. However, unfavourable winds drove the fleet east, forcing it to relocate to Saint-Valéry-sur-Somme in Guy's county of Ponthieu.[19] This was fortuitous, for Saint-Valéry offered a number of advantages over the Dives. It possessed a large natural harbour and lay much closer to English shores. Already, William's earlier alliance-building was paying off.

The winds remained against William all through July and August, and well into September. Further efforts may, however, have been made to cross. The E version of the *Chronicle* reports a naval conflict, and a stray reference to the same event made its way into Little Domesday.[20] Still, most of the army lay holed up in Ponthieu. Keeping discipline through these months of inactivity must have been an immense challenge; so, too, would have been provisioning such a large force.[21] That William achieved this is nothing short of amazing – indeed, it was probably his greatest achievement of the year.

Harold knew of William's ambitions and made sure to keep a close eye on his southern coast. It was impossible to keep the mustering of such a fleet secret for long; and news soon reached English shores. Here Harold already had his hands full. His brother Tostig had appeared off the Isle of Wight in late April, then proceeded to ravage along the southern and eastern coasts, before seeking shelter at the court of the king of Scots. With Tostig's first foray over, Harold raised an army and fleet 'larger than any king had assembled before in this land', ready to meet William. This he stationed on Wight and along the southern coasts, where Tostig had made landfall earlier (and just opposite the site at which Edward had landed in 1041). Yet Harold had no more reckoned with the weather than had William. And as one month stretched into the next, provisions started running dangerously short. Eventually, on 8 September Harold was forced to disband the army, relocating the navy to London.

Yet scarcely had Harold returned to the Thames river metropolis than he heard troubling news from the North. Tostig had joined forces with the Norwegian king, Harald Hardrada, who held a residual claim to England as the would-be heir of Harthacnut. They had met at the Tyne, then proceeded to put Tostig's old enemies Edwin and Morcar to flight, occupying the Northumbrian capital of York. In response, Harold undertook one of the great feats of medieval logistics. He raised an army and marched north at breakneck speed, reaching the enemy force at Stamford Bridge in less than two weeks – a pace of over 25 miles (40 km) a day! Harold caught Harald and Tostig unawares – their troops apparently didn't even have time to don their armour – on 25 September and soon put them to flight. In the resulting slaughter, both Harald and Tostig fell.

But there was no time to rest for Harold and the English. For only two days after this stunning victory, the winds changed on the Channel, allowing the overnight passage of William and his men on 27–28 September. Ironically, the lengthy weather delay had played into the duke's hands. He now found himself largely unopposed. He landed at Pevensey, then headed east to Hastings, where Iron Age earthworks afforded an element of defence. Here William set up camp, ordering the construction of a Norman-style motte – a raised earthwork topped with a wooden fortification – to provide further protection. Then William ravaged the surrounding countryside. In part, this was a matter of necessity. William and his men could not have crossed with more than a few days' rations, so would have to live off the land. But it was also a shrewd tactic, designed to draw Harold into an engagement. Harold's father hailed from Sussex and William was laying torch to traditional Godwin family lands. It was already late in the campaigning season and the duke was keen to bring matters to a head. If winter came, it would favour Harold and the native English, for William could scarcely provision such a force in hostile territory across the lean months.

Fortunately for William, Harold took the bait. After riding south to London, he raised another army. Elements of this may have fought at Stamford Bridge, but the bulk must have been fresh forces, probably drawn from the army disbanded a month earlier. This army then headed south, setting up camp close to the modern town of Battle, about seven miles (12 km) north of William's army at Hastings. The scene was set for a show-down. Why Harold was willing to offer battle remains something of a puzzle. Battles were risky affairs at the best of times; and Harold could ill afford a loss. Perhaps the decision to strike at Harold's ancestral homelands riled the otherwise composed king. More likely, Harold was hoping to repeat his success at Stamford Bridge, catching William unawares. Either way, the mistake proved fatal.

Harold and William joined in battle on the morning of 14 October. As in earlier months, William was keen to secure divine assistance – and just as keen to be seen doing so. He therefore began the day by hearing Mass, then bore relics with him into battle – reportedly those on which Harold had sworn his oath two years previously. Whatever the reality of Harold's promises, this was a PR victory, which served to remind William's men that God was on their side.

Despite the many accounts of the battle, our knowledge of its details remains patchy. None of the surviving narratives were produced by a combatant; and the two most detailed, those in the poetic *Song of the Battle of Hastings* (or *Carmen*) of Guy of Amiens and the encomiastic prose *Deeds of William* of William of Poitiers, were written some time later for an audience at the Norman ducal court. What's clear, however, is that the forces were roughly evenly matched. Harold's army was arrayed on a hill, probably the raised ground running through the heart of the modern town of Battle. This placed them at a strategic advantage against William's mounted men, who might otherwise have had the best of things. There was, however, little else to distinguish the armies, tactically or technologically.[22] Where William may have had a slight edge was with his archers. On the Bayeux Tapestry, the Normans have considerably more of these than the English, while later sources claim (rather improbably) that the English knew nothing of archery. It may be that Harold's bowmen were still marching south from London when the armies joined battle, or that he'd struggled to recruit sufficient numbers in his haste. Archers are particularly effective against massed infantry; and, since Harold's best chance lay in defending the higher ground, this left them exposed. Still, it's unlikely that archery was the decisive factor in the battle. Thanks to their elevated position, the English were protected from the worst of the Norman bowmanship, at least initially.

William first sought to soften the English up with his archers. Then he moved his infantry forward to attack, but they made little headway against the tightly packed English shieldwall. William's cavalry fared little better when they joined the fray, and were soon forced to retreat in disarray. William of Poitiers suggests that the Bretons led the flight, but the *Carmen* places the blame (more plausibly) on the Normans. There now threatened to be an all-out rout. Rumours spread that William himself had fallen, and discipline began to disintegrate. In response, the duke famously lifted his helmet and addressed his men, rallying them to turn on the pursuing English, who now suffered significant losses of their own. In formation on top of the hill, the English lines were all but impregnable; dispersed across the plain, they were now easy pickings for the Norman knights. According to Poitiers, this became the cornerstone of Duke William's tactics. He and his cavalry twice more attacked the English on the ridge, then feigned retreat, before cutting their pursuers down on the slopes.

It was well into the afternoon and Harold's men were tiring. Their numbers depleted, they became increasingly isolated from one another and vulnerable. It was now that the Norman archers began making serious inroads. Still, as long as Harold lived, the long-term prospects of the English remained good. The Normans thus pressed on, going (quite literally) for the kill. The decisive moment came with Harold's death, at some point mid- to late afternoon. The circumstances remain shrouded in mystery. Our earliest source, the *Carmen*, has Harold cut down by a Norman 'death squad' led by Duke William, Eustace of Boulogne, Hugh of Ponthieu and Robert Gilfard. And one of the two possible death scenes on the Tapestry may depict this. But it is suspicious that such senior figures should be directly involved in Harold's demise, suspicions only deepened by the fact that Guy of Amiens (the poet) places his own brother Hugh among the group.[23] By the early 1080s, an alternative – perhaps more accurate – version of events was circulating. This is the famous tale of Harold meeting his fate with an arrow in the eye, the tale still taught in most British schools. The first to record this is Amatus of Montecassino, writing within the Norman domains of southern Italy *c*.1080. Amatus' text only survives in an early fourteenth-century French translation (and thus at one remove from the Latin original) and is often dismissed on this account. But the translation is quite accurate – the translator's main interventions take the form of occasional glosses and omissions. What he does include demands respect. And this death scene, too, seems to be depicted on the Tapestry, though the section in question has been subjected to restoration.[24]

In the end, the fact of Harold's death is more important than its manner. With the king dead, defeat became a rout – and here the Norman knights came into their own. Alongside Harold, two of his brothers fell, as well as a significant cross-section of the English aristocracy. Most importantly, the English army was prevented from regrouping. This was as decisive as victory could be in the Middle Ages. Little now stood between William and the crown he coveted.

6

Court Propaganda: The Case
for Conquest, 1066–84

It was with great satisfaction that William marched into London in December 1066, ready to be crowned and anointed king of the English. Since disaster at Hastings, the English army had all but vanished – and with it, English resistance. Still, the road to London had not been entirely smooth. After his victory, William had initially waited at Hastings, expecting the English to submit. Only when this didn't transpire, did he set about further ravaging the Home Counties and planning a march on the capital.

In London, rival plans were being made. Harold and his brothers may have fallen, but the earls Edwin and Morcar – who'd been mopping up in the North during the Hastings campaign – remained alive and well. Along with Archbishops Stigand and Ealdred, they now put forward Edgar the Ætheling as king. What Edgar lacked in age, he more than made up for in legitimacy. That some – perhaps many – anticipated Edgar going on to enjoy a long and fruitful reign is revealed by the actions of the monks of Peterborough, who'd recently lost their abbot. They now elected one of their own, a certain Brand, and sought the Ætheling's assent for the appointment, which the newly elected king readily gave (an act William would not forget).

Yet even if Edgar's prospects did not appear too bad at the time, there could have been no doubt that he faced an uphill fight. The English had just suffered a major defeat and remained on the back foot. What was needed was swift and decisive action. The wider William ravaged, the more the local English magnates started weighing up their options. Most would have preferred Edgar; but backing the wrong horse was a dangerous game, and pragmatism trumped idealism. Edgar's youth and inexperience did little to help the matter. There may also have been divisions within the English camp, for

William of Malmesbury reports that Edwin and Morcar had designs of their own on the throne.[1]

With the Conqueror edging ever closer, such divisions sealed England's fate. Only William offered realistic prospects of stability – a stability for which many yearned. Once William crossed the Thames at Wallingford and encircled London, most of the English agreed to submit at Berkhamsted in Hertfordshire.[2] This was not quite a 'national' submission, for the simple reason that the English lacked clear leadership. But it included almost all of those who'd backed Edgar in the intervening weeks: Edwin and Morcar; Archbishop Ealdred of York; Bishops Wulfstan of Worcester and Walter of Hereford; the men of London; and Edgar himself. Resistance would rumble on in some regions. But the heart of the realm was now William's.

One significant absence is worth registering: Archbishop Stigand. Stigand had been appointed following the flight of Robert of Jumièges in 1052. At the time, this represented a major victory for the Godwin clan. However, it created an almighty uproar in Rome. It was against Church regulations to remove a bishop from his post without papal approval and due procedure. King Edward was hardly going to go out of his way to help the man who'd replaced his dear friend. And so the situation remained unresolved at the time of Edward's death in 1066, with Stigand *de facto* archbishop, still unacknowledged by the pope. The English were well aware of the problems. And this lingering stain is presumably why Harold chose to be consecrated by Ealdred of York.[3] Typically, it would have been the archbishop of Canterbury who anointed a new ruler. But a new king, whose own dynastic credentials were open to question, could ill afford to take a risk here.

Mindful of these blemishes, Stigand had submitted to William a few weeks earlier at Wallingford. But William was not one to be fooled. He knew full well the nature of the archbishop's appointment; he also knew that Stigand had been Harold's creature. William's supporters were probably already spreading rumours that Stigand – and not the unimpeachable Ealdred – had overseen Harold's coronation. Here was one usurper, illegally anointed by another. This is the version of events recorded *c.*1070 by the Conqueror's chaplain,

William of Poitiers, and it almost certainly goes back to the duke's own attempts to secure papal support in early 1066. By associating Harold's accession with this earlier act of usurpation, William and his sympathisers ensured a sympathetic hearing in Rome. They presented Alexander II with a simple solution to a thorny problem: Duke William should replace Harold and bring order to the English Church.[4]

As such rhetorical gymnastics reveal, William's central problem after Hastings was how to present an opportunistic land-grab as an act of rightful succession. And if Stigand's appointment offered part of the solution, another was presented by the Confessor's prior promises. Again, William of Poitiers offers the most direct insights into thinking at and around the ducal court. He reports that in 1051/2 Edward held an important assembly, at which the king promised the throne to William *in absentia*, then made all the leading English magnates swear oaths to uphold the duke's rights. We have no evidence of earlier English kings designating heirs in this fashion. And indeed, the details of the ceremony conform suspiciously to the practices of Norman ducal succession, as recorded by Dudo of Saint-Quentin and William of Jumièges. But what matters is less the deception than that such deception was deemed necessary. Both before and after Hastings, William and his advisers worked hard to justify the Conquest.[5]

In case the point might be missed, William of Poitiers – never knowingly subtle – returns to the subject of Edward's promises in the context of Harold's visit to William *c.*1064. According to his version of events, the English king wanted to strengthen his earlier commitments by binding Harold to them. He therefore sent the earl of Wessex to Normandy to swear a solemn oath to uphold William's right to the kingdom.[6] Again, what matters is less the inaccuracy of the tale – Edward was in no position to be ordering Harold around in the 1060s – than that it was spread around at all. For a duke seeking to raise an army, such stories were a powerful recruiting tool. Harold became an anti-king, an inversion of all that was right and proper. Those who helped replace him could therefore expect to benefit not only in the here and now, but also in the hereafter. For any doubters within the Norman camp, victory at Hastings proved once and for all that God was indeed on William's side.

Further insights into William's claims emerge from the so-called Penitential Ordinance, issued upon his return to Normandy in 1067. This was composed by the local Norman bishops and promulgated with the approval of the papal legate (i.e. representative) Ermenfrid of Sion. The text details the penances due from those who'd served William in England. It does not exonerate them entirely from guilt – killing was a sin, even in a just cause – and we remain a few steps away from the kind of thinking that would inspire the First Crusade a few decades later. Nevertheless, there can be no doubt as to the fundamental justice of William's cause. All those who served the duke in good faith are offered reduced penances for killing; and only those who acted out of avarice, or committed violence after William's consecration on Christmas Day 1066, are to be treated as run-of-the-mill murderers. This is a powerful affirmation of papal support for the Conquest. It is also significant that the period of just war is conceived as lasting from Harold's usurpation in January 1066 to William's consecration at the end of the year. Between these dates, the English were effectively in revolt against their rightful lord (i.e. William) and thus fair game.[7]

As the Penitential Ordinance reveals, the need to justify William's claim did not pass with the Conquest. If anything, it became more pressing. As Cnut had discovered, it was one thing to win a realm; it was another to hold onto it. A first step was to place loyal men in positions of power and influence. But lasting rule rested on legitimacy; and here there was much work to be done. It's no coincidence that William of Poitiers wrote his history in these years, furnishing something close to an 'official' version of events. It was also around this time that William of Jumièges updated his imposing *History of the Dukes of Normandy* in the light of the Conqueror's stunning successes.

The most important and enduring records of William's efforts to legitimise his new regime come from England, however. The first of these is a document (or writ) issued for the people of London, shortly after William's coronation. This assures the citizens of their rights and commits to upholding the laws of the realm as they were 'in King Edward's day'. This may all seem rather unspectacular. Cnut had committed to upholding the laws of Edgar in 1018, and the Confessor himself had promised to maintain Cnut's laws when he landed in

1041. Now William was simply doing the same. Yet what's significant here is the omission of Harold. The implication, soon to be articulated more fully, is that Harold was never a true king, and that William succeeded directly from Edward.[8]

But try as William might, Harold remained the elephant in the room. Everyone knew Harold had been king; and in the eyes of most, he'd been a perfectly legitimate one. If there was a usurper, it was William. Yet it was precisely this disjunction between political reality and legal theory that led William and his supporters to assert their case so stridently. Harold may have been king for the better part of a year, but there was now a concerted effort to ignore this. Harold is almost never mentioned in William's official documents; and only under exceptional circumstances are his acts confirmed. Indeed, of all the many hundreds of documents Harold must have issued, only one survives: a writ for the Francophone (Lotharingian) Bishop Giso of Wells, who went on to enjoy the Conqueror's favour.[9] For churches seeking to secure their rights in the years after 1066, charters in Harold's name were worse than useless – they were actively detrimental.

The greatest monument to William's claims, however, is the Domesday Survey: a massive compendium of information about the king's new realm, drawn up swiftly between Christmas 1085 and 1086. As those who have dipped into its pages will know, the survey is anything but a riveting read. Often simply called 'Domesday Book', it actually compromises two separate volumes: Little Domesday, covering Norfolk, Suffolk and Essex; and the larger Great Domesday for the rest of England south of the Tees. The two are clearly companion pieces; and one scribe has been responsible for the entire text, which runs to over 2 million words, across 832 large manuscript pages or folios, each covered on both sides in a small but clearly legible hand. Since the conversion of the English in the late sixth century, only bibles had ever been produced on this scale – and then rarely. In part, the survey's size was a necessity if the material was all to be included. But it's also clear that Great Domesday was meant to impress.[10] And impress it did. In later years, it was known as 'the great book'. And eventually, it became 'the book of the Day of Judgement' – or Domesday Book, for short.

A typical Domesday entry lists the estates held by a particular lord in a given region 'at the time of King William' (i.e. in 1086; *tempore regis Willhelmi*, given as 'TRW' for short), typically grouped and listed within the region by who held them at the time of Edward's death (i.e. on 5 January 1066, or 'TRE' – *tempore regis Edwardi*). To take a random example, royal holdings in Tiverton in Devon (where the king was the main landholder), read as follows (listed under the lands once held by Countess Gytha, Harold Godwinson's mother): 'TIVERTON. TRE paid geld for 3.5 hides. There is land for 36 ploughs. There are 35 villeins and 24 bordars and 19 slaves with 30 ploughs. There are 3 swineherds paying 10 pigs. There are 2 mills paying 66d.'[11] Read at any length, the survey soon becomes an insomniac's dream remedy. But behind such dry, dusty figures lie fascinating insights into local life and society. In Tiverton's case, it reveals a bustling town of local significance, with two mills and a population in the hundreds. Such records have much to tell us about pre-Conquest England, the nature of William's regime and the transformations between 1066 and 1086. William's motives in commissioning the survey remain a matter of debate, but a deep concern for landholding, lordship and dues owed to the king is clear throughout.[12] Together, Little and Great Domesday furnish the most comprehensive surviving survey of any pre-industrial society – a veritable treasure trove for the modern historian.

From our standpoint, the survey's interest lies in its presentation of the Conquest. Though the actual process of conquest and colonisation is never described in any detail, it pervades the material. In the majority of cases, the holder TRW was not the same as that TRE – hence the need for the survey. And even where this was so, as in the case of many royal and ecclesiastical estates, the caesura of Conquest is clear. Yet as with William's other official documents, the Domesday Survey carefully avoids acknowledging the reality of Harold's reign or the events of the Conquest, maintaining the pretence that William directly succeeded Edward. For example, when touching on two estates of Regenbald, who served Edward, Harold and William successively (perhaps as chancellor), Great Domesday comments elliptically that 'two men held [these] as two manors in the time of King Edward; Earl Harold joined them into one.' Clearly it was

Harold who, as king, united the estates and granted them to Regenbald. But the unwitting reader would be forgiven for thinking that Harold simply acted as earl of Wessex.[13] Only occasionally does Homer nod: in over 1,600 sides of meticulously copied text, just twice does our scribe acknowledge the reality of Harold's reign (and even then, Harold is called usurper).

The most fundamental effort to write Harold out, however, is reflected in the survey's framing. The points of reference throughout are Edward's death and the present (TRE and TRW), creating the impression that William's reign began when Edward's ended. It was not simply William's claim to the throne which was at stake here. The premise for confiscating the lands of the English was that they had been oath-breakers – they'd treasonously accepted Harold as king over William. This is why William of Poitiers is so insistent that the English consented to Edward's offer of the succession to William in 1051/2; it's also why the Penitential Ordinance treated them as rebels up to the point of William's coronation.

If from the vantage point of almost a millennium the tendentious nature of William's claims is clear, it must have been even more so at the time. The point, however, was not to persuade, but to assert. And once asserted firmly enough, political lies slowly became legal fact. Long before the advent of modern propaganda, William understood that if you're going to tell a lie, you might as well tell a big one. The problem was, once you started embroidering history, you were unlikely to stop.

7

The Bayeux Tapestry:
Embroidered History, 1066–97

Visit Bayeux in the height of summer, and you'll be confronted by crowds. The town may be home to only 14,000 people, but it receives that number of visitors many times over each summer. Some come for the well-preserved Gothic cathedral, others for the Museum of the Battle of Normandy. But the biggest draw is to be found in a dimly lit but well apportioned room in the Musée de la Tapisserie, in the heart of the town. Here the crowds are thick and you're advised to arrive early. Pay your entrance, join the growing queue, and soon enough, you'll be confronted by a treasure far greater than any manuscript, war memorial or cathedral.

This is, of course, the Bayeux Tapestry. Despite its modern designation, the Tapestry is an embroidery, produced in the final third of the eleventh century to commemorate the dramatic events of 1066. By far the most iconic monument to the Conquest, it adorns objects from ties to greeting cards the world over. It's also the medium through which thousands of school children learn about William and the Norman Conquest every year, in Britain and beyond. Consciously or not, the Tapestry frames the way we all think about these events. It has, therefore, attracted the interest of hundreds of scholars, from dyed-in-the-wool historians to literary critics and art historians. Scarcely a year passes without a new interpretation being offered.

Yet for all its fame, we know remarkably little about the Tapestry's early history. Our first record of its existence comes from an inventory of 1476 from Bayeux. At this point, the Tapestry was being displayed annually at the cathedral for eight days (the octave) before the Feast of the Relics (5 November), a tradition alive as late as 1728. Thereafter, the Tapestry led a rather chequered existence. It narrowly escaped destruction during the French Revolution and was almost carted off to Berlin by the Nazis in the Second World War. Thankfully, it emerged from these scrapes (largely) unscathed, finding its present home at the Musée de la Tapisserie in 1983, where it has welcomed over 14 million visitors.[1]

Tapestries and embroideries were extremely popular in medieval Europe. They adorned the walls of castles and noble residences, commemorating past feats and inspiring future ones. Yet in scale and ambition, the Tapestry exceeds all other surviving textiles of the era. In its present form, it stretches to an imposing 68 m (or 224 feet). And since a number of scenes have been lost towards the end, it must once have exceeded this. Given the scale of the enterprise, it's scarcely surprising that those responsible chose to produce it as an embroidery rather than a woven tapestry. Embroideries are sewn directly onto a background, making them much quicker to produce, if no less elegant in the right hands.

Our knowledge of the Tapestry is fragmentary, much like the textile itself. Part of the problem is that we know so little about its early history. It was almost certainly produced in England but has been in Bayeux more or less continually since 1476. And the presumption is that it arrived there probably early in the reign of the Conqueror (and certainly before the loss of Normandy by King John in 1204). There are many conceivable routes by which the Tapestry may have been passed to the cathedral, but by far the most likely intermediary is Bishop Odo, the Conqueror's half-brother and close associate.

The key evidence for Odo's involvement comes from the Tapestry itself. Its artwork reveals close associations with manuscript illumination from Canterbury; and the most likely place of production (or at least artistic inspiration) is the abbey of St Augustine there.[2] We are thus dealing with an artwork produced within Odo's Kentish earldom, celebrating the Conquest, and preserved at his cathedral. Recent work suggests that the tapestry's original dimensions would have fitted perfectly into the nave of the new eleventh-century cathedral church at Bayeux, just behind the choir screen.[3] It was probably designed for display there, by someone who knew the dimensions of the cathedral well. We know that Odo enjoyed good relations with the monks of St Augustine's – unlike the neighbouring cathedral canons of Christ Church, with whom he repeatedly locked horns – making his patronage all but certain.

Just as significant is the narrative presented within the Tapestry. Odo is far more prominent here than in any other account of the Conquest. Only the Tapestry presents Odo playing a leading part in preparations for the invasion, and it's also unique in having Harold swear his oath to Duke William at Bayeux (other sources place this at Bonneville-sur-Touques or Rouen). The Tapestry is likewise alone in depicting Odo's involvement at the Battle of Hastings, where he helps steady the ranks at the decisive moment when the first Norman cavalry charge is repulsed. And if that weren't enough, three of Odo's tenants are mentioned by name in the text: Turold, Wadard and Vitalis. Besides the mysterious Ælfgyva (Ælfgifu), these are the only minor figures to be named.[4]

The production of the Tapestry must post-date the Battle of Hastings and presumably precedes 1082, the year Odo would be politically disgraced. Given the likelihood that it was designed for display at Bayeux, it was probably produced shortly before or after the consecration of the new cathedral there in 1077. This period falls conveniently within the abbacy of Scotland (1072–87) at St Augustine's in Canterbury, the first Norman abbot of the abbey. Scotland had previously been a monk at Mont-Saint-Michel, a monastery with its own proud tradition of artwork and manuscript illumination, and has long been identified as the probable artistic vision behind the composition.[5]

In many respects, the Tapestry is an encomiastic account of the Conquest, a propaganda piece which compares well with the narratives of Guy of Amiens and (in particular) William of Poitiers. It's clearly designed to celebrate the events it depicts, opening with Harold's Norman expedition of c.1064 and closing (probably) with William's coronation on Christmas Day 1066. At a number of junctures, it takes the 'Norman' line on events, presenting Harold early on swearing a solemn oath to William (at Bayeux!) and having the controversial Stigand preside over Harold's later coronation. Other details also speak of Norman sympathies. William is presented in exalted terms throughout; and the depiction of the duke's efforts to stem the flight of his cavalry, lifting his helm and addressing his men, closely recalls the accounts of William's Norman panegyrists.

At other points, however, the Tapestry reveals more 'English' sympathies. William may be the star of the show, but the focus is largely on Harold, at least in the extant sections: the Tapestry opens with the earl's expedition to Normandy and then follows Harold back to Edward's side, only returning to Normandy after Harold's accession. And Harold himself is depicted with a sympathy entirely out of step with our other Norman narratives. On the Breton campaign, he heroically saves one of William's men, earning knight-hood at the duke's hands – details recorded by neither William of Poitiers nor William of Jumièges. More significantly, the artists and designer leave no doubt that Harold was a *bona fide* king. In his final hours, Edward is presented conferring with his wife and leading men, then reaching out and touching Harold's hand in what is apparently an act of designation. This closely recalls the account in the *Life* of Edward the Confessor, commissioned by Queen Edith (Harold's sister) and completed in the years following the Conquest. (So closely, in fact, that it may rely on this.) And while Stigand's presence at the ensuing coronation may subtly undercut this act, Harold is accorded the full royal title (Latin: *rex*) throughout.

In fact, what impresses most about the Tapestry is its studied ambiguity. In part, this is a function of its form. As a visual depiction, only furnished with minimal narrative gloss, it is open to interpretation. Take Harold's famous oath. Viewers acquainted with the tales spun at the ducal court would swiftly see this as confirmation of the Norman version of events: here Harold promises William the English throne. Yet the Tapestry does not actually say this, and the accompanying text simply states that 'Harold made an oath' (but concerning what?). The Tapestry thus looks both ways. This can also be seen in the scene of Edward's death and Harold's consecration. A Norman audience would have been quick to read this as a *coup* on Harold's part, the terrible consequences of which are soon presaged by the appearance of Haley's Comet.[6] Yet an English audience might simply see Edward's designation of Harold and the latter's ill-fated (but entirely lawful) accession.

Of all the accounts of 1066, the Tapestry is probably the most important – and certainly the most compelling. Precisely because of its visual form, it furnishes details that no written narrative can. Thanks to it, we know of the English custom of sporting long moustaches and the Norman preference for shaving the lower part of the hair, immediately above the neck. The Tapestry also furnishes precious evidence for the early Romanesque abbey at Westminster. The most famous (and controversial) scene of all is that of Harold's death. The difficulty here is that two figures are shown at the decisive moment: first, a man standing, clutching what seems to be an arrow in his eye; and second, a man who's in the midst of being cut down by a mounted horseman. Above the first is written the name 'Harold', while above the second are the words 'was killed' (Latin: *interfectus est*). Normally, we might expect other sources to come to our aid here. But they, too, are divided on the nature of Harold's death. The earliest account (that in the *Carmen*) has him cut down by a group of William's leading magnates, led by the duke himself. The next to provide any detail, Amatus of Montecassino (*c.*1080), has the famous arrow-in-the-eye story. To make matters worse, this section of the Tapestry has been heavily restored. It's conceivable that the first figure originally had a spear or javelin in his eye (rather than an arrow) – but if so, it's hard to explain why so many early written sources report an arrow.

A popular solution has been to accept and combine both reports. Harold was *first* struck by an arrow in the eye, *then* cut down by a cavalry charge led by the duke. Yet no written source reports a twofold death scene, and there are grounds to doubt that this is what the Tapestry's designers had in mind either. To start with the obvious, the two dying figures are depicted very differently. The falling man's socks are of a different colour from those of the figure with an arrow to the eye; and the former bears a shield and spear, while the latter has just dropped an axe. Unless we are to imagine a mid-death wardrobe and weapon change, it's hard to believe that these are indeed meant to be the same man. Which of the two is Harold is, of course, the million-pound question. While certainty is impossible, there remains a strong case in favour of the man with the arrow in his eye. It is his head which interrupts the name Harold in the text; and it is he whose fate mirrors that reported in the largest number of early sources, including Baudri of Bourgueil, who was writing for William's own daughter Adela.[7]

The search for a single solution may, in any case, be misguided. Medieval battles were chaotic affairs and few of those present at Hastings would have had any idea what was going on outside their immediate field of vision. It's entirely possible no-one knew who'd been responsible for Harold's death or how it had transpired.[8] Yet because this was the decisive moment of the battle, competing tales soon emerged to fill this gap.

If the Tapestry has much to tell us about the events of 1066, it has even more to say about the career and ambitions of Odo, its patron. As noted, Odo was William's half-brother, probably the first child born of Herleva's marriage to Herluin, the viscount of Conteville. It's clear that Herluin and Herleva were figures of independent means; and throughout his reign, William drew readily on the support they and their children (his half-siblings) proffered. An early vote of confidence was the appointment of Odo to the strategic see of Bayeux in 1049, and Odo remained one of William's most trusted supporters over the next three decades.

As his early elevation to episcopal dignity revealed, Odo was not a world-shy prelate. He was a courtier bishop, a man equally comfortable in secular and ecclesiastical circles. This is not to say that Odo was not pious after a fashion: he donated generously to the Church and oversaw an impressive building programme at Bayeux. But he combined religious and secular duties in a manner later reformers would find troubling. For William, this was a boon. Odo had been appointed to help secure ducal authority in the Bessin; from the start, it was his job to be active beyond the cathedral cloisters.

We know little of Odo's early activities, but all indications are that he performed them well. Orderic Vitalis reports that he and Guy of Ponthieu were the commanders during the conquest of Le Talou, Bray and the Pays de Caux in 1054.[9] And Odo starts coming into sharper focus during the Hastings campaign. The Tapestry may exaggerate his role here, but other sources confirm that he played an important part. Ducal charters place Odo in regular attendance on William during the spring and summer of 1066, often alongside his younger brother Robert of Mortain.[10] And the list of the ships supplied to William at this point records that Robert and Odo furnished 120 and 100 vessels respectively – more than any other

Norman magnate. (By comparison, Roger de Montgomery and Roger de Beaumont – two of William's longest-standing allies – only provided sixty each.)[11]

Odo was one of two Norman bishops to march with the army, the other being Geoffrey of Coutances. Together, they were William's spiritual advisers during the campaign. The Tapestry presents Odo blessing the first meal the army enjoyed upon arrival in England. And William of Poitiers famously reports that Odo and Geoffrey jointly celebrated Mass on the morning of the fateful battle. Whether Odo's involvement extended beyond the spiritual sphere is less clear, however. The Tapestry presents Odo alongside William steadying the ranks, when the first cavalry charge wavered. And it's often been suggested that he wields a mace here in order to circumvent Church restrictions on clerical combat and bloodshed. Yet the Tapestry is careful not to depict Odo as part of the mêlée and he's simply said to have 'comforted the lads' in the accompanying text – an act of encouragement, not of combat. Moreover, the object Odo brandishes is not a mace but a staff (or at least so the text claims), the traditional symbol of episcopal authority. But if Odo is not in the midst of the fray, he certainly is wearing armour and a helmet – indeed, he has to be labelled here because we cannot see his distinctive tonsure. And there may well be an element of studied ambiguity, since the same type of staff (or perhaps mace, after all?) is also wielded by Duke William at points in the battle. These were not the bishop's first military manoeuvres, nor would they be his last.[12]

Following the Conquest, Odo was generously rewarded for his service. In the Domesday Survey, he is England's wealthiest magnate after William. And as earl of Kent he controlled the strategic castle of Dover, overlooking the sea passage to Boulogne, the home of the restless Count Eustace.[13] The D version of the *Chronicle* presents Odo as one of William's *de facto* regents in 1067, when the duke returned to Normandy.

Like his elder half-brother, Odo directed much of the wealth won in England back to his Norman homeland. He probably embarked on his ambitious building project at Bayeux before departure; but it's only in the years following 1066 that the new cathedral began to take shape. Relations with William remained strong; and in the summer of 1080, Odo led a force to ravage the region between Tees and Tyne on the king's behalf.

Such evidence of continuing cooperation makes Odo's sudden downfall in 1082 all the more surprising. In this year, the bishop is said to have been deposed from his earldom in Kent, deprived of his English lands and imprisoned at the ducal capital of Rouen. Odo's betrayal apparently lay in syphoning off men from William's service, in order to pursue his own ambitions on the papal throne. It's difficult to credit these reports. But the sources nearest the events all agree. And the only alternative explanation, offered by Guibert of Nogent, is even less credible: Guibert has Odo deposed for seeking to deprive William himself of the crown.[14] What connects all these reports, however, is that they have Odo brought down by his own pride.

Like William, Odo was an unusually ambitious man, willing to risk everything for fame and fortune. Odo was well aware that his countrymen had been making inroads into southern Italy in recent years, and he may have hoped to find support for his prospective papacy from these circles. More to the point, there were worrying signs for him in England. By 1082, William was an old man and factions were beginning to form around his sons. Odo was a partisan of the eldest of these, Robert Curthose. But Robert was only to be William's successor to Normandy, a situation which risked depriving Odo of rich lands and offices in England. Just the previous year (1081), Matilda had deputised for William in England, a role previously performed by Odo. Add to this Odo's strained relations with the reform-minded archbishop of Canterbury, Lanfranc, and the writing was very much on the wall.

Odo would spend the next five years in prison. Only on his deathbed would William release his half-brother, restoring him to his former position of dignity. But Odo was now a man with few friends. The following year, he threw in his lot with the rebels against William Rufus, who'd succeeded to the Conqueror's English domains. The plan was to replace Rufus with his elder brother Curthose. But the rebellion was a failure, and Odo soon skulked back to Bayeux a much diminished man. Still, he was not an entirely spent force. When the First Crusade was announced a few years later (1096), Odo took up the cross with Duke Robert, enticed by new prospects of plunder and conquest. By this point, however, Odo was in his sixties, and the journey took its toll. While wintering with his Norman kinsmen in Sicily, he died in early 1097, without having reached the Holy Land. An adventurer to the last, he found his final rest in the cathedral of Palermo.

Contemporary opinion on Odo was divided. Until 1082, his loyalty had been unswerving, and his acumen and generosity were the stuff of legend. But he forgot the old proverb: pride comes before the fall. He was not, however, alone in rebelling against his brother. In the years following 1066, the English would rebel, repeatedly, against their new monarch.

8

The Fate of the English: Conquest
to Colonisation, 1066–84

In the spring of 1068, William received troubling tidings. Edwin and Morcar, the only English earls to have survived the Conquest unscathed, had raised the flag of rebellion in the West Midlands and in the North. The local population flocked to their cause and they were soon joined by the rulers of Gwynedd (in northern Wales) and Scotland. There were also rumours of a Danish invasion. All of William's enemies were converging, and even Edgar the Ætheling may have briefly joined their ranks.

William responded with his typical steely determinism, marching straight to Warwick as soon as he got wind of the insurrection. His speed caught the rebels unprepared, preventing them from linking up with their Welsh allies. Having won a first victory, William proceeded to build a castle – a gesture as symbolic as it was strategic. The tide was already beginning to turn. By this point – if not before – Edgar the Ætheling had gone into exile at the court of Malcolm III in Scotland. Outmanoeuvred, the earls Edwin and Morcar now sought terms. As in 1066, they submitted to the king in return for pardon. William himself headed north, securing further rebel lands and building castles at Nottingham and York. On his way back south, he did the same at Lincoln, Cambridge and Huntingdon. Slowly but surely, the castle was becoming *the* symbol of Norman lordship – and the key to controlling the new colony. For castles could be held by a handful of trained men, enabling the small Norman elite to dominate a much larger English population with relative ease.

The Conqueror had seen off the threat, but only just. Had he waited any longer; had Edwin and Morcar met up with their Welsh allies; had the Danish fleet arrived sooner, the result might have been very different. William's conquest still hung by a thread. As he was discovering, land won by the sword can just as easily be lost by it.

~

That William's regime was far from secure in these early years is revealed by the handling of Edgar and the other leading English magnates. These men had submitted at Berkhamsted in December 1066. The following spring, William took them with him *en masse*, when he returned to Normandy. The fear was that the English would not stick by William's side with a throne-worthy candidate on the loose – fears that soon proved well founded. The real surprise, in fact, is not that William kept Edgar, Edwin and Morcar under lock and key, but that he let them live at all. When Cnut had conquered England, he swiftly despatched the remaining son of Æthelred who'd tarried there (Eadwig the Ætheling); he did likewise with a number of leading English magnates. The Norman duke now took a very different tack.

That William did so reflects developing ideas about chivalry in mainland Europe. In pre-Conquest England – as in much of early medieval Europe – it was the norm to slaughter or enslave rebels and opponents captured in battle. By the mid-eleventh century, however, conventions had begun to change on the continent. Noblemen there now preferred to spare and ransom each other in battle (though such courtesies were not extended to non-aristocratic combatants).[1] From this perspective, it would have been deeply dishonourable for William to kill Edgar in cold blood. It also wouldn't have done much to help his cause. William may have promised his men riches in England, but he had to work with the local powers, at least initially. The nature of William's claims further militated against executing Edgar. Unlike Cnut, William had cast himself as the rightful heir to his English predecessor, Edward; to execute Edgar risked acknowledging that the emperor had no clothes. Contemporaries were well aware that William was breaking with tradition, and his panegyrist William of Poitiers underlines William's contrasting this clemency with Cnut's brutality.[2]

If William, initially, succeeded in neutralising Edgar's threat, he was not able to stifle opposition closer to home. Shortly after his departure, Eustace of Boulogne seized the opportunity to strike at Dover on the Kentish coast. Eustace was not Norman and had enjoyed mixed relations with William to date. He'd played a major part in the Hastings campaign, earning praise from Guy of Amiens in this connection; and it may be that he was disappointed by the rewards on offer. It's also conceivable that Eustace was eyeing up his own prospects of acquiring the throne. (As the second husband of Godgifu, the Confessor's sister, he held at least as strong a dynastic claim as the Conqueror.) But whatever the grounds, Eustace's venture failed thanks to the stiff opposition offered by Odo of Bayeux (the new earl of Kent), and he was stripped of his rights in England. By 1071, however, he was back fighting at William's side, and he was one of the wealthiest magnates in England come the Domesday Survey.[3]

A greater threat soon emerged among the English. Towards the end of 1067, a rebellion began to foment in the West Country. Harold's mother Gytha was a wealthy landholder in Exeter, the most important town south and west of Winchester. In William's absence, she and her associates began advocating the succession of Harold's sons, who'd gone into exile in Ireland, just a short boat ride away from the north Devon coast. This was a threat William couldn't ignore. The moment he got wind of the growing insurrection, he took to the campaign trail, risking a Channel crossing and military operations in the heart of winter.

William was already back in England in early December and soon moved against Exeter. Gytha was, however, able to escape as the siege commenced. William now sought to cow the city into submission, ravaging the surrounding countryside and blinding an English hostage within sight of the walls. But Exeter was a hard nut to crack and the siege dragged on for another three weeks. When the town finally submitted, it did so conditionally.[4] The people of Exeter agreed to swear loyalty to William on the agreement that taxes and dues would remain at pre-Conquest levels. That the townsfolk were able to dictate terms reveals how precarious William's position still was. With Gytha on the loose and the return of Harold's sons on the cards, William could ill afford to offend the main city (and key fortress) of the south west. This rapprochement between ruler and town found expression in a charter of the following year for the bishopric of Exeter. At a glance, this looks almost identical to one of the Confessor's diplomas, as indeed was the intention; here William is every inch Edward's heir. Yet beneath such apparent continuity lie important differences: the royal entourage is now largely Norman, with Odo appearing above any of the native English bishops in the witness list and Robert of Mortain attesting first among the earls. As in Domesday Book, this is change dressed up as stasis.[5]

William may have given ground, but this was an important strategic victory. He'd secured the support of Exeter; and from here, he might hope to extend control over the rest of the south west. To speed up the process, he began work on a castle within the old town walls. Thereafter, William marched into Cornwall – a demonstrative show of strength in a region unaccustomed to royal visits – before returning to Winchester to celebrate Easter. Then William proceeded to London for Pentecost (Whitsun), where his wife Matilda was formally crowned queen.

The threat to his rule, however, had not passed. The summer months saw an attempted landing by Harold's sons, who travelled up the Severn Estuary to Bristol. After being repulsed by the townsfolk there, they proceeded to harry the north Somerset coast before being decisively defeated by Eadnoth the Staller, one of a small but significant number of English aristocrats who'd thrown in their lot with the new regime.[6]

Still, the new Norman overlords could do little to paper over the reality of conquest. And trouble was also brewing in the Midlands and North where, as we've seen, Edwin and Morcar soon found a warm reception. The problem for William was that he couldn't keep Edgar the Ætheling and the leading English magnates under lock and key forever. Yet almost as soon as they were left to their own devices, they began fomenting discord. The ringleaders were the brothers Edwin and Morcar. Neither had taken kindly to the enforced Norman jolly of the previous year. More immediate grounds for grievance were the appointment of a host of new Norman earls and sheriffs within their old domains. Edwin and Morcar remained earls in name, but their wings had been decisively clipped.[7]

Once Edwin and Morcar committed to resisting their new lords, rebellion spread fast. They were able to tap into existing grievances, for the West Midlands magnate Eadric the Wild had raised a smaller rebellion in 1067. Both Eadric and the Welsh ruler of Gwynedd, Bleddyn ap Cynfn (Eadric's old ally), now joined the cause; and soon the entire West Midlands and the North were up in arms. This rebellion was much larger than those of Eadric or the Godwins and posed a direct threat to William's regime, not least since it secured the support of the Scottish king, Malcolm III, at whose court Edgar sought refuge at some point in the year (sadly we do not know whether before or after the rebellion).[8] But alive to the danger, William was able to nip the rebellion in the bud by his forced march to Warwick,.

Once more, decisive action had steadied the ship. But if the situation looked stable – and William and Matilda felt secure enough to return to Normandy in the autumn of 1068 – such illusions were soon dashed. Late in the year William sent the Fleming Robert de Comines north to replace Gospatric as earl of Northumbria. Gospatric had been part of the previous year's rebellion and was now in exile at the Scottish court with Edgar. Yet what was supposed to mark the end of the rebellion prompted its renewal. For soon after his arrival, Robert was killed at Durham on 31 January. What ensued was effectively a repeat of the previous year's rising. A bad situation was made worse by revolt against William's authority in Maine. William sensibly decided to focus his energies on the greater prize (and greater threat) in England. Again he moved fast, arriving at York in February, where the local Norman commander had holed himself up in the castle built the previous summer. Catching the besiegers unawares, William inflicted a major defeat on the rebels, before proceeding to sack the city, reportedly desecrating the cathedral in the process. The contrast with Exeter's merciful treatment a year earlier is striking. William was losing patience with the English.

The Conqueror may have quashed the northern rebellion. But the political situation remained volatile. This probably explains Matilda's return to the relative calm of Normandy at Easter, while William settled down to ride out a summer of revolt. For the second year running, Harold's sons now returned. They sailed up the Bristol Channel, this time landing in northern Devon, before being defeated by William's men, probably near Northam. There were also disturbances on the Welsh frontier, as English rebels in the West Midlands once more called on support from across the frontier.[9] William's regime was looking decidedly shaky, and many were keen to reap the rewards of toppling it.

The situation was further complicated over the summer by the arrival of a large Danish fleet. The English rebels had been appealing to the Danish king, Svein, for support for some time. As a descendent of Cnut, Svein had his own claims to the English throne. Now the Danish threat finally materialised, and a large fleet commanded by Svein's brother Osbjorn and two (or possibly three) of his sons sought out English shores. They initially struck at Dover, Sandwich, Ipswich and Norwich, before sailing north. Here they joined up with the rebels of previous years, and the united force marched on York, where the garrison offered battle but suffered a resounding defeat.

As previously, William responded decisively, marching north. Faced with the Conqueror's full force, the invaders decided that discretion was the better part of valour and retreated from the city of York. This was the third northern rebellion in quick succession, and William was now determined to stamp his authority on the region. He again let his men ravage York, doing even greater harm than earlier in the year (the Domesday Survey reports that two-thirds of housing there was still uninhabitable). For Christmas – the anniversary of his triumphant consecration at Westminster three years previously – William called for his crown, which we can imagine him wearing triumphally in the wreckage of the city. This was a show of brute force.

It was over these winter months that William undertook his most infamous act: the Harrying of the North. This was partly an effort to hunt down his enemies in the aftermath of the rebellion. But it was also a symbolic show of strength. William's men systematically devastated the surrounding countryside, seeking to inflict maximum damage. Even the king's sympathisers were appalled by the resulting destruction. William of Malmesbury, writing half a century later, reports that in many regions the soil remained barren.[10] As this statement suggests, what mattered besides the loss of life and livestock (and this was considerable) was the damage to the region's ecology. Far more died of famine than ever had at the swords of the Norman knights. This was the politics of terror, a concerted effort to crush the will to resist.[11] This was also a strategic move. Medieval armies marched on their bellies, and William was ensuring that the rebels would find no sustenance in the North. In political terms, the Harrying had the desired effect. Most of the rebels submitted early in the New Year, and the North would not rebel again. In human terms, it was a catastrophe from which the region was still recovering decades later.

Despite the submission of the English, the Danish fleet remained intact into the New Year. William had initially bought them off in December, when his main energies were focused on the English rebels. This only secured a temporary reprieve, however, and Svein soon sailed over from Denmark to join the fleet. Yet without local support, the Danish king's prospects were now poor. He sought to link up with the remaining rebel elements, who'd begun to coalesce around the Fenlands. It was here that Hereward the Wake, the inspiration for many later legends, had been agitating against the abbey of Peterborough. The previous year, William had removed Abbot Brand from his post – an act of revenge for the latter's appointment by Edgar the Ætheling. Brand was now to be replaced with a Norman, Turold of Fécamp. Not all were pleased by this move, however, and in response Hereward and his men proceeded to sack the abbey before the arrival of the new abbot.

It was to join up with these rebels that Svein now sent Osbjorn south to Ely, which soon became the main rebel base. But Hereward and his small band of outlaws could hardly provide an adequate camp from which the Danes could operate. When William later offered Svein terms (which may well have included money), he was only too happy to accept. Such was William's confidence, that he now returned to Normandy for Christmas. After almost two years in England – William's longest stay in the region – he was ready to come home.

Yet rebellion continued to rumble on at Ely. Thanks to its easily defensible location – at this time, still an island in the fens – it proved a thorn in the side of the Normans. And it soon became a lightning rod for further resistance. In the winter of 1070/1, Edwin and Morcar carried out what was to be a final rebellion. When this failed to gain traction, they fled – Edwin north to Scotland and Morcar east to join Hereward's forces in Ely. En route, Edwin was betrayed by three of his men and killed; Morcar, however, successfully joined the Fenland rebels. He was not the only one to do so. Æthelwine, the bishop of Durham, who'd been implicated in the previous northern revolts, now made his way south from exile at the Scottish court. What had started as a regional revolt was threatening to become something much larger. William therefore returned to England in 1071 and led a successful attack on the Isle of Ely. Æthelwine and Morcar submitted and would live out the rest of their days in confinement. Not all the rebels fared so well. Some – the commoners, one suspects – had their hands cut off and eyes gouged out. As in York, William was making a statement.

William emerged from these conflicts with his power considerably enhanced. There was no way of knowing that the revolt in the Fenlands would be the last. But the direction of travel was now clear. None of the later risings had managed to match that of 1068 in scale; and with Svein out of the picture, there was little immediate threat to William. His later years would not be entirely free from troubles – one of the few remaining English earls, Waltheof, plotted rebellion in 1075, and Odo was apparently guilty of undermining William's rule in 1082 – but never again would the Conqueror's control of England itself be challenged. The crown the Norman duke had won, against the odds, in 1066 would remain his. But if William's regime survived largely unscathed, this is not to say that he remained unfazed by these events. There is a palpable anger and frustration to William's actions in 1069 and 1070 out of keeping with the cool-headed reason of earlier years, an anger and frustration which explain other developments at this juncture.

For it is in these years that we start to see sustained efforts to replace the English ruling elite. To an extent, this represents the natural course of the Conquest. William could not have hoped to reallocate all the lands of the rebel English in the three months between his consecration on Christmas Day 1066 and his departure to Normandy the following March. That further confiscations loomed was clear. Nevertheless, the comprehensive nature of Norman settlement owes much to William's experiences in the years 1067 to 1070. By 1070, every English earl had turned coat; and many less prominent figures had done so, too. It's not difficult to see why William now sought to replace such men with Normans and Flemings. In doing so, he killed two birds with one stone, rewarding those who'd been loyal and punishing those who continued to threaten his regime. It's only upon William's first return in late 1067, that we start to see Normans replacing Englishmen in the middle to lower ranks of the royal office holders, a process that intensified over the coming years.[12] One of the central justifications for the Conquest had been the dissolute ways of the English; it was all too easy to make the case for a clean slate now.

English resistance and Norman settlement thus went hand in hand. The more the native aristocracy rebelled, the more determined William became to extirpate it. The result was the most complete replacement of a ruling elite in British history. The results can be seen in the Domesday Survey. By 1086, less than 8 per cent of land (at most) was in native hands – a staggering transformation. This was, however, not simply a matter of replacing like with like: the very nature and distribution of landholding was changed in the process.[13] The fiction was born that all land was held of the king. It was the conquering William who now distributed lands and offices to his men (or, more rarely, confirmed them in the hands of the English). Henceforth, he was to be the lord of all. Similarly new were the forms of military service demanded. Though the obligation to serve in the king's army had a long history in England, now this was recast to meet the Norman need for heavy cavalry (in what is known as knight service). Royal landholding itself was left considerably enhanced. For while William rewarded his men generously, he ensured that none could rival him. Indeed, more wealth was now concentrated in the hands of the ruling elite, but its numbers had grown, so on average Norman earls held slightly less than their English forebears. There would be no more supermagnates like Godwin and Harold. In general, the rich had got richer and the poor – and moderately wealthy – poorer. For the English, who were now relegated to the latter two groups, this was very bad news indeed.

If the rhetorical framing of the Domesday Survey asserts continuity, its contents thus reveal the harsh reality of conquest and colonisation. In practice, this was achieved by brute force, as must have been clear across the countryside. For every Norman magnate or prelate who claimed that William was the Confessor's true heir (and Harold an oath-breaking rebel), there were many more who simply believed that they had won their lands by right of conquest. This was certainly the view of the Warennes, one of the many Norman families now catapulted into the circles of Europe's ruling elite. When, in the late thirteenth century, John de Warenne was asked for the basis of his landed claims, he famously produced a rusty old sword, exclaiming: 'Look, my lords, here is my warrant. For my ancestors came over with William the Bastard and conquered their lands with the sword; and I will defend them with the sword against anyone wishing to seize them!'[14] John's message was simple – to the victor the spoils. So, ultimately, was William's. If he had played Edward's heir at Westminster at Christmas 1066 – appearing more English than the English – three years later at York he cut a very different picture. Surrounded by wanton destruction, he called for his crown, so that he could wear it in proud defiance in the wreckage of the Anglo-Saxon city. Few images better sum up the nature of the Conquest. With York Minster nothing but a smouldering ruin, the rest of the English Church now awaited its fate with bated breath.

9

Church and State in Conquered England: Romancing the Stone, 1066–87

Few features better reveal the history of a country than its built environment. And few buildings are so eloquent in this regard as religious houses. Northern France stands out for its ornate Gothic architecture, embodied in the hulking Notre-Dame in Paris, the shining brilliance of the nearby Sainte-Chappelle, and the imposing majesty of Chartres. By contrast, Italy, Austria and southern Germany are striking for their embrace of the Baroque, exemplified by St Peter's Basilica in Rome, St Stephen's in Passau and Salzburg Cathedral. Here we see Counter-Reformation bulwarks against the growing influence of Protestantism. England, by contrast, is characterised by the elegant simplicity of the Romanesque – an architectural style developed in continental Europe in the ninth and tenth centuries and characterised by its thick walls and large, rounded arches. With the exception of St Paul's – rebuilt following the Great Fire of 1666 – almost all of England's great cathedrals bear Romanesque features; and many are Romanesque through and through. These were all built within a short span of years following the Conquest. And they are part of a wider set of changes in the institutional Church. In 1066, only four of fourteen English bishops hailed from the continent; by the time of the Conqueror's death, it was fourteen of fifteen.

To modern eyes, conquest and colonisation may seem like acts of military might and political nous. But in an era before the separation of Church and State, conquest was inevitably a moral affair – a process as much religious as it was political. This was doubly true of England after 1066. From the start, William had been keen to secure papal support for his invasion; and one of his first acts as king was to found an abbey at Battle (as the name suggests, the site of the carnage in October 1066). The latter was partly a gesture of thanks and reconciliation, but it was also an attempt to expiate the sins incurred in the course of conquest.

Such acts were part of a wider programme of religious transformation. Just as William and his men ushered in a tenurial revolution in the countryside, so they were catalysts of change within the Church. In part, this reflects the logic of William's case for invasion. An essential element of this had been the claim that the English and their Church were venal, irregular and schismatic. And while such caricatures may be unfair, they exploited real differences between Church structures in England and its continental neighbours. It was common for English bishops to hold multiple sees (as had Stigand), a practice long since abandoned elsewhere as being contrary to canon law; the small number and uneven distribution of the English dioceses was also most unusual from a European perspective.[1] At a time when stricter ideas about ecclesiastical life were gaining ground across western Europe, these variations were bound to become a problem at some point – and William was only too happy to speed on the process. He positioned himself as the brush needed to sweep clean the English Church.

William's case was strengthened by the associations he'd developed with the papacy in the years preceding 1066. For although the duke's marriage to Matilda (a distant relative) had briefly raised heckles in Rome, William had been a firm supporter of the Church and its leading pontiff.[2] He was helped by the strong Italian element within the Norman Church, which opened channels to Rome. Another important point of contact were the councils held by Pope Leo IX in France and Germany in 1049 and 1050. These played a key part in spreading new reformist ideas. The most visible consequence in Normandy was a run of similar councils (on a smaller scale), starting in the early 1050s. These concerned clerical marriage and the purchase of ecclesiastical office (simony), faults the Norman episcopate now stood beside the pope in seeking to eradicate.

Once William had established himself in England, it was but a matter of time before similar initiatives would be introduced. It must always have been the plan to replace Stigand; and a more thorough-going reform of the Church was clearly the end goal. William's initial caution is illustrated by his coronation. Although Archbishop Ealdred of York presided, much as he had at Harold's, Stigand was also present and may have played a more active role than later sources let on. It's clear, however, that William did not trust the archbishop – and with good reason. Stigand was Harold's (and Godwin's) creature; he could scarcely be expected to support William wholeheartedly. After the disaster at Hastings, Stigand had initially backed Edgar, and only submitted to William once the writing was on the wall. In the name of continuity, the Conqueror now tolerated Stigand's presence. But as English rebellions spread, the archbishop's position became untenable. Thanks to William's own propaganda, Pope Alexander II was calling for Stigand's deposition. The king was only too happy to oblige.[3]

The opportunity was presented by a visit from papal legates in 1070. Their intention was to survey the situation within the Conqueror's new realm and set about righting the purported wrongs of the English Church. As the pre-eminent symbol of these ills, Stigand had to go. At an important council held at Winchester at Easter, the archbishop was formally deposed by the legates and other bishops in attendance. This was followed by a second council at Windsor at Pentecost.[4] Stigand was not the only figure to suffer as a result of these developments. With papal support – indeed, at papal request – William now conducted a cull of the English episcopate every bit as ruthless as that of the kingdom's secular aristocracy. Alongside Stigand, the archbishop's brother Bishop Æthelmær of Elmham (in East Anglia) and three unnamed abbots (one of them probably Brand) were removed from office at the first of these gatherings. Leofwine of Lichfield was also called to answer charges of clerical marriage on this occasion; and when he refused to appear, was excommunicated, freeing up another see. It was around this time, too, that the former bishop of Durham, Æthelric, was imprisoned, while Æthelric's brother (and successor) Æthelwine was outlawed. By the time the second council deposed Æthelric of Selsey on accusations of irregular appointment, over a third of the episcopate had been forcibly removed. If we add to this the two English prelates who'd died of natural causes since 1066 (Ealdred of York and Wulfwig of Dorchester), half of the kingdom's sees had changed hands in just four years. In all cases, English bishops were replaced with continental (typically Norman) ones. This was a move as political as it was religious.

Clearly the determination was to start afresh, on the basis of the best models available in mainland Europe. In this respect, it is no coincidence that of the seven surviving bishops, one was already Norman (William of London) and four hailed from (or had received their training within) the Francophone region of Lotharingia, on the western frontiers of the German Empire (Leofric of Exeter, Herman of Sherborne, Walter of Hereford and Giso of Wells). The other two were Wulfstan of Worcester and Siward of Rochester. The latter was an old man in charge of an inconsequential see, while the former seems to have survived on account of his saintly reputation.

Yet it is not simply the depositions which warrant our attention. The councils of 1070 set in motion a series of more fundamental changes. It was probably on these occasions that the possibility of relocating many English sees was first raised. The first two canons of the Winchester council also prohibit the possession of more than one bishopric (pluralism) and simoniacal ordination, crimes of which the recently removed bishops stood accused. The remaining canons go on to touch on other reformist themes, including ecclesiastical ordination, the payment of tithes and the regular holding of diocesan synods (smaller gatherings on the level of the individual bishopric). While councils and synods had been known throughout the Anglo-Saxon period – and were probably more common than our sources reveal – regular local and national gatherings had not been common since at least the early ninth century.[5]

From the early 1070s, a run of councils and synods can be observed which sought to confront a similar range of subjects to their Norman counterparts. The ambitions of the legatine councils were soon fulfilled. Spearheading these efforts was Lanfranc, the new archbishop of Canterbury. Lanfranc had been one of the leading lights of the Norman Church for some time. An Italian by birth but a Norman by choice, Lanfranc had made a name for himself at the newly founded monastery of Bec in the south-western Roumois. He'd settled here in 1042 and swiftly established a reputation as one of the leading teachers and intellectuals of northern France. He played an important part in early reforming efforts within the duchy. Lanfranc's reputation soon made it to the ducal court. When William came to pick an abbot for his prize foundation of Saint-Etienne at Caen – the duke's counterpart to his wife's La Trinité – the choice naturally fell on Lanfranc.[6]

As a man on good terms with both duke and pope, Lanfranc – or an associate – had probably been responsible for securing Alexander II's support for William's invasion of 1066.[7] It thus made sense that he should take the lead in transforming the English Church: having persuaded the pope of the sins of the English, it fell on Lanfranc to put these to rights. Lanfranc's appointment was clearly on the cards at the Winchester and Windsor councils of 1070. Stigand's removal created a vacuum at the top of the English ecclesiastical hierarchy, which it was in William and Alexander's interests to fill. Lanfranc was the ideal figure to do so.

The only problem lay in persuading Lanfranc to take the job. William had already tried to make Lanfranc archbishop of Rouen – the most senior ecclesiastical post in Normandy – in 1067, to no avail. Now once more, the learned abbot sought to avoid such responsibilities, expressing his desire to remain in monastic solitude. This time, however, William had the pope on his side. According to Lanfranc's letters, it was Alexander's legate Erminfrid of Sion and a Roman cleric named Hubert who finally persuaded him – in the pope's name – to accept the office.[8]

Lanfranc's arrival in England in summer 1070 was met with pomp and ceremony. He was formally appointed on the feast of the Assumption of Mary (15 August), then consecrated on that of the Beheading (or Decollation) of John the Baptist (29 August), two weeks later. The latter event was witnessed by a veritable who's who of the English episcopate: William, the longstanding Norman bishop of London; Walkelin, Stigand's Norman successor at Winchester; Remigius, a monk of Fécamp who'd been appointed bishop of Dorchester on the death of the English bishop, Wulfwig, in 1067; Siward, the elderly English prelate of Rochester; Herfast, the Norman successor to Æthelmær at Elmham; Stigand, the Norman ducal chaplain made bishop of Selsey (who shared a name with the disgraced English archbishop); Herman, the longstanding Lotharingian bishop of Sherborne; and Herman's fellow countryman Giso of Wells.[9]

Lanfranc came to the job well equipped. He was on excellent terms with king and pope, and had been involved in earlier reforming initiatives within Normandy. He was also an experienced ecclesiastical administrator, having been abbot of the wealthy foundation of Saint-Etienne for over half a decade. In the latter guise, Lanfranc had initiated the construction of the massive new church, whose consecration he would oversee during a rare visit back to Normandy in 1077. Still, Lanfranc faced a number of challenges at Canterbury. At the time of his appointment, he was an old man by medieval standards (probably over sixty) and had no prior experience of English Church or society. He also almost certainly didn't speak a word of English.

As archbishop, Lanfranc's priorities were three-fold: to clarify the position of Canterbury at the head of the ecclesiastical hierarchy; to secure the archbishopric's landed assets; and to drive forward the initiatives against simony, clerical marriage and other failings of the English Church, as outlined at the Winchester and Windsor councils. All three could be subsumed under the umbrella of reform. What Lanfranc conceived of in terms of restoration was in practice an exercise in bringing local traditions more closely in line with those of mainland Europe (and, in particular, Normandy).

It was not only the personal administrative structures of the English Church that were transformed. For the Conqueror's new Norman episcopate proved just as interested in rebuilding the nation's churches as they were in reforming its practices. As a result, the seventy-five years following the Conquest witnessed an unprecedented boom in church building. This was the heyday of the Romanesque style, which had been developed in mainland Europe in the ninth and tenth centuries. The replacement of earlier English church architecture was almost complete: by 1130, every cathedral had been rebuilt or relocated (sometimes both – and sometimes more than once). None of the resulting structures owes more than its location and orientation to its Anglo-Saxon forbear, and many are completely new creations. In the majority of cases, the Norman church still stands, often as first constructed in these years. The replacement of the English clerical and secular elite was thus accompanied by an erasure of native architecture every bit as thorough. Modern tourists have to go out of their way to find an Anglo-Saxon church, but they can scarcely avoid catching sight of one (or more) of England's great Romanesque masterpieces.

Building a church was, of course, a much longer process than replacing an abbot or bishop. But even so, the speed of this reconfiguration of the ecclesiastical landscape is startling. By the Conqueror's death, construction had been commenced (and in some cases completed) at Christ Church and St Augustine's in Canterbury, York Minster, the Old Minster in Winchester, Rochester, Salisbury (Old Sarum), Worcester, Lincoln, St Albans, Glastonbury, Abingdon, Ely, Bury St Edmunds, Evesham and Battle. By the time of William Rufus' death in 1100, these were joined by St Paul's (London), Chichester, Durham, Norwich, Gloucester, Bath, Pershore, Crowland and Tewkesbury – not to mention a second, larger Christ Church Cathedral at Canterbury.[10] This construction boom was new. With the exception of the Confessor's foundation at Westminster – itself inspired by Norman models – the half-century prior to 1066 had witnessed remarkably little church building in England. And even if we go back to the activities of the monastic reformers of the later tenth century, who'd refounded religious houses across southern and eastern England, we find nothing approaching this in scale and ambition. In 1066, almost all the English cathedrals and major abbey churches were centuries old; fifty years later, they were all of recent vintage.

In part, this was an extension of developments in Normandy. The duchy had witnessed major building undertakings at Jumièges, Rouen and Caen before 1066. At the latter, William and Matilda's joint foundations of Saint-Etienne and La Trinité offer particularly fine (yet starkly contrasting) examples of the early Norman Romanesque.[11] This was also part of a wider European trend, evocatively described by Raoul Glaber in the 1040s as a new 'white mantle of churches' cladding the landscape.[12] Yet the scale and speed of church building in England after the Conquest was not the organic growth seen in much of France and Germany; it was frenetic and ambitious. Christ Church, Canterbury, trumped Battle in size (both c.1070), only to be bettered by St Augustine's (also c.1070), which was then matched by Lincoln (c.1072 × 1075), soon to be outdone by St Albans (c.1077), before Winchester (c.1079) topped them all.[13] With the exception of

Rochester (c.1077) – a small and poor see, traditionally dependent on neighbouring Canterbury – each new church was as long or longer than the one before, and the resulting structures were far larger than those of William's Normandy – indeed they were among the largest in western Christendom.

Bigger was, however, not always better. Many of the earlier Anglo-Norman churches show signs that their artisans and architects were operating at the limits of their abilities. Bishop Walkelin's new cathedral in Winchester may impress in size (at the time of its completion, it was the longest in western Europe), but this cannot hide the shoddy quality of much of the stonework. Similarly, there is a marked improvement in the quality of execution between the two phases of work on Ely: that undertaken before an abbatial vacancy in 1093 is solid but unexciting, lacking the ornate mouldings popular in Normandy at the time; the second phase following 1100 matches in quality that seen anywhere else in Europe. Yet the problems were not simply aesthetic. Only five days after its consecration in 1092, the bell tower at Old Sarum was blown down by a storm. More dramatic was the experience of the monks of Winchester, whose cavernous new cathedral came crashing down in 1107, only a few decades after its completion. Similar experiences were had at Abingdon, Gloucester, Ely, Evesham and Lincoln, all of which had towers collapse in these centuries.[14]

Still, not all the architecture and stonework was so shoddy, nor would it be right to see this simply as an extension of the Norman Romanesque. Architects in England borrowed ideas and approaches from the Rhineland as well as northern France, combining these with native traditions. If at its worst Anglo-Norman ecclesiastical architecture was crude and fleeting, at its best, it set standards for the rest of Europe. Among the finest early achievements are the innovative structures at St Albans and Bury St Edmunds. But the jewel in England's Romanesque crown is Durham Cathedral. Construction here began in 1093 and extended well into the twelfth century. Due to its site crowning the Durham peninsula, flanked on either side by the meandering Wear, the cathedral could never have rivalled its largest English, French or German counterparts in scale. But what it lacks in size, Durham more than makes up for in skill.

The new cathedral church made the most of its unique setting. It is as long as the natural rise on which it stands allows, towering over the Wear. Its layout conforms closely to established norms, taking the form of a cross running west to east. The smaller apse and main altar are separated by a transept running north–south from the longer nave in the west. The ultimate model here is that of Saint-Etienne, though this was probably mediated via St Albans and Bury St Edmunds. Arches flank the nave and apse, serving to define the main internal space. These were finished with complex mouldings, the first of their kind in England. Equally innovative was the use of ribbed vaulting over the east arm (and perhaps also the transept and nave) – again one of the first examples of this from the British Isles (indeed, one of the earliest anywhere in Europe). Similarly novel are the elaborate decorations on the arches, columns and piers (as square or rectangular columns are known), which are likewise among the first (and finest) of their nature.[15] Above all, it is the consistency of execution which impresses, and Durham has (quite rightly) been dubbed 'the culminating achievement of the Norman Romanesque school in England'.[16]

Alongside the Romanesque church, the castle was the most striking (and enduring) Norman contribution to English architecture. Whether the simple wood motte and bailey, or the rarer (but sturdier) stone keep, these fortifications were an essential part of the Normanisation of the landscape. They were in large part functional. A newly imposed aristocracy was in need of bolt holes, and castles provided these in abundance. Yet they were also symbolic. Typically constructed *after* regions had been subdued (violently or otherwise), castles were the projections of royal and lordly power *par excellence*.[17] When the Peterborough Chronicler, one of our few English voices on William's reign, came to write a poetic epitaph for the king, he began with the themes of fortification and domination: 'He [William] had castles constructed / and wretched men greatly oppressed.'[18] The novelty of the Conqueror's interventions is underlined by the poet-chronicler's choice of words; he employs the new Franco-Norman loan-word *castelas* ('castles'), in favour of the native English *burig* ('fortifications') here. This was a new concept as well as a new structure.

Though later Anglo-Saxon lordly towers anticipate the Anglo-Norman castle in important manners, it too was a fundamentally new phenomenon.[19] The most famous of the resulting structures is the Tower of London, where the Crown Jewels reside to this day. Yet far more important were the more workaday castles, constructed in wood from Exeter to Durham, and Cambridge to the Welsh marches. Few people would have been more than half a day's walk from the nearest of these, and it's estimated that a staggering 600 had been erected in England and Wales by the turn of the century.[20] The impact of the Norman aristocracy on the English countryside could scarcely be clearer. But having whetted their appetite for conquest, would the Normans really stop at England's frontiers?

IO

Settling the South:
Ironarm in Italy, c.1030–45

In the middle years of the eleventh century, the Conqueror's fellow countryman, Robert Guiscard made a name for himself in Italy. Thanks to a series of daring military ventures, he'd been able to secure control of much of the southern half of the peninsula, and had come to personify Norman achievement there. According to William of Malmesbury, Duke William was envious of these achievements, proclaiming that it would be shameful were he to be surpassed in strength and courage by a man of lesser birth.[1] The Conqueror's jealousy was not ill-founded. From relatively humble origins in the Cotentin, Robert and his brothers came to control vast tracks of land in Italy. Their exploits began in the later 1030s, and may have been the inspiration for William's own fateful gamble in 1066, as Malmesbury implies. And they were to cast a similarly long shadow, with the independent Sicilian realm they founded enduring up to the unification of Italy in the 1860s.

For much of his early career, Robert played second fiddle to his elder half-brothers, foremost among these being Count William 'Ironarm'. William was the eldest of twelve sons of Tancred de Hauteville with two successive wives. Tancred was a figure of middling stature in Normandy – an aristocrat of local note in the Cotentin, but not a man capable of supporting so many sons in the manner to which they'd become accustomed. As the eldest, William was well aware of his straitened prospects. Partible inheritance was the norm within the Norman duchy, and William faced a stark choice between poverty at home and seeking his fortune abroad. Not surprisingly, he chose the latter.

As William de Hauteville's experiences suggest, population pressure was one of the factors which drove Norman expansion in these years. The population of the duchy was growing steadily, and the more sparsely populated regions of southern Italy – where recent conflicts had taken their toll – offered rich prospects. But though our accounts place considerable emphasis on this factor, it's unlikely to have been the overriding incentive for Norman ventures abroad. Overpopulation is a common trope among medieval chroniclers, routinely wheeled out to explain migration and settlement. And while population was growing in Normandy, the same was true almost everywhere in France (and western Europe); yet only Normandy saw such an exodus. Another important factor was the increasing popularity of pilgrimage. Many sources report that the first Normans came south as pilgrims, and there are signs of a particularly strong Norman interest in the cult of the Archangel, whose leading shrine was at Monte Gargano (Monte Sant'Angelo) in northern Apulia. But again, these developments were not unique to Normandy – Count Fulk Nerra of Anjou went on pilgrimage to the Holy Land four times – and the Archangel's cult was also popular elsewhere, so we must look further to explain the Norman settlement.

The decisive factor was almost certainly the political situation in Normandy.[2] Norman activity in the south gained momentum in the 1030s and 1040s, during the troubled years of Duke Robert's reign and (in particular) the Conqueror's minority. A number of accounts have political exiles among the earliest settlers, and these years produced no shortage of such men. It's also likely that others – men such as the Hauteville brothers – deemed this an inauspicious moment to seek their fortunes locally, so looked further afield. Southern Italy offered excellent prospects here. It was wealthy, but politically divided, and smaller groups of Norman mercenaries had already been plying their trade in the region for a few decades.

At what point William arrived in southern Italy is not entirely clear. Our most detailed report is furnished by Geoffrey of Malaterra, a Norman monk writing in Sicily in the late 1090s.[3] Geoffrey states that the elder Hauteville brothers decided to seek their fortune as mercenaries, upon which God guided them to Italy. Here they entered the employ of the Lombard prince of Capua, before jumping ship to join the prince of Salerno to Capua's south.[4] Geoffrey says nothing about what drew the brothers south (save the guiding hand of the Almighty), and his silence is significant. For Geoffrey's work is a panegyric on the Hauteville clan, culminating in the conquest of Apulia, Calabria and Sicily by Robert and his younger brother Roger (the real hero of Geoffrey's story). As we know from other sources, the Hautevilles were not the first Normans to come to southern Italy. But by passing over such precedents in silence, Geoffrey was able to present William and his brothers as the founding fathers of the Norman colony.

Other sources help round out this picture, though the gaps in our knowledge remain large. The problem is that, much as in Rollo's Normandy, the advent of the Normans only took on its full significance many years later. There was no reason to believe that the earliest Norman incomers would stay, let alone flourish. Only once they had, did this require explanation. The main challenge for modern historians is that none of our early sources agrees with another; and on many points, they actively contradict each other. Pride of place is traditionally given to Amatus of Montecassino, who furnishes our earliest narrative. According to Amatus, writing *c.*1080, the Normans came to the region shortly before the year 1000 (*avan mille puis que Christ*). First to arrive was a group of pilgrims on their way home from the Holy Land. Whether they'd been travelling by land or sea is unclear; but either way, they stopped off at Salerno, which they found besieged by Saracens. Grasping the gravity of the situation, the pilgrims asked the local prince, Guaimar III, for weapons and horses (as pilgrims, they were travelling unarmed). They then set the Muslim force to flight. So impressed were Guaimar and his people, that they begged the Normans to stay on. When the pilgrims politely refused, the Salernitans sent them on their way with rich gifts and the request to send more of their fellow countrymen south. This wish was soon fulfilled when the Norman duke (Richard II) exiled a man called Gilbert, who set off south with his four brothers. They formed the first permanent Norman presence in the region, immediately joining the rebellion of Melus within Byzantine Apulia in 1017, which aimed to achieve independence from Byzantium for the local Lombard population.[5]

Our next account is that of William of Apulia, writing in Latin verse in the 1090s. He places the arrival of the Normans exclusively in the context of Melus' rebellion. Here, too, they arrive as pilgrims, albeit ones en route to the shrine of the Archangel in Monte Gargano.

Upon arrival they (rather implausibly) bump into the rebel Melus, who persuades them to join his endeavour.[6] Despite differences in the detail, Amatus and William agree that the Normans arrived in Italy early (no later than 1017), initially as pilgrims. The situation is complicated, however, by the fact that two other earlier accounts, those of Adémar of Chabannes and Raoul Glaber writing north of the Alps, have the Normans come south at the behest of the pope, whom they'd met in Rome. Only thereafter did they join Melus' rising.[7]

There are enough recurring features across these reports to encourage prudent speculation. Pilgrimage was becoming increasingly popular in the late tenth and early eleventh centuries, and Norman involvement here is well attested. It's quite likely that the Normans first became acquainted with southern Italy as pilgrims – and the shrine of the Archangel was a frequent staging post to the Holy Land. Likewise, it's clear that these incomers soon became implicated in Melus' revolt, perhaps with papal blessing (or even on papal instruction). It's harder to know what to make of Amatus' remarks about earlier Norman activity at Salerno. On the one hand, he's unique in mentioning this; on the other, Amatus speaks as a Salernitan, and Salerno did boast a major Norman mercenary force in later years. In fact, a number of other Italian sources – some more garbled than others – record traditions of a Norman arrival just before (or after) the year 1000, so this is unlikely to be an outright invention.[8]

In the end, it would be wrong to look for a single moment of Norman settlement. Unlike in England, the conquest and settlement of Italy was a piecemeal affair. The earliest Normans came as mercenaries, only slowly putting down roots; and there was almost always more than one group active at a time. This process of settlement was well on its way by the 1030s and 1040s, when external observers such as Adémar and Glaber started to take note. It's also around this time that the Hautevilles seem to have appeared. In this sense, Geoffrey of Malaterra is right to place the brothers at the start of his narrative. The Hautevilles may not have been the first Normans to come to the region, but their arrival marks a qualitative change in the nature of Norman activity. It was now that the incomers went from being occasional mercenaries to being lords and settlers in their own right.

The Normans encountered a very different social and political order to that of northern France. Southern Italy was composed of a complex web of political players, from the Byzantine governors in the south east and south west (Apulia and Calabria), to the Lombard princes of the north and west (Campania), to the Muslim amirs of Sicily. The Normans' cause was aided by local social and political developments. The power of the Lombard principalities of Capua and Salerno was ebbing in favour of that of the landed aristocracy.[9] The Byzantine Empire was entering a phase of decline, as large swathes of Asia Minor (the old imperial heartlands) were lost to the Seljuk Turks.[10] As a consequence, the local governors (or catepans) of Italy were often left isolated and underfunded. Similar processes were under way in Sicily. Such divisions played into the hands of the Normans. Not only did they ensure a ready market for their martial skills (the Normans were still first and foremost mercenaries), but they made any co-ordinated response difficult.

Still, it's important not to exaggerate the importance of early Norman settlement in Italy. Norman mercenaries constituted but a small part of Melus' force in 1017/18; and even once they entered Lombard service thereafter, they did so as auxiliaries. Only in 1030 was the first permanent base established, by a certain Rainulf at Aversa under the auspices of the local Lombard prince, Guaimar IV. Further Norman incursions were then enabled by a fresh round of revolts against Byzantine authority in the early 1040s. One of the leaders of these, a dissident Lombard officer named Arduin, who'd previously led Norman mercenaries in the Byzantine army, inflicted a series of major defeats on the imperial forces. The Normans were just one element in his army, though a more significant one than in Melus' revolt. After initial victories under Arduin, the Normans transferred their allegiance, first to the Lombard lord Atenulf, then to Argyros, the son of Melus. Argyros himself soon turned coat, perhaps realising the Normans posed a greater threat than his old Byzantine overlords. In response, the Normans now decided to go it alone, electing William de Hauteville – later known as 'Ironarm' – as their leader. No longer would they serve Lombard lords and Byzantine rebels; now the Normans were their own masters.

Before this point, we know little of William and his brothers. Malaterra reports that they'd served under the Lombard princes of Capua and Salerno in the 1030s. They almost certainly joined Rainulf's settlement at Aversa and were part of a scion of Aversa Normans that joined a Byzantine expedition to retake Sicily from the increasingly divided Saracens in 1038.[11] (It was in this connection that the Hautevilles encountered Arduin, who would draw them into revolt against the Byzantines a few years later.) William de Hauteville was thus an established presence within the Norman ranks; and by Malaterra's (admittedly encomiastic) report, he gained considerable acclaim for his actions in Sicily. When the time came to elect a leader in 1042, William was the natural choice.

It's clear that many of the Aversa Normans had been chomping at the bit to carve out their own territories; and Rainulf was more than happy to see the back of the Hautevilles and their men in 1038 and again in early 1041. Yet as such actions reveal, the Italian Normans were still far from unified. Unlike in England, where conquest was planned and directed by a single will, in Italy it evolved slowly and organically from a series of loosely associated initiatives. Some men first came as pilgrims, others as mercenaries; some wanted land, others were (for the time) happy to make do with financial reward. No-one set out to conquer the south, and it was only a confluence of unforeseen circumstances which led to this result.

William's election in 1042 was an essential step along the way. It marked a first tentative move towards independence for those Normans who'd participated in the revolts against Byzantine authority in Apulia. They still deferred to Rainulf of Aversa on some matters. But it was now clear that they would pursue their own interests, if needs be against Rainulf and their erstwhile Salernitan allies. Their ambitions were evidently growing – and the Hautevilles were the most ambitious of all of them.

That the count was no more than first among equals, however, is reflected in the nature of his election. As Amatus notes, this was part of a much wider territorial settlement. Twelve other leading Norman barons are mentioned in this connection, each of whom was assigned authority over a town or region. These ranged from William's younger brother Drogo, who was given Venosa (William's future resting place), to the family's future rival Peter, son of Amicus, who received Trani. The division itself was less a matter of rewarding loyal service than a programme of conquest, since many of the lordships lay outside Norman hands at this point.

These events thus stand at the start of the Norman conquest proper. Initial progress in the following years was slow. The Normans held on to their base at Melfi, along with other cities taken in the early 1040s, but were able to add little more. In 1044, William decided to change tack, leading an expedition into Calabria, where he established a new outpost at Scribla. The following year, Drogo is reported to have secured Bovino, opening the way into the Capitanata in central to eastern Apulia. Incursions were also now starting to be made into the Lombard principality of Benevento to the west.

In late 1045, however, William fell ill and died in the winter months. His death was a major blow to the Hauteville clan, but had little discernible effect on the course of Norman conquest and settlement. William's oversight during the past four years had been largely nominal, so a change of leader was little cause for concern. Moreover, in his brother Drogo, William had an obvious successor. Drogo had come to Italy with William in the 1030s and was already one of the leading men in the Norman camp at the time of the 1042 settlement. He was now able to inherit his brother's mantle. The situation remained fragile, however. The Normans only held parts of Apulia and a small toehold in Calabria; a Byzantine revival remained very much on the cards. Nor could the danger posed by the Lombard princes be ignored. The Apulian Normans remained nominally under the authority of Guaimar IV of Salerno, who'd yet to flex his muscles. Still, William's achievements were considerable. He'd united the Normans and given them purpose. The only question was whether his brothers would prove worthy of William's legacy.

11

Robert Guiscard: A Cunning
Count, c.1040–85

In the Abbey of Santissima Trinità ('the Most Holy Trinity') in Venosa, a modest Apulian town about 20 km (12 miles) south east of Melfi, lies the Hauteville family tomb. An imposing monument of the Baroque style of the sixteenth century, this brings together the remains of William Ironarm, his brothers Drogo (d. 1051) and Humphrey (d. c.1057), and their younger half-brothers, Robert Guiscard (d. 1085) and another William (d. 1080). Agostino Barba, the early modern sculptor responsible for the tomb, wanted to underline the degree to which the Norman settlement of southern Italy was a familial affair, directed and overseen by the Hautevilles. He also wished to emphasise the role of Venosa, the family's favoured monastery, in this endeavour. In doing so, however, Barba obscured as much as he revealed. For in the eleventh century, the Hautevilles were just as much rivals as allies; and it was, to a large extent, fraternal competition which drove Norman expansion in the south.

Frustratingly for modern historians, Barba's interventions destroyed almost all evidence for the original Hauteville tombs. We know that Santissima Trinità was indeed a family mausoleum in the Middle Ages. But each brother was originally buried separately, as befitted their distinct interests and careers. Only the tomb of Robert Guiscard's first wife, Alberada (in the left aisle opposite the new sepulchre), escaped Barba's 'improvements'. Thankfully, William the Conqueror's jealous interest in the exploits of his southern countrymen has ensured that some details of the most important of these lost tombs, that of his rival Guiscard, have not been lost. For William of Malmesbury, in recounting the Conqueror's rivalry with Guiscard, reports that the latter's tomb bore the following inscription:

Here lies Guiscard, terror of the world.
He drove from the City [Rome] the king of the Ligurians,
    Romans and Germans.
Neither Parthians, Arabs nor the army of Macedon could save
    Alexius,
Only flight; and neither flight nor the sea could save Venice.[1]

This is a eulogy, and we must naturally allow for a degree of poetic licence. Nevertheless, the sentiments are not out of place. Of all the Hauteville clan, Robert did most to establish Norman rule in the south; and more than once, his enemies were indeed left quivering before him.

The 1040s had seen the Hautevilles come to prominence in Italy. In Melfi, they'd gained an essential toehold in the south, and by the middle years of the decade, the family and their associates were extending control over ever larger swathes of Apulia. Here Drogo, the second of the brothers (who'd been assigned Venosa in 1042), picked up where Ironarm had left off. William had received a personal mandate to lead the Apulian Normans in 1042; yet it was far from certain they would accept the succession of his brother. The fact that Drogo had been involved in recent conquests certainly helped. But there were plenty of others with equally strong credentials. Foremost among these was Peter, son of Amicus, one of the most powerful of the lords created in 1042. Peter increasingly saw the Hautevilles as a threat to his own interests, and William of Apulia reports that conflict broke out between Peter and Drogo soon after Ironarm's death. However, while Drogo prevailed, the centrifugal tendencies within the new Norman polity remained undiminished.

During Drogo's half-decade at their head, the Normans made steady, but unspectacular, progress in Apulia. More important were new developments in Calabria. For it was in this period that Drogo's younger half-brother Robert appeared on the scene. Malaterra reports, plausibly enough, that Robert had been drawn south by tales of his elder siblings' exploits. Robert was the eldest of Tancred's second set of sons. With six younger brothers of his own, Robert could expect little more by way of an inheritance than William or Drogo, so the appeal of such ventures for him was unsurprising.

Yet if Robert had hoped for a warm welcome, he was soon disappointed. In part, this was a matter of internal family dynamics. William, Drogo and Humphrey – Humphrey being the younger brother of William and Drogo – had grown up together and come south as a team. They were a tight-knit band. By contrast, Robert was a decade or so younger. He would have shared little by way of childhood experiences with his half-brothers; moreover, as a son of Tancred's second wife, Robert was a potential competitor as well as ally.

Robert's timing did little to help his cause. He came to Apulia shortly after William's death (probably c.1046–7), when Drogo's own position was far from secure. Even if Drogo had wished to grant his younger half-brother lands and titles – and he probably didn't – he was in no position to do so. So initially Robert's fraternal entreaties were rebuffed. Soon thereafter, he was sent packing to Calabria. William and Drogo had started to make inroads here in recent years. The problem for Robert was that without land he could not establish a substantial following; and without men, he stood little chance of securing land. Robert could expect little help from Drogo, who had his own work cut out for him in Apulia (and who, in any case, was wary of Robert's motives). Robert was understandably frustrated by this catch-22. According to Amatus, he soon returned to Drogo and told him of his poverty, begging for support. But Drogo and his household demonstrably turned their backs on Robert.[2]

In later years, Robert's exploits in Calabria became the stuff of legend. Amatus reports that the turning point came when Robert arranged a meeting with Peter, one of the leading men of the town of Bisignano. At the time, Robert's base was S. Marco Argentano, an elevated site just west of the Crati Valley in northern Calabria. Bisignano lay to the south and east, about equidistant from the Crati. The men met on the east bank of the river, slightly nearer the settlement. Having lured Peter away from the town walls, however, Robert now dragged him from his steed and forcibly took him back to S. Marco to await ransom. The result was a substantial financial windfall, which enabled the cash-strapped young Hauteville to expand his operations considerably.[3]

As important as the material rewards was the reputation Robert was beginning to win for himself. When he next came to request forces from Drogo, his half-brother was no more inclined to support Robert than he had been previously, but others now flocked to Robert's banner. Foremost among these was Gerard of Buonalbergo, the leader of a group of Normans who'd established themselves at Telese (Terme Telese), about 30 km (20 miles) north west of Benevento. Gerard brought with him some 200 knights, probably more than doubling Robert's force. Gerard was to prove a staunch ally, and the alliance was formalised when Robert took Gerard's aunt Alberada (a younger sister of Gerard's father) as his wife, a union to which Drogo only grudgingly consented. According to Amatus, it was Gerard who gave Robert his famous moniker, 'Guiscard', meaning 'the cunning' or 'the crafty', when he heard of Robert's exploits at Bisignano.[4]

Suitably reinforced, Robert began to make more headway. But just as things were looking up, clouds gathered. Many of the local Lombards were starting to resent their new Norman overlords, while the popes in Rome looked on with growing dismay. The papacy had a long-standing interest in the Lombard principalities of the south, which bordered on papal lands. By the 1040s, the Normans were becoming a menace. No longer satisfied with carving out lands from Byzantine Apulia, they'd begun to threaten their erstwhile Lombard employers in Campania. A decisive moment came in the spring of 1051, when the citizens of Benevento expelled their own prince and submitted to Pope Leo IX, in the hope that he would be able to offer better protection against the Normans.

Leo came to the Benevento region in July, where he encountered Drogo and Guaimar IV of Salerno. Both agreed that attacks on Beneventan territory would cease. But implementing such promises was really not in their powers. And in the case of Drogo, whose loose overlordship had been contested from the start, any attempts to carry out such promises were negligible. Attacks from Apulia therefore continued unabated. Leo and the Beneventans were not the only ones concerned by recent Norman encroachment. The local Lombard population of Apulia who had once welcomed the Normans as liberators, now found them no more accommodating than their erstwhile Byzantine governors. Drogo himself would feel the full brunt of this resentment when he came to stay at Monte Ilaro (near Bovino) in the summer of 1051. On the morning of 10 August, Drogo went to pray in church, as was his custom. One of his supposedly loyal companions, Riso, however, lay in wait for the unsuspecting count. And as Drogo entered the church, Riso struck him down. Many of Drogo's men were also killed in the ambush.[5] This was but one of a series of assassinations of high-profile Normans.

A broad anti-Norman alliance was emerging. The Byzantine emperors had long been looking for suitable allies against the northern interlopers. And with Pope Leo now on the side of the Lombard princes (and keen to build bridges with the Byzantine Church in the East), there was the chance to build a wider coalition. The process took time, in part because Guaimar IV – who still maintained close ties to the Apulian Normans – was hesitant to join. But Guiamar and his brother were killed in 1052, opening the way for a grand alliance. By early 1053, the German emperor Henry III, Pope Leo, the Lombard princes of Capua and Benevento, and the Byzantine emperor had all committed to the cause. Things were starting to look grim for the Normans.

With their backs to the wall, the Normans chose to fight. The various Norman forces now united under the banner of Humphrey, the youngest of the older branch of the Hautevilles, who'd succeeded Drogo as count of Apulia in 1051. The Norman strategy was clear: prevent the papal army from combining forces with the Byzantine expedition in the south east. William of Apulia reports that Humphrey's Normans comprised 3,000 knights, supported by a smaller band of foot soldiers. If these figures are to be believed – and they sound plausible – it was a respectable force. This was, however, far smaller than Leo's army. For although German support proved minimal – a few hundred infantry from Swabia had been all that Henry III could spare – the pope marshalled an impressive army from the Lombard principalities, which had suffered so sorely from the Normans in recent years. Leo now led this in person.

The papal and Norman armies met near Civitate, a small town overlooking the River Fortore. Noting their numerical inferiority, the Normans sought to parley. They offered to hold their lands as dependents of the pope, much like the Beneventans. But efforts to placate Leo failed; and the Normans, left with little room to manoeuvre, chose to fight. This was a high-risk strategy, but a sensible one. The Normans were short on supplies and time was on Leo's side. The longer they waited, the greater the chances that papal and Byzantine forces would join. Battle, by contrast, was a most unpredictable affair, in which a determined force might prevail against superior numbers.

So it proved at Civitate. The Norman army was drawn up with Humphrey and the Apulian Normans on the left flank and Richard (Rainulf of Aversa's cousin) and his knights on the right. The former met stiff resistance in the form of Leo's Swabian infantry, but Richard managed to put the Lombards to flight, then circled around to attack the Germans from the rear.[6] The result was annihilation – a victory every bit as complete as that at Hastings. Its consequences were no less momentous. Pope Leo fell into the hands of the Normans. And while they did not immediately press their advantage, efforts to revive the alliance were hindered by internal divisions within the Byzantine camp and by Leo's death soon thereafter.

In the aftermath of victory, Norman advances were rapid, and nowhere were they quicker than in Calabria.[7] The heart of Byzantine power in Italy lay on the opposite coast in Apulia, those regions closest to the imperial heartlands of Greece. Here, resistance remained fierce. By contrast, Calabria – the doorway to Sicily – was left vulnerable. By 1056, Robert was securely in control of the entire province north of the Crati; he was also receiving tribute from important centres further south, including Bisignano, Martirano and Cosenza. The following year, Humphrey died and Robert was able to make good his claim to overall leadership of the Apulian Normans.

With new resources at his disposal, Robert was able to make quick work of the rest of Calabria. By the early summer of 1057, he was already leading a daring raid as far as Squillace. Thereafter, he proceeded along the east coast up to Reggio, the Byzantine capital of the region. A revolt by Peter, son of Amicus, required Robert's return to Apulia for the rest of the summer. But by the autumn of 1057, Robert was back in Calabria, where he launched an abortive attack on Reggio.

At this point, division began to dog the Norman advance once more. Robert had recently been joined by his younger brother Roger, who took to deputising for him in Calabria. In a repeat of Robert's own experiences, however, Roger was now disappointed by the lack of rewards on offer. Malaterra is our only source for these grievances, and he writes from the perspective of Roger's later Sicilian court. Not surprisingly, he accuses Guiscard of jealously and stinginess. But like Drogo before him, Robert had little to give. Major gains had been made in Calabria, but the situation remained extremely precarious. Robert also had to balance interests in Apulia, where the Byzantines continued to hold out and where Peter, son of Amicus, had recently challenged his authority.

These divisions, combined with a serious famine in Calabria, served to bring the Norman advance to a standstill. Late in 1058, a solution was found. Robert promised Roger half of Calabria, but the half still under Byzantine control. This prevented any diminution of the count's own resources, while giving Roger an active stake in future conquests. Robert also married the Lombard princess Sichelgaita. She was the daughter of Prince Guaimar IV, who'd been responsible for the establishment of the first Norman outpost at Aversa. Salerno itself had weathered the storm of the early eleventh century better than most of its neighbours, thanks in part to Guaimar's firm leadership. Following Guaimar's death and the battle of Civitate, however, the principality had entered a phase of rapid decline. As in Capua and Benevento, the ultimate causes were internal, but the situation was not helped by the ascendancy of the Normans.

A marriage alliance had much to offer both sides here. For the Salernitans, it provided support and security from the new lords of the south. For Robert, it served to legitimise recent gains and integrate him into the local aristocratic scene (much as Cnut's marriage to Emma had for the Danes in England). The importance of the match is revealed by Robert's willingness to set aside his first wife, Alberada, in order to achieve it. The latter was still alive and well, and had borne Robert an heir, Bohemond of Taranto. She was also the aunt of one of Robert's closest allies, Gerard. Evidently it was worth risking a great deal for Sichelgaita's hand.[8]

With domestic issues settled, Robert and Roger were able to make swift progress in Calabria.[9] A Byzantine attack was seen off by Roger in early 1059, and by early 1060 Reggio itself had fallen to a joint strike by the two brothers. Byzantine resistance now crumbled; and the last remaining garrison, at Squillace, fled upon Roger's approach. Similar gains were now being made elsewhere. Most notably, Richard of Aversa took Capua and secured control of the Lombard principality of this name.

These successes explain another important development of these years: rapprochement with the pope.[10] Although Leo IX and his successors had tried to revive the anti-Norman alliance of 1053, their efforts failed in the face of Byzantine weakness and German lack of interest. In 1058, a papal schism loomed, as the reform party in Rome backed Nicholas II, while the urban aristocracy sought to enthrone Benedict X.[11] If the pope was to maintain any influence in the south, he would have to work with the region's new masters. Moreover, if he wanted allies – and Nicholas II certainly did – there were few other places to turn.

The decisive moment came in 1059. That spring, the papal archdeacon Hildibrand – the archdeacon being the pope's deputy – travelled to newly conquered Capua, where he secured the support of Richard, who sent 300 knights north to help Nicholas II re-establish himself in Rome. In exchange, Hildibrand recognised Richard as the legitimate prince of Capua, accepting his oath of fidelity on behalf of the pope. This new relationship offered significant benefits to both parties.[12] Nicholas gained the military support he so desperately needed, while Richard received formal papal acknowledgement of his status as prince of Capua. So successful was the alliance that Nicholas soon made contact with Robert. In August 1059, the pope travelled south in person, holding an important council at Melfi. Here Robert swore fealty to Nicholas before being formally invested as 'by the grace of God and St Peter duke of Apulia and Calabria and, in the future, with the help of both, of Sicily.'[13]

As this august title indicates, the pact was not simply a matter of acknowledging Robert's gains; Nicholas also now provided papal approval for future conquests. Sicily remained Muslim territory and Nicholas evidently hoped Robert and Roger would help win this back for western Christendom. Scarcely had Robert taken Calabria, than plans were being laid for Sicily. This was not the only speculative element of the title. For though Nicholas had invested Robert, matter-of-factly, with the title 'duke of Apulia and Calabria', significant parts of the former still lay in Byzantine hands, while recent gains in the latter had yet to be consolidated. Much like the original settlement of 1042, the oaths of Melfi gave Robert rights he would now have to assert, often at spear point.

Still, this pact was a milestone in the Norman conquest of Italy. It acknowledged that Robert and his men were here to stay and accorded them complete authority south of Capua and Aversa. It also tells us much about Robert's ambitions. Robert was already thinking well beyond Calabria, where the last Byzantine outposts at Reggio and Squillace would only fall the following year. There were doubtless pragmatic reasons for extending his authority further south into Sicily, not least, the need to secure lands with which to reward his younger brother Roger. But one suspects there was a deeper reason for this interest. Apulia, Calabria and Sicily comprised the traditional regions of Byzantine authority in Italy, and Robert seems to have been increasingly committed to recreating the Eastern Roman Empire in his own image.

After the dramatic successes of the late 1050s, the 1060s saw Norman progress slow once more. The parameters of activity were largely set by the oaths of Melfi. And once Reggio fell in early 1060, Robert and Roger began making plans for Sicily, as we might expect. The Kalbid amirate on the island, established over a century earlier, had been dissolving for some time. Out of the resulting chaos had emerged two main factions, those of Ibn al-Ḥawwās and Ibn al-Thumna. The former had recently started to get the upper hand; and in early 1061, Ibn al-Thumna (whose base lay in the east, nearest to the mainland) appealed to Robert and Roger for assistance. The Hauteville brothers were only too happy to oblige. A full invasion was launched that May. This soon secured Messina, the most important city in the north east of the island. Thereafter, however, progress stalled.

Robert's problems were much as they had been in the previous years. He had two fronts on which to fight – Sicily and Apulia – yet only the resources to dedicate to one at a time. Moreover, the Norman camp itself remained deeply divided. The problem here was not so much the relationship between Robert and Roger – though this remained fraught at times – as that between the Hautevilles and the other Apulian Normans. Robert may have been the fourth successive brother to take on the mantle of leader, but the family's elevation remained a recent development, still resented by others. Both of these problems converged when revolt broke out in Apulia in 1067. This was financed by the Byzantines, who were keen to sow seeds of discord among their enemies, and involved Robert's own nephews. The threat was considerable and much of late 1067 and early 1068 was spent supressing it. Rebellion would break out again in 1072, further undermining Robert's efforts to consolidate control of the mainland and support operations in Sicily.

Between risings, however, action remained possible. And if the conquest of the south took longer than one might have predicted it would in 1059, revolts and resistance largely delayed the inevitable. An important moment was marked by the long and hard-fought siege of Bari, starting in the autumn of 1068. A populous and heavily fortified city on the eastern coast of Apulia, Bari was the centre of Byzantine operations in the region. The Normans had repeatedly struggled to take well-defended cities in the past, so Bari posed a real test. This was not the only difficulty. As a port, Bari could be supplied by sea. And once it became clear that force alone would not suffice to take the town, Robert had to contemplate a blockade. The Normans were even less experienced at sea than they were with siege craft. However, Robert recruited ships in Calabria, then sat down for a long blockade.

The Byzantines faced a desperate situation. Turkish pressure was building on the empire's eastern frontier, with raids now penetrating deep into Asia Minor. And defensive efforts were hampered by a major revolt, spearheaded by the Norman mercenary, Robert (Roger) Crispin and his followers. Thanks to this Norman connection – Crispin had served in Sicily under Roger before entering Byzantine employ – Guiscard almost certainly knew of these problems. The upshot was that few resources (and even fewer men) could be spared for Apulia. The men of Bari would have to fend for themselves.

And fend for themselves they did. Despite the difficulties, they held out for over two and a half years. Byzantine messengers were able to escape early on and an attempt to raise the blockade proved partially successful in 1069, ensuring that much-needed supplies reached the defenders. A second attempt was made in early 1071, by which point the city was on its knees. This was led by Joscelin of Molfetta, one of the Norman rebels of 1067, who'd fled east to Constantinople as a political exile. In the end, however, it was the cunning count who had the last laugh. Joscelin tried to run the blockade under cover of night. But he was intercepted by Roger, who'd recently brought naval reinforcements from Sicily. The result was a rout, in which Joscelin himself was captured. With all prospect of supplies and relief lost, the city soon submitted. The importance of this victory went beyond the fate of Bari itself. To defeat an established sea-power on its own turf (or rather, surf) was a major accomplishment, one which inspired a new-found confidence in Norman seafaring capabilities. As William of Apulia notes, 'the Norman people had known nothing of naval war up till now.'[14]

Much as with the fall of Reggio in Calabria, the fall of the provincial capital of Apulia led to the collapse of further resistance. The one other Byzantine outpost, Brindisi, had fallen shortly before this. And with the exception of the Lombard principalities of Capua and Salerno (the former now under the control of Richard of Aversa) and the small city-state of Amalfi, all of the south was now Robert's.

Robert was quick to take advantage of the situation, relocating his navy to Sicily. In Robert's absence, Roger had been making slow but steady progress here. He'd won set-piece battles at Cerami (1063) and Msilmeri (1068). The north-east was now securely in Norman hands, as was the north coast as far as Palermo. Like Bari, however, Palermo was proving a hard nut to crack. An early attempt on the town had foundered in 1064. And since then, Roger had been laying the foundations for a more concentrated effort. Fresh from victory and with a navy at hand, the time had come for a second siege.

Bari surrendered in April, and by late summer Robert and Roger were in a position to invest Palermo. The resulting siege was another protracted affair, though notably swifter than that at Bari. The combined naval and land forces of Robert and Roger were able to establish an effective blockade, repulsing at least one relief attempt by Sicilian and North African ships. The blockade soon started to take effect, and in January 1072 Robert and Roger decided to risk an assault. The latter led the main force, which sought to storm the walls

by land. This was, however, a decoy, intended to distract the defenders from the smaller force with which Robert made for the walls on
the seaward side. The ruse worked. Roger was repulsed, but while
the defenders were occupied with his force, Robert and his men
managed to scale the walls and open the gates. The defenders then
retreated to the city's inner walls (those of the Old City or al-Kazar).
But realising the game was up, they surrendered to Robert the following day, on agreement that their lives be spared and they be allowed
to continue practising the Muslim faith.

Shortly thereafter, Robert entered the Old City with much pomp.
His men removed all features of the Islamic faith from the main
mosque, which was transformed (back) into a Christian cathedral – a
symbolic act of regime change. The ruling elite would henceforth be
Christian, so the main place of worship was also to be Christian. But
much of the population remained Muslim, and were free to continue
practising their faith. Nothing better underlines the pragmatism of
Robert and Roger. They were happy to parade their Christian
credentials when convenient (and their new papal allies certainly
cheered on their successes), but this was not a holy war. Like Duke
William's conquest of England, it was an opportunistic land-grab
under papal licence. And if William of Apulia and (in particular)
Geoffrey of Malaterra were later to play up the religious element in
these conflicts, it's because they were writing after the First Crusade
had been launched.[15] Holy war was now all the rage, so it was natural
to recast Robert and Roger's conquests in such terms.

After the capture of Palermo, it was a matter of time till the
Normans secured the rest of the island. Yet as in Apulia, the process
dragged on.[16] The challenges were similar. Norman numerical superiority remained slight; and Robert's attentions now shifted back to
the mainland, where his own domains lay. Sicily had always been
Roger's prize. And since it was now clear the island would (eventually) fall, Robert had little to gain from further engagement. Roger's
own efforts were complicated by continuing upheaval on the mainland. In 1075, Roger was called back to help put down a rebellion by
his cousin Abelard, who as the son of Humphrey was frustrated to
find himself locked out of the corridors of power (and line of succession) within the nascent duchy.

When Roger returned to Sicily in 1076, he was able to make better headway. In 1077, he secured Trapani and with it control of the west of the island. In 1078, the fortress at Castronovo (in the centre of the island) followed, which had been a thorn in Roger's side in recent years. Such progress was maintained the following year, which saw Taormina surrender after a six-month siege. Taormina lies on the eastern coast of Sicily, some 50 km (30 miles) south of Messina. With it, the conquest of the island north of Etna was complete. At Trapani and Taormina, the Norman navy played an essential part in siege operations, revealing Roger's growing confidence in seaborne operations. Yet just as everything seemed to be going Roger's way, events elsewhere again conspired to slow his advance. The year 1079 had seen a major Muslim revolt in the west of the island, which kept Roger busy following his success at Taormina. In 1080, Roger was then recalled to the mainland to help hold the fort while Guiscard tried his hand in the Balkans. In 1084, Roger had to return to cover for his brother once more. He also began to experience some of the same problems Robert had encountered. During his absence from the island in 1084 and 1085, Roger's own son rebelled, apparently in frustration at the limited rewards on offer.[17]

Robert's death in 1085 required further absences from Roger, who now helped shore up the ducal regime on the mainland under Robert's son, Roger Borsa. Only in 1086 could Roger focus his attentions fully on Sicily, resuming the conquests of the later 1070s. His first move now was to strike at Syracuse on the south-eastern coast, one of the largest remaining cities in Muslim hands. As previously, Roger's fleet proved essential to the operation, driving off the navy of the Islamic amir. Four months later, the city surrendered. The following spring saw the fall of Agrigento, another important centre on the south coast. And this paved the way for the submission of Castrogiovanni (modern Enna), a well-fortified city in the centre of the island.

Muslim resistance was beginning to crumble. Only the south-east corner was still securely in Islamic hands, and this was under threat. Roger spent much of the campaign season in 1088 on the mainland, assisting Roger Borsa in putting down a revolt by Bohemond, Guiscard's son with Alberada. The following year, however, he succeeded in capturing Butera, near the coast on the far south-west of the island. The remaining Muslim enclaves were now under intense pressure. Finally Noto, the last outpost, just inland of the eastern coast, some 30 km (20 miles) south of Syracuse, surrendered in early 1091.

The Hautevilles had now secured the south. For while Roger had been busy in Sicily, Robert made one final conquest on the mainland: Salerno. Robert had been extending his influence into the principality for some time, and his marriage to Sichelgaita in 1058 had been made with an eye to this prize. After victory at Bari in 1068, Robert was initially kept busy putting down revolts. But once he was in a position to campaign again in 1076, Salerno was his first target.

Later chroniclers go to considerable efforts to justify Robert's invasion of the principality, claiming that he was responding to prior attacks by the local prince Gisulf II (his own brother-in-law). In reality, this was an act of naked aggression. The city-state of Amalfi had submitted to Robert in 1073, so Salerno now stood isolated. It withstood the resulting siege valiantly, but over the night of 12/13 December 1076 a turncoat opened the gates. Awaking to find a section of the walls in Guiscard's hands, the citizens finally submitted. Between them, the sons of Tancred de Hauteville had won the south.

It had been a slow, piecemeal process, but we should not underestimate the Hauteville achievement. For the first time in almost half a millennium, all of southern Italy stood under a single banner. The Hauteville successes did not, however, stand alone. For Norman influence was also being felt in other parts of the Mediterranean.

12

Under a Byzantine Banner:
Into Asia Minor, 1038–77

Of all the empires of the European Middle Ages, Byzantium was without a doubt the grandest. The direct descendant of the Roman Empire, it could claim an antiquity unequalled by its rivals. Here was a truly eternal empire, or so its inhabitants liked to think. The rulers called themselves 'emperor of the Romans' and their domains were known as 'Romania', the land of the Romans. (Not to be confused with the modern eastern European state – though this, too, is named after ancient Rome.) Most importantly, the eastern emperors continued to inhabit Constantinople (modern Istanbul), the greatest of the late Roman cities, founded by Constantine the Great in the early fourth century. Ideological and material claims to antiquity thus met in the lived environment of Byzantium.[1]

The pomp of the Byzantine court was the stuff of legend. This was a place of elaborate etiquette and conspicuous consumption. Above all, it was the tremendous wealth of the Byzantine rulers which impressed their neighbours. Here was a state still running on the Roman model, capable of generating large tax revenues and redistributing these to faithful servants and allies. Given this, Byzantium was a much-coveted prize. Constantinople itself survived successive sieges by the Sassinid Persians (626), Umayyad caliphs (654, 674–8, 717–18), Slavic Bulgars (813) and the Kievan Rus' (860, 907, 941) – sometimes by the skin of its teeth.

The century before Guiscard's arrival in southern Italy had been one of the most successful in Byzantine history. The empire expanded on all fronts, securing Asia Minor and moving deep into the Middle East.[2] It was this optimism which inspired the empire's attempt to retake Sicily in 1038, in which Ironarm and his brothers, fighting as mercenaries for the Byzantine general George Maniakes, first won acclaim. Yet as we move into the middle years of the century, cracks in the imperial regime begin to show. Some of these were the result of structural tensions within the Byzantine polity, which was characterised by intense internal competition for power and influence. The biggest problems, however, lay beyond the frontier. The arrival of the Seljuk Turks had destabilised the Middle East, starting in the late 1030s. By the 1060s, Turkic groups were raiding deep into Anatolia. And in 1071, Emperor Romanos IV Diogenes himself was defeated and captured at Manzikert.[3] The empire now entered a period of sharp decline; the only question was whether this would prove terminal.

It was in this context that the Normans came close to toppling Byzantium. Although they'd first come to southern Italy as enemies of the Byzantines, almost from the start the Normans found themselves fighting both for and against them. Impressed with what they'd seen of the newcomers, local Byzantine generals recruited Normans into their ranks. The first recorded instance of this is in the attempt to reconquer Sicily in 1038. This came at a time when the Kalbid amirate had begun to splinter. George Maniakes was an experienced general with considerable resources, not least a large cohort of mercenaries. These comprised between 300 and 500 Normans, under the oversight of the Lombard general Arduin; Varangians (Viking mercenaries), under the leadership of the fearsome Harald Hardrada; and further Lombard forces from the north.

Among the Normans were William Ironarm and Drogo (and perhaps also Humphrey) – ambitious young men with bright futures before them. Their exploits are doubtless exaggerated by Amatus of Montecassino and Geoffrey of Malaterra, who are keen to see signs of later greatness here. But the invasion certainly went well, as we know from Byzantine sources; and we can be confident that the Normans pulled their weight.[4] Maniakes won decisive victories at Rometta (1038) and Troina (1040). His army succeeded in capturing the strategic city of Syracuse and looked set to take the rest of the island. However, Maniakes' campaign is a lesson in the dangers of depending on mercenaries. For after the second of these battles, the Normans were unhappy with their share of the spoils. And when Arduin raised the matter with Maniakes, the general had him beaten around the camp, humiliating him for all to see (not Maniakes' only reported act of vengeful sadism). The Normans now took umbrage, upping sticks for the mainland, where they started to foment revolt with Arduin.

That this was the beginning of the end for Byzantine Italy could scarcely have been foreseen. Maniakes' Norman mercenaries numbered no more than 500, and there are reasons to suspect that not all of these defected. For though John Skylitzes, our main Byzantine source for the expedition, has the entire group leave, he later speaks of the continuing service of at least one of the Norman leaders, Hervé. Moreover, a Norman mercenary unit known as the Maniakatoi – named after Maniakes – is attested in imperial service well into the 1070s.[5] This strongly suggests that some (perhaps most) of the Normans remained loyal. And for his part, Maniakes was not overly troubled by the defection. Indeed, it was not this which brought his campaign to a halt, but rather intrigue at the imperial capital. Rumours that Maniakes was disloyal had started to circulate here. And soon enough, orders came that he was to be brought back in chains to Constantinople. In Maniakes' absence, the imperial advance faltered.

If the Sicilian expedition had not been a complete success, the Normans had proven their worth. The Maniakatoi were apparently redeployed to Constantinople, perhaps in connection with the appointment of Argyros, a Lombard general, to senior office in 1046. Certainly Norman mercenaries were involved in putting down the revolt of Leo Tornikios (a Byzantine general) there the following year.[6] Thereafter, they are a regular presence among Byzantine armies.

The Normans – invariably called Franks in Byzantine sources – quickly gained a reputation for fearlessness and ferocity. The court historian Michael Psellos reports that they were impetuous and overwhelming in their onslaught, sentiments echoed by Anna Komnena, the Byzantine princess whose history of her father's life and times furnishes our most detailed (if tendentious) narrative of the later eleventh century.[7] As these reports suggest, the Normans were prized as heavy cavalry, and it was the force of their charge that most impressed observers. Anna notes, with grudging admiration, that they were undefeatable in the charge, though easier prey on foot. Psellos similarly observes that while their charge was unique in its ferocity, if this could be weathered, their stamina soon gave way. Evidently by the later years of the eleventh century, the Normans were enough of a fixture in Byzantine armies for them to have earned such stereotypes.

These anecdotes help explain the stationing of the Norman forces. Most of these were based in central and eastern Anatolia, regions under growing pressure from the Turks. The latter also fought on horseback, albeit as part of lighter and nimbler forces; the Normans offered a natural foil here. The clearest sign of growing Norman repute comes from Byzantine efforts to recruit more of them. William of Apulia reports that in 1051 Argyros, the Lombard general recorded leading Norman troops in Constantinople four years earlier, was sent on a recruiting drive to Italy. Here he offered great riches in exchange for service 'against the Persians' (i.e. the Turks). William sees the trip as a ploy to sap Norman forces in Apulia. But given the growing military plight in Anatolia (and the Pecheneg threat in the north), the Byzantine need was genuine. Indeed, William of Poitiers claims that the Byzantines even tried to secure support from the Conqueror in these years.[8]

Despite their popularity, Norman recruits proved no more reliable in Asia Minor than they had in Sicily. A mercenary's first loyalty is to his paymaster. And though the Normans were a useful counterweight to regular imperial forces, they added a degree of additional instability to the mix. We can see this in the career of Hervé, one of the first Norman leaders. Hervé had been part of the original force recruited in 1038 for the attack on Sicily. However, he hadn't followed the Hautevilles into rebellion in the 1040s and, thereafter, secured a position of trust within the imperial regime, serving successive rulers. In 1049/50, he commanded the left flank of the 'Roman phalanx' (apparently comprised of Norman cavalry) in a battle against the Pechenegs, a steppe people resident along the northern and western shores of the Black Sea. The battle ended disastrously for the Byzantines, and Skylitzes – our main source for Hervé's career – accuses Hervé of having instigated the flight, an accusation probably informed by knowledge of Hervé's later infidelity. Certainly, for the time being, Hervé remained in imperial employ, his career apparently unaffected by the loss.[9]

In 1057, however, Hervé was one of a number of men snubbed at the emperor's Eastertide rewards ceremony. He'd requested promotion to the status of *magistros*, an elevated (but largely honorary) title. When rebuffed, Hervé took up arms against the Byzantine emperor. This rebellion came at the same time as that of two other Byzantine generals, Isaac Komnenos and Katakalon Kekaumenos (who had similar grievances). But Hervé doesn't seem to have considered cooperation, choosing instead to make a common cause with the Turkish leader Samouch. The plan was to lead raids on imperial territory from eastern Anatolia. But disagreements soon emerged between Hervé and Samouch; and despite defeating Samouch in battle, Hervé found himself imprisoned by the Turkish amir of Chliat (modern Ahlat).

Though Skylitzes leaves matters here, this was not the end of the line for the Norman mercenary. We possess two seals in Hervé's name, which throw further light on his later career. The better known of these gives Hervé's name in its Greek form, as Erbebios Frangopoulos ('Hervé son of a Frank'); it also accords him the honorifics *magistros*, *vestēs* and *stratēlatēs* (the last two being honorary titles akin to *magistros*). Since Hervé is called *magistros* here, the seal can scarcely pre-date 1057, when he was denied promotion to this office. It would seem to follow that Hervé had returned to Byzantine service at some later point, earning those honours he'd previously been denied. Confirmation of this comes from the other seal in Hervé's name. This accords him the even more exalted title *proedros*; it also states that he was charged (in all likelihood temporarily) with oversight of all Byzantine forces in the East. This would have been an astronomic rise indeed, and a plausible context is offered by the disastrous battle of Manzikert in 1071. In the aftermath of this, Emperor Romanos IV was imprisoned and the eastern army left in disarray; Hervé would have been well-placed to step in.[10]

Two other Norman leaders figure prominently in Byzantine politics of the 1060s and 1070s: Robert Crispin and another mercenary Roussel de Bailleul. Unlike Hervé, both of these men are mentioned by Amatus, who includes them in an aside on Norman activities in the East.[11] Michael Attaleiates, writing in the late 1070s, reports that 'a certain Latin man from Italy' called Crispin had entered imperial employ shortly before Romanos' eastern expedition of 1069. Like most Norman recruits, Robert was sent to the eastern front, where the threat from the Turks was greatest. But scarcely had he arrived than he started causing problems. Believing that he'd been insufficiently rewarded by the emperor, he began to harass local tax collectors. When Romanos got wind of this, he ordered an attack on the upstart mercenary. An initial strike by local forces was defeated, so Romanos sent five western *tagmata* (the *tagma* being the kind of professional unit which formed the core of the imperial army) to deal with Robert. They attempted a surprise attack on a Sunday, knowing that the God-fearing Robert and his men would be at rest then. But they bungled the ruse – tripping over the Norman tents, according to Attaleiates – and soon found themselves driven back. Once the Normans were able to mount their horses and regroup, the imperial *tagmata* were routed. This was no longer a local tax revolt – it was a direct threat to imperial authority. In response, Romanos marched to Dorylaion (Şarhöyük), where the main Byzantine army was starting to assemble. Sensing the danger, Robert decided to submit in exchange for amnesty. Soon after doing so, however, he was arraigned on further charges of conspiracy. Hearing of this, the bulk of Robert's troops, who'd stayed behind during the affair, went on the rampage.[12]

Robert's revolt bears many similarities to Hervé's. The core issues were again honour and remuneration. And Robert's hope was clearly to make terms with the emperor, much as Hervé had done. Indeed, while conciliation proved impossible under Romanos, Robert was soon restored. In 1071, he returned from exile to join another rebellion led by Byzantine generals, thereafter earning a place of honour in the regime of the usurper Michael VII Doukas.[13] Still Robert's initial rebellion against Romanos represents a significant escalation of Norman troublemaking. Hervé's forces only numbered a few hundred and his revolt petered out without direct imperial intervention. Robert's, by contrast, removed significant territory from Romanos' control, subverting imperial taxes. It also defeated a retaliatory expedition, probably numbering thousands of men.[14] In the end, it had taken the emperor's own involvement to bring him to heel.

If Crispin's revolt had revealed the prospects awaiting a sufficiently brazen Norman commander, these were fully realised by Roussel de

Bailleul a few years later. Amatus mentions Roussel in the same breath as Robert, and it's clear that contemporaries saw him as Crispin's successor. Evidently Norman involvement in Asia Minor was now beginning to attract comment back in Italy. If Amatus is to be trusted, Roussel had first served the emperor in 'Slavonia'. This probably means that he was involved in putting down the Bulgar revolt of 1071; he may also have been charged with guarding the region against the Pechenegs.[15] Following Robert's death (c.1073), Roussel seems to have inherited command of his men (doubtless reinforced by Roussel's own) in north-eastern Asia Minor.

This was an extremely difficult time for the empire. Defeat at Manzikert had not only opened the way for the Turks to make inroads into Anatolia; it also represented a massive ideological blow. For almost a century, the empire had been on the front foot, securing and expanding its frontiers in the Balkans and Middle East. This latest defeat now created a crisis of confidence, and when Romanos was captured by the Turkish leader Alp Arslan, a *de facto* vacancy emerged on the imperial throne. It was problems such as these which were to prove most intractable, and the following years saw successive waves of internal revolt and rebellion. The first (and most successful) of these brought Michael VII Doukas to the throne (with Crispin's assistance). But Michael VII was immediately faced by further disruption in the Balkans, where efforts were being made to resurrect the old Bulgar state.

Only in 1073 was Michael in a position to attend to his eastern frontiers. The aim now was to claw back recent losses. In this connection, Isaac Komnenos was placed in charge of a large expeditionary force alongside his younger brother Alexios. Among this was the Norman detachment now headed by Roussel, which reportedly numbered some 400 heavily armoured knights.[16] Much like four years earlier, tensions soon emerged between the mercenaries and the main imperial force. In this case, the cause was the treatment of one of Roussel's men, who'd been charged by Isaac of mistreating a local. According to Nikephoros Bryennios – our main source, who probably draws on a lost historical account about (or by) Michael VII's brother[17] – Roussel had been looking to rebel for some time, so this may have been no more than a pretext. In any case, the Normans now struck out on their own, defeating a small Turkish force at

Melitene (Malatya) or perhaps Sebasteia (Sivas). Isaac and the depleted main army, meanwhile, were defeated by the Turks at Kaisareia (Kayseri) in the central Anatolian plateau.

Isaac's defeat presented Roussel with a golden opportunity. With the empire in disarray, central Asia Minor was ripe for the picking. And like the Hauteville brothers before him, Roussel was swift to seize the chance. He immediately began setting himself up as an alternative to imperial rule, offering the long-suffering people of Anatolia protection in exchange for payment. This may have been little better than a racket, but it was not so different from imperial rule; all it involved was redirecting taxation from Constantinople to Roussel. From a local perspective, this arrangement had the singular advantage that Roussel was on hand and ready; he may also have demanded less tax. Certainly the offer found many takers, and a Norman state began to emerge in the eastern reaches of the empire.

We know little about the nature of Roussel's polity, but the threat was taken seriously in Constantinople. Early in 1074, the last remaining imperial forces in Asia Minor were assembled to stamp out the revolt. These were joined by Varangian and 'Frankish' (i.e. Norman) mercenaries and placed under the overall command of John Doukas, the emperor's brother (Bryennios' source). The entire army probably numbered only a few thousand – a sign of the straits in which the empire now found itself. This marched through Dorylaion, south east of Constantinople, to the bridge at Zombou. This was a strategic crossing point over the Sangarios (Sakarya), the river which divides north-western Anatolia from the rest of the peninsula. Alerted to John's advance, Roussel and his men rapidly secured the opposite bank, seeking to prevent further progress into their newly annexed territories. The sides now began to draw up lines for battle. At this point, John's Normans, who comprised the left flank of the army, decided that their interests would be better served by joining their fellow countrymen. And as was so often the case, one act of subordination led to another. Nikephoros Botaneiates, the commander of John's rear guard, also decided to withdraw as soon as the battle began to go against the imperial forces. The result was a comprehensive and humiliating defeat. John and his son, Andronikos, were captured, the latter badly wounded.

John's defeat marked the effective end of Byzantine authority east of the Sangarios. The loss of Asia Minor, begun at Manzikert three years earlier, was all but complete. Roussel, by contrast, was at the height of his powers. With no active army between himself and the capital, he marched on Constantinople. He encamped at Chrysopolis (Üsküdar), on the Anatolian side of the Bosporus, directly opposite the metropolis. Here Roussel demonstratively razed the town in full sight of the city walls. Roussel had now won almost all the Norman mercenaries to his cause – a total force numbering perhaps between 2,000 and 3,000 heavily armed men. This was enough to make a splash, and was far larger than the imperial armies available. But it was not nearly strong enough to take the capital by storm. Roussel knew this, and seems to have hoped that internal divisions would bring Michael VII down. He'd miscalculated, however.

Unable to take the city, Roussel was forced to improvise. He now proclaimed his captive John Doukas emperor, seeking to create a puppet imperial government. That Roussel was set on replacing Michael is revealed by his curt response to the emperor's offer of generous gifts and the title of *kouropalates* (literally, 'in charge of the palace'), should Roussel and his men submit. Yet Roussel had overplayed his hand. A Norman-led regime in the heart of Asia Minor may have been a viable prospect. But by setting himself squarely against the Byzantine state, Roussel made it impossible to find any middle ground. Sensing that the Normans were now the greatest threat to the empire, Michael reached out to his erstwhile opponents, the Turks. He hired a prominent Turkish general, who was able to make swift work of the Norman force. The Turks captured both Roussel and John, but were happy to ransom the former back to his wife and men. Chastened, and certainly diminished, Roussel remained a potent force.

Michael now sought out support from his brother-in-law, George II of Georgia. George placed 6,000 men at the service of Nikephoros Palaiologos, the emperor's chosen general. And with these, Nikephoros marched west (from Georgia) to Pontos, on the northern Turkish coast. Yet soon Nikephoros ran out of funds and his troops began deserting. Roussel was then able to dispatch the remnants. Desperate and depleted of men, the emperor finally entrusted the task of bringing Roussel down to the up-and-coming young Alexios Komnenos, who'd led the expeditionary force of 1073 alongside his brother Isaac. Given his future career – Alexios would be Michael's successor but one – it's hardly surprising that later writers glamourise Alexios' capture of Roussel. They present him waging a valiant guerrilla war against the odds with a skeleton force.

The reality was more prosaic. Alexios let gold do the work of steel, putting out a bounty on Roussel's head among the Turks of Asia Minor. Soon enough Tutak, who'd been an ally of the fledgling Norman state to date, turned traitor, arresting Roussel at a feast. He then turned Roussel over to Alexios at Amaseia (Amasya) in northern Anatolia. Interestingly, Bryennios records that the local population was so upset by the prospect of a return to Byzantine rule that Alexios had to pretend to blind Roussel – rendering him unfit for rule – in order to leave with his skin. The tale has a legendary air to it – and Bryennios was married to Alexios' daughter, Anna Komnena – but it preserves a kernel of truth. Roussel had proven a reliable protector and many were unhappy about the prospect of returning to rule from Constantinople.

While Norman state-building proved abortive in Anatolia, its legacy was considerable. The loss of the region had been on the cards since Manzikert, but it was sealed at Zombou Bridge. For two years thereafter, large parts of Asia Minor had been under Norman sway. And while future generations of Norman mercenaries were to prove more pliable – more Hervé than Roussel in disposition – such westerners continued to be a disruptive element within the imperial forces. Indeed, the same Alexios who earned acclaim for bringing Roussel to heel, would later seek to harness the power of the western 'Franks' for his own purposes.

13

Bohemond and the Balkans:
'A Marvel to Behold', 1081–5

When Anna Komnena, the Byzantine princess and historian, came to write of Guiscard's eldest son Bohemond, it was with awe, fear and grudging respect. He was 'a marvel to behold', a man whose appearance inspired admiration and whose name struck terror in his foes. Bohemond towered above his fellow men, with broad shoulders and a wide chest. His hands were large and his neck and back compact. Though he possessed a rough charm, there was a savage side to his demeanour. Even his laugh was more a threat than an invitation to merriment. Bohemond was also arrogant and cunning, his words carefully chosen for their ambiguity. Only the emperor himself was Bohemond's match.[1]

In many respects, Bohemond is the antihero of Anna's work – the antithesis of her great father, Emperor Alexios Komnenos. That Bohemond should loom so large is no accident. For in Alexios' thirty-seven-year reign, no-one troubled him so often (or so seriously) as Bohemond. The fall of Roussel de Bailleul may have spelt the end of Norman state-building in Asia Minor, but it was just the prelude to more serious threats from the Hautevilles. Once Bari had fallen in 1071, responsibility for Sicily was delegated to Roger. Guiscard then spent nearly a decade quelling rebellions and vying for power and influence with the pope, whose conciliatory attitude had hardened since the fall of Apulia. But soon enough, Robert began to turn his attentions to more daring ventures.

The obvious target was the Byzantine Empire. The Byzantines had long been Robert's main rivals. And core provinces of the empire lay in Greece and Illyria, just a short boat trip across the Adriatic. As the emperor's attention was drawn ever more firmly to the Turkish threat on the eastern frontier, these regions presented an easy target. Yet

Robert might hope to do more than just pick off another Byzantine province or two. If he played his cards correctly, he stood a chance of replacing the emperor outright. In the aftermath of the Battle of Manzikert and Roussel's rebellion, the empire was teetering on the verge of collapse. All it would require to bring it down was a gentle nudge (or so it seemed).

Robert had another, less lofty, reason for wanting to carve out domains in Greece and the Balkans. Guiscard had married twice, first to the fellow Norman Alberada, then to the Salernitan princess Sichelgaita. The latter match was the more exalted, and it was probably always foreseen that any sons from it would be Robert's main heirs. Yet this left the question of what would happen to his son with Alberada, Bohemond. With three younger sons with Sichelgaita to accommodate, Robert had little to offer in Italy. Yet if he failed to satisfy Bohemond, the risk was that the latter would take matters into his own hands. Sichelgaita was well aware of the threat. When Robert fell severely ill in early 1073, she rushed to call an assembly, at which she secured support for the succession of her eldest, Roger Borsa.[2] New conquests in Greece and the Adriatic promised to solve this knotty problem: these could be left to Bohemond, leaving Robert's Italian domains undiminished in the hands of his younger sons.

For much of the 1070s, Robert avoided antagonising his Byzantine neighbours. After the fall of Bari, Romanos IV had reached out to Guiscard, hoping to secure his western frontier at a time when new threats (some of them of Norman making) were presenting themselves in the East. Though initial efforts failed, in August 1074 Romanos' successor Michael VII Doukas established a formal treaty with Robert. This was to be sealed by a dynastic union and one of Robert's daughters was now pledged to the young son of Michael VII. The marriage itself never came to pass, but the engagement alone brought considerable kudos to the fledgling Hauteville dynasty. There was also another side to the pact. Robert was granted the highest court rank available to non-members of the Byzantine royal family, that of *nobilissimus* (literally, 'most noble'); and similarly high ranks were offered to one of Robert's sons and many of his followers. Besides prestige, these roles came with large annual stipends. This was tribute by any other name, and Robert and his men stood to gain to the tune of over 200 pounds of gold per annum.[3] One can see why they were keen not to throw this away.

By the early 1080s, however, the situation had begun to change. In 1078, Michael VII was ousted by Nikephoros III Botaneiates, who was replaced in turn by Alexios Komnenos I three years later. This effectively meant the end of the alliance. It also created political instability on the Bosporus, which Robert might hope to exploit. It didn't take long for him to respond. As soon as he'd put down a rebellion at home, Robert began making plans. His interests coincided with those of the pope, who was keen to re-establish contacts with the eastern Church; and they now began to hatch a joint plan for an eastern invasion.

The key figure in the coming campaigns, however, was Bohemond himself. Bohemond would become a legend in his lifetime. His given name was Mark, perhaps because he'd been born at San Marco Argentano, Robert's early base in Calabria. Mark itself is a Graeco-Italian name, not a Norman one, and the young boy's parents evidently saw his future in the south. As significant as his given name, however, is the designation by which Mark went: Bohemond. This was originally the name of a giant, about whom Robert had heard during a banquet. Struck by the similarities between this legendary figure and his own larger-than-life son, Robert henceforth took to calling the young prince Bohemond.

The name stuck – and aptly so. For in almost every respect, Bohemond loomed over his contemporaries. Anna Komnena remarks that he towered over a cubit (about 1.5 feet or 0.44 m) above the tallest of other men. He was also perfectly proportioned (so Anna continues) and stood out on account of his pale complexion and light hair (a product, perhaps, of his Scandinavian heritage).[4] We do not know Bohemond's precise date of birth. Robert wed Alberada in 1050 and separated from her in 1058, so a date in the early to mid-1050s is likely. This means that he would have come of age in the early 1070s, around the time that Robert's illness threatened to overturn Sichelgaita's succession plans. It's in these years that Bohemond had his first experience in battle, perhaps in connection with the rebellion of 1079.[5] Certainly by the time Robert began to turn his attentions to Byzantine Illyria, he had considerable faith in the capabilities of his first born.

In early 1080, a Greek monk arrived in southern Italy, claiming to be the deposed Michael VII, with whom Robert had been on such good terms. Pretenders were a common phenomenon in the ancient and medieval world. In an age before mass media and rapid transportation, it was easy to claim an exalted lineage.[6] In this case, it was in Robert's interest to suspend disbelief. In reality, Michael VII had entered a monastery after his deposition. And far from seeking restitution, Michael enthusiastically embraced religious life, eventually rising to the post of metropolitan of Ephesus – one of the most senior offices within the Byzantine Church. Robert must have known all this and one suspects a degree of calculated cynicism on his part. Indeed, later sources suggest that the duke had put the false Michael up to the task, and there may be some truth to this. In any case, with 'Michael' in tow, Robert and Bohemond could position themselves as the restorers of their old friend and ally, the rightful emperor.

In March 1081, Robert placed a fleet under Bohemond's command, with instructions to strike at Corfu and, if possible, secure bases on the mainland. Over the next two months, Robert gathered further forces. By now, the pope was starting to have misgivings about the venture. But Robert pressed on with his plans. He had Roger Borsa designated heir, then proceeded to Corfu. Robert arrived in May, and together with Bohemond, soon secured the main city on the island. He then moved over to the mainland, establishing a base at Buthrotum (Butrint), in the south of modern Albania. From here they travelled north to Valona (Vlorë). Their target was Dyrrachion (Durrës), the most important administrative centre in the region (and to this day Albania's second city). Before investing the town, however, Robert and Bohemond had 'Michael' crowned, staking their claim to the empire in suitably ceremonial form. The siege itself was under way by 17 June.[7]

Our main Byzantine source for these events, Anna Komnena's panegyric of her father (the *Alexiad*), claims that Robert was out to take the entire eastern empire. Her testimony must be treated with caution. Anna wrote many decades after the events from an avowedly pro-Byzantine (and pro-Komnenian) perspective. Alexios had just seized the throne, and it was in her interest to exaggerate the Norman threat, so as to make her father's eventual success all the more remarkable.[8] However, Anna is not alone in making this claim. Amatus also reports that Robert dreamt of conquering Constantinople. This would indeed have been a bold move. But in the context of the early 1080s, it was far from inconceivable. Over the previous decade, military failures had spawned factional divides, and every emperor since Constantine X Doukas (r. 1059–67) had been violently removed from the throne. Having just taken southern Italy against the odds, Robert must have fancied his chances. Even if he failed to secure the whole empire, he might still hope to carve off valuable territories in northern Greece and the Adriatic.

The siege of Dyrrachion was a protracted affair. The city was well defended and Norman efforts were hampered by repeated attempts to lift the siege. Alexios made contact here with his Venetian allies, who had every reason to be concerned by the emergence of a new naval power to their south. They planned to encircle the Normans, with the Venetians attacking by sea and Alexios approaching by land. But co-ordinating forces was a tricky matter at the best of times. And while the Venetian force may have had some success, any sign of it was long gone by the time the emperor appeared in mid-October. Alexios engaged Robert in battle on 18 October, but was decisively defeated. Even so, the siege dragged on deep into winter. In the end, Dyrrachion was taken by deception rather than force, when a Venetian nobleman called Dominic, who commanded one of the towers, was bribed to betray the city.[9]

Robert and Bohemond were in no position to press their advantage. Dyrrachion had fallen in February, in the heart of the winter months which made campaigning difficult in the Balkans. In the spring, they moved inland, initially on a route along the Diabolis (Devoli) valley, taking Kastoria in northern Greece. This was a detour from the Via Egnatia, the main road from Dyrrachion to Constantinople, and may have been intended to catch Alexios off guard. Robert and Bohemond were now making good progress (all things considered), and Geoffrey of Malaterra reports that those at the capital began to tremble. We may suspect a degree of exaggeration, but Byzantine sources also speak of growing unease. Certainly large swathes of Greece looked set to fall. But just as the campaign was gathering steam, troubling news reached Robert. The German ruler

Henry IV was poised to march on Rome, a move which not only threatened Robert's papal allies but also exposed his own domains in southern Italy. Even more disturbing were reports of renewed revolt in Apulia, perhaps encouraged by Alexios' agents.[10]

In face of this dual threat, Robert returned to Italy. He had not, however, given up on the Balkans. Bohemond was left behind with the main force, with instructions to press on towards Constantinople. And soon after Robert's departure, Bohemond dealt decisively with a counterattack led by Alexios near Ioannina. In the aftermath of victory, Bohemond struck north and east, back along the Via Egnatia. Here he defeated Alexios a second time. But while the Normans might best the Byzantines in battle, they struggled to make much of a dent in the well-oiled machine that was the Byzantine state. Bohemond was able to secure the strategic city of Lychnidos (Ohrid), but the citadel held out, barring further passage along the Via Egnatia. In response, Bohemond tacked south once more, striking at Thessaly. The intention was probably to force an alternative route through to Constantinople, though the prospect of further conquests in Boeotia, Euboea and the Peloponnese may also have been alluring.

Travelling down the Salvarias valley, Bohemond took Triakkala, then made for Larissa, not far from the Aegean Sea. The Byzantines, however, avoided battle, leaving Bohemond with the prospect of another long siege. Norman supplies now started to run short, and Alexios approached with a new army. He once again offered battle. But this time, it was a decoy. Alexios drew out Bohemond's men, only to have a smaller force sneak behind and sack their camp. The following day, the Normans were defeated outright, though not decisively. Trapped deep in enemy territory with morale ebbing (and supplies running low), Bohemond was forced to retreat. In his absence, the Venetians had taken Dyrrachion, depriving him of his main base of operations on the Adriatic. The Normans therefore returned to Valona. Soon, however, Kastoria was lost, making Bohemond's position untenable. And so Bohemond withdrew once more – this time, all the way back to Apulia.[11]

Robert had been kept busy with the Apulian revolt for much of 1082 and 1083. And just as he might have hoped to regroup with Bohemond, pressing matters demanded his attention in the north.

For in early 1084, Henry IV had finally seized Rome. So far, Robert had been unable to heed the pope's pleas for assistance. But now, the time had come for action. Robert marched north, arriving to find an abandoned Rome in late May. Here he was able to free the pope, who'd holed up in the Castel Sant'Angelo, just outside the medieval city. But the cost of victory was high. Much of the city was put to flame by Guiscard's men, and the pope's (long fraught) relations with the urban aristocracy never recovered.

Only in October was Robert in a position to turn his attentions to the Adriatic once more, launching a belated invasion with Bohemond. But if Robert's first foray had posed a real threat to the empire, his second never did. Alexios was now well established in Constantinople; the emperor was also becoming a deft hand at dealing with Norman troublemakers. Robert came with a large force, this time including his younger sons. Initially, Roger Borsa and his brother Guy were sent with a reconnaissance force to secure Valona, much as Bohemond had in 1081. Robert then followed with the main army, joining up with them between Valona and Buthrotum. Roger's presence is significant. This suggests that Guiscard now felt more secure in his southern Italian domains and did not feel the need to leave his son behind; it's also a sign that any lands won for Bohemond were to be held under Roger's aegis.

Autumn invasions were always risky affairs; and in this case, the risk did not pay off. The intention was to relieve the remnants of the first expeditionary force, who had been holding out in the citadel of Corfu since May 1081. Storms, however, prevented operations for the first two months after landing. And when the weather finally improved, allowing a crossing, Robert almost immediately faced opposition from Venetian and Byzantine naval forces. As previously, Robert managed to get the better of his opponents. But the cost of victory was high (Roger is said to have been wounded). Robert then raised the siege of Corfu. But with further rough weather on the horizon, there was little way of exploiting the victory. So Robert laid up the fleet for the winter on the Acheron, taking up quarters himself with the main force at Vonitsa to the south. This southwards move is reminiscent of Bohemond's tactics in 1083. It points toward Robert's strategy for the coming year, when he would leave the well-defended Via Egnatia and strike at the empire's soft Grecian underbelly.[12]

Whatever the plan, it was soon overtaken by events. Keeping large armies safely encamped in hostile territory is always a challenging affair. In this case, plague struck. As important as the resulting loss of manpower was the psychological blow this represented. While the Normans' enemies' forces grew steadily stronger, their own army was wasting away. A particular loss was Bohemond, who fell so ill that he had to return to Salerno for treatment.

Apparently undeterred, Robert pressed on south in the summer. The first prize was to be Cephalonia, which would open the way into the Gulf of Corinth. An advance force under Roger and Sichelgaita had already secured the island's capital. But by the time Robert met them, he was severely ill himself – perhaps with the same plague that had struck his men over the winter months, or perhaps with malaria (the traditional Mediterranean illness of the summer). Whatever the cause, Robert died on 17 July, soon after his arrival on the island.

Robert's death spelt the end of Italo-Norman adventures in Greece and Illyria for over a generation. A power vacuum beckoned back in Apulia and Calabria, which Roger and Sichelgaita rushed to fill. But Robert's dream of an eastern empire would live on in his eldest son. Alexios may have won the first engagements, but Bohemond was not about to leave matters at that.

14

The First Crusade: Eastern
Promises, 1096–1108

Few events of the Middle Ages are better known than the storming of Jerusalem on 15 July 1099. Inspired by the preaching of Pope Urban II, a rag-bag group of adventurers had taken up the cross three years earlier with the promise of redeeming Christianity's most holy city from the hands of the Muslims. After years of toil, which saw their numbers diminish fourfold, they'd now achieved the unthinkable. Their success would send shockwaves throughout Europe, North Africa and the Middle East, and leave a legacy which is felt to this day.

The story is a good one, regularly recounted in tones either triumphal or censorious by modern historians.[1] But what often gets lost along the way is the specifically Norman dimension of the First Crusade. For not only did a large proportion of the crusaders hail from Normandy and southern Italy, but the very endeavour itself was informed by earlier Norman activity. It was the successes of the Conqueror and Guiscard which had first shown the western European aristocracy what could be achieved by risky ventures in foreign lands. And often a direct connection can be drawn between these early Norman conquests and the First Crusade.[2] One of the most prominent of the crusaders was Bohemond of Taranto, whose exploits stand centre stage here. Denied an appropriate inheritance in Italy and the Adriatic, Bohemond was only too happy to march east in search of fame and fortune.

Yet the Norman contribution went well beyond Bohemond and his men. Another leading figure was the southern French count Raymond of Saint-Gilles, who had been married to Matilda of Sicily, Bohemond's cousin. Raymond looked jealously on at the Hauteville successes, and crusading offered an opportunity to match them. Equally prominent are participants with connections to the duchy of Normandy. Foremost among these are Robert Curthose, the

Conqueror's eldest son, and Odo of Bayeux. Robert's cousin, Robert II of Flanders, was another important recruit. This latter Robert enjoyed ties of his own to the Hautevilles, as his sister had wed Roger Borsa. And two other prominent crusaders, the brothers Godfrey and Baldwin, were the younger sons of Eustace of Boulogne. Finally, Stephen of Blois, perhaps the grandest of all the princes to join the expedition, was married to the Conqueror's daughter Adela.

Earlier Norman exploits thus furnished the model for the First Crusade. This is not to say that the movement was crudely materialistic. For most participants, religious zeal and material gain (not to mention fame and honour) were either side of the same coin.[3] This is what made the venture so enticing – it allowed knights and noblemen to seek their fortune in the name of God. The Conqueror had already sought papal endorsement for his invasion of England, and Guiscard and Roger had similarly framed their Sicilian campaigns in terms of the defence and expansion of the faith. The crusades represent a development of such practices, with papal approval now taking on a decisive role.

Yet if ideas about holy war had been percolating in Europe for some time, the immediate impetus for crusade came from the East – more specifically, from Alexios' Byzantium. In the 1070s, Pope Gregory VII had already contemplated sending a papally endorsed army to relieve the emperor. The situation became even more critical in the early 1090s. At this point, a wave of attacks from the nomadic Pechenegs served to draw Alexios' attention to the western provinces.[4] In response, Abu'l-Qasim and the Seljuk Turks struck at the rich imperial lands to the north and west of their base at Nicaea (İznik). Sensing weakness, other Turkish groups began to raid deep into the remaining provinces of Anatolia. Matters turned from bad to worse in late 1092, when the Baghdad-based sultan Malik-Shah died. Alexios had enjoyed good relations with Malik-Shah, but the ensuing succession dispute created considerable instability, which the increasingly independent Turkish rulers of Asia Minor were happy to exploit.

As failure followed failure, the mood in the capital darkened. Unrest was already visible in the early 1090s and came to a head in 1094, when conspirators began plotting to oust Alexios and replace him with his nephew, John Komnenos. It increasingly looked as though Alexios would go the way of his predecessors. It was in this context that the emperor made the fateful decision to appeal to Pope Urban II for aid.[5] In a sense, this was an extension of the tactics long employed by the Byzantine emperors, who'd successfully pitted Norman knights and Anglo-Scandinavian Varangians against eastern Turks for many years. Yet the results were to prove very different indeed. Neither Alexios nor Urban could have predicted the enthusiasm with which their call would be taken up, nor could they have imagined the long-term consequences of their actions.

Alexios' request arrived at a large church council at Piacenza in early March 1095. Urban responded favourably to the initial entreaty, and by summer was starting to drum up support for an expedition in his native France. These efforts were crowned by the Council of Clermont later in the year, at which Urban gave a stirring speech calling those present to march east to free the Holy Land.[6] The pope had good reason for backing the expedition. It promised to distract attention from interminable conflicts between himself and the German emperor (the so-called Investiture Contest). It also offered the prospect of rapprochement between the eastern and western churches, which had long been a papal aspiration. Amid the growing popularity of pilgrimage, eastern affairs became even more pressing, as disruption in Asia Minor now threatened to cut Christianity's most holy city off from its most devout worshippers.

Precisely because Urban's appeal proved popular, it took time for the crusading forces to assemble. Not all, however, were willing to wait. Inspired by the apocalyptic preaching of a man called Peter the Hermit, a group of minor noblemen set out before the main armies in the so-called People's Crusade of 1096. These groups committed a series of gruesome Jewish pogroms before departing Europe – a reminder of the perennially fine line between religious zeal and bigotry.[7] Despite clashes with fellow Christians in Hungary, they arrived in Constantinople in early August and were ferried across the Bosporus. Shortly thereafter, however, the motley army was cut down by Turkish forces outside Nicaea. Many died or were enslaved. Some of the survivors now opted to await the arrival of the main force.

Of the four princely armies to follow, three came from France and the Low Countries. One of these – that of Robert Curthose – was

Norman through and through, and many of the crusaders that made up the other armies enjoyed Norman associations. But perhaps the most significant Norman contribution would come from southern Italy, in the form of the restless Bohemond. Much like Curthose, Bohemond had drawn the short straw where dynastic succession was concerned, so stood to gain much from the expedition. The 'Deeds of the Franks' (*Gesta Francorum*) – an account of the crusade, written by an anonymous associate of Bohemond – reports that the Norman prince first got wind of the movement while besieging Amalfi, in early summer 1096, with his lord (and half-brother) Roger Borsa. Inspired by the news, Bohemond immediately pledged his involvement, cutting up his own cloak to form crosses for the men who flocked to join him. Modern historians have long suspected that this impressive *coup de théâtre* was premeditated. But we should not be too cynical. The anonymous report is corroborated by that of Geoffrey of Malaterra, who says that Roger was forced to abandon the siege because Bohemond diverted so much of his army. Geoffrey was a well-informed observer (and no fan of Bohemond). Moreover, it's not until August of this year, that we see Bohemond liquidating his landed assets to help fund the expedition.[8] Urban's preaching in support of the crusade had been focused on France, so it may well have been spring or early summer 1096 before the full details reached southern Italy.

While Roger Borsa must have been happy see the back of his brother, the circumstances cannot have pleased him. The anonymous chronicler claims that the two parted on good terms, but Geoffrey records the duke's frustration (as well as that of his uncle Roger I). That Bohemond was able to recruit so much of the army should not come as a surprise. Italo-Norman aristocrats knew full well the wealth and prestige to be won from foreign ventures. And with the conquest of Sicily now complete, there was little prospect of further gains in Italy. Fame and fortune would now be won in the East.

Bohemond probably always had more in mind than saving the Holy Land. After the failure of the Balkan campaigns of the 1080s, he had unfinished business with Alexios. Geoffrey reports that Bohemond embarked on the expedition precisely because he'd long had designs on the eastern empire (*Romania*, as Geoffrey calls it, in keeping with

Byzantine tradition). Taking imperial service may seem like an unusual way to bring the empire down. But Bohemond knew how easily gamekeepers could turn poachers, particularly in the volatile world of eleventh-century Byzantium.

If the decision to join the crusade had been spontaneous, Bohemond was sensible enough to spend the coming months preparing for the expedition. He had less far to travel than his northern counterparts and knew the route well, so there was no rush. Bohemond left from Brindisi in October 1096 and, in a striking repeat of the campaigns of the 1080s, landed near Valona on the Ilyrian coast. In doing so, he parted ways with the other crusading groups which travelled through Italy. They all sailed straight to Dyrrachion, where they met up with imperial forces and traversed the Via Egnatia. Bohemond's deviation is significant, particularly in light of Geoffrey's testimony. He may have been weighing up a strike against the emperor. One account has it that Bohemond requested Godfrey of Bouillon (Eustace's son) not to enter into friendship with Alexios, but rather to join him in moving against the capital. And Anna Komnena similarly recalls Alexios' suspicions that Bohemond and Godfrey were scheming.[9] If Bohemond had yet to declare – or even commit to – his peaceful intentions, this would also state why his men clashed with the emperor's Pecheneg auxiliaries, when they first joined the Via Egnatia.

In the end, Bohemond decided to stick with Urban's plan. If Godfrey could not be diverted, there was little hope of removing Alexios. The emperor was, however, right to be suspicious of Bohemond's motives. To allay such fears, Bohemond now left his men in the hands of his nephew Tancred and headed straight to the capital. Both Bohemond and Alexios had reason to be wary; but both needed each other. By means of deft diplomacy, the emperor convinced Bohemond that it was in both of their interests to cooperate; and Bohemond, for his part, committed to the Byzantine cause, swearing an oath of loyalty. This oath reportedly contained a provision that any traditional Byzantine territories would revert to Alexios, but that Bohemond could expect to receive lands of his own beyond Antioch.

For Alexios, such promises were essential. From his perspective, the crusade remained first and foremost a mission to save the empire. More men may have arrived than he'd anticipated – and more fuss made of Jerusalem as their final destination – but the westerners were still exalted auxiliaries, the heirs of Hervé, Robert Crispin and Roussel de Bailleul. He was therefore insistent that they swear oaths of loyalty, committing to restore any old Byzantine territory they were to conquer. For the idealistic incomers, Alexios' expectations were uncomfortable (and often resisted). Godfrey only agreed to oaths similar to those sworn by Bohemond under pressure, while Raymond of Saint-Gilles refused to swear outright. Bohemond, however, was playing a different game. He had no fear of subordination to Alexios. Previous Norman leaders had taken similar oaths; and even Guiscard had entered into (nominal) Byzantine service when he'd become *nobilissimus* in 1074. So rather than avoid swearing, Bohemond sought to wring the greatest possible concessions for doing so. Initially, he may have floated the possibility of being made commander-in-chief of the imperial army in the East. In the end, he seems to have extracted the promise that he would receive substantial lands beyond Antioch. Here we see Bohemond's aims in their purest form: for him, crusade was a means to an end.[10]

With the oaths sworn (or not, in the case of Raymond), the massive crusading army was ready to lumber into action. Their first target was Nicaea. The city had been lost to the Turks in the early 1080s. In recent years, it had been a thorn in Alexios' side, enabling attacks deep into the remaining Byzantine lands on the western Anatolian coast. Yet it was not simply Alexios' interests which dictated the move. If the crusading forces were to receive supplies from Constantinople in the coming months, they would need to control the city. Nicaea was the key to Asia Minor.

Nicaea was a large and important centre, now the capital of Kilij Arslan's Sultanate of Rum (one of the many splinters of Malik-Shah's massive empire). Kilij's forces had already seen off the People's Crusade the previous year, but the main force presented an altogether more serious challenge. When the crusaders arrived, the sultan was off campaigning against the Danishmends in the East. But he soon returned, attempting a relief of the city on 16 May. This was driven back. Even so, it took another month before Nicaea capitulated. Alexios carefully stage-managed the entire operation. Nicaea's submission was agreed in advance; however, imperial forces were allowed to scale the walls, creating the impression that the Byzantines had won the day. The concern was that the western troops would otherwise resent the generous terms offered to the city's inhabitants (most of whom were old Byzantine subjects), particularly after a hard-won siege.

Victory at Nicaea was crucial. It opened the Anatolian plateau to the crusaders; it also marked the first significant expansion of Byzantine territory in a generation. For Alexios, it was an opportunity to cement control of the crusade. A master of carrot-and-stick politics, he now rewarded the army's leaders generously, securing oaths from many of those who'd previously escaped or resisted these. Among this group was Bohemond's nephew Tancred, who'd stayed with the main Italo-Norman force when his brother hurried on to the capital.[11]

As the army marched further inland, it divided in two. The crusading force was far larger than most western and Byzantine armies of the era, and would be easier to provision if divided into constituent parts. Yet division was not without risks. Smaller forces risked being picked off. And sure enough, Kilij Arslan soon sought to exploit the situation, attacking the smaller vanguard led by Bohemond near Dorylaion (Şarhöyük). The fearsome Norman charge initially checked the Turkish attack, but it was the arrival of reinforcements from the second (larger) force that finally turned the tide. The battle had been a close-run thing, particularly for Bohemond and his men. But victory left the crusaders free to march unopposed through central Anatolia.

Alexios' gamble had paid off – or so it seemed. The main Byzantine enemy, Kilij Arslan, had been decisively defeated; Nicaea had been won; and the rest of the Anatolian plateau would soon follow. Yet with territorial gains came complications. The towns and cities captured reverted to Byzantine control, as per the earlier oaths and agreements. Yet many of the crusaders started to become frustrated by the lack of spoils. The first to part ways with the main force here was Baldwin of Boulogne, the youngest son of Eustace. Baldwin helped secure Tarsos for Alexios against the wishes of Tancred, who'd initially secured the city. Soon thereafter, Baldwin received his quid pro quo, when he took Edessa. Though Baldwin may initially have acknowledged Alexios' loose overlordship, he clearly had his sights set on greater things, and Edessa would soon become an autonomous polity – the first crusader state in the Middle East.[12] It may seem odd for Baldwin to abandon the expedition so early. Yet here we must bear in mind that freeing Jerusalem was just one of the aims of the crusade; only from the perspective of 1099 did this become the defining goal of the expedition. It had been Alexios' plea which spurred Urban to action, and Baldwin had played a key role in liberating the Christians of Asia Minor. He may well have believed that he could best serve the Christian cause from here.

It's clear that Alexios remained an active player in developments. For while the crusaders had been bulldozing their way through the Anatolian plateau, his own forces were securing the western and southern coasts. This was a carefully co-ordinated operation, which brought almost all of Asia Minor back under the imperial banner. Yet, with the (partial) exception of Bohemond, the crusaders had not signed up to be imperial stooges. And Baldwin's own gains provided a model for any looking to break ranks.

These tensions came to a head during the long siege of Antioch. The ancient city lay about halfway between Constantinople and Jerusalem, just south of the fulcrum between Asia Minor and the Middle East, where the crusader army tacked south after its long eastward march. Having made steady progress in 1097, they arrived outside the city walls in October. Antioch was one of the largest and best fortified cities of the Middle Ages, and even the massive crusader army couldn't invest the entire perimeter at once. Supplies therefore continued to stream in to the defenders. The only options available to the crusaders were to risk assault, hope for an enemy traitor or wait for submission.

The result was a war of attrition – the longest and most trying episode of the First Crusade. The problem for the crusaders was that they were now far beyond Alexios' supply lines. This meant that while the defenders continued to receive regular sustenance, they did not. In the New Year, they saw off a large relief force from Damascus, but were still left facing starvation. The living resorted to eating their horses; and when these ran out, reportedly turned on their fallen comrades. Many died. Many more deserted, including the Conqueror's son-in-law, Stephen of Blois.

It was in this context that relations with Alexios finally broke down. Byzantine efforts to secure supplies for their allies repeatedly failed – whether through want of trying or sheer difficulty is unclear. In January 1098, Alexios' representative, Tatikios, left the army, never to return. Bohemond was quick to exploit the situation.[13] In Tatikios' absence, Bohemond painted Alexios as a traitor, blaming him (not entirely without reason) for the army's present predicament. Because Alexios had failed to keep his side of the bargain, Bohemond argued, the crusaders were no longer bound by their oaths. This was essential for Bohemond's purposes, for he now had his eyes set firmly on Antioch, a city he'd committed to restoring to Alexios.

Having undermined the emperor's authority, Bohemond made contact with the captain of a portion of the wall, an Armenian called Firuz, who agreed to let the crusaders in. Bohemond then suggested to his fellow leaders that whichever of them could secure the city should receive it in reward. Some were wary – and rightly so. Bohemond was not a man to be trusted. But desperate to break the deadlock, they eventually relented.

With all the arrangements in place, Bohemond now made good his plan. He and his men entered the city via Firuz' section of wall on the night of 2/3 June, then threw open the gates to their fellow crusaders. The result was a bloodbath second only to that witnessed at Jerusalem the following summer. Yet scarcely had the crusaders entered the city than they found themselves facing the prospect of being under siege themselves. For a large force under the command of Kerbogha was rapidly closing on Antioch. Kerbogha was the governor (or atabeg) of Mosul to the east, and the army had originally been intended to relieve the siege. It was much larger than the depleted crusader force; what's more, it was fresh and well-provisioned. Initially, the crusaders sought to defend the walls. But they were desperately short of provisions and Kerbogha was more than happy to starve them out.

Running out of options, the crusaders decided to risk everything on a battle. Their spirits were raised by the discovery of the Holy Lance – the spear that pierced Christ's side upon the cross. Not all were convinced of the relic's authenticity (the German and Byzantine emperors both already claimed to possess the Holy Lance). But for an army in need of a miracle, it provided much-needed encouragement.

For three days, the crusaders embarked on a barefoot procession from church to church within the city, entreating divine favour. Spiritually prepared, they then marched out with the lance on 28 June. Initially taken aback, Kerbogha gathered his forces and struck. Yet the nerve of the crusaders held. Facing fiercer resistance than they'd anticipated, the Turks began to panic; and soon enough, they'd broken ranks, leaving the field to the determined westerners. The latter had been heavily outnumbered – perhaps by as much as two to one. Yet thanks to divine intervention – or so it seemed – they'd triumphed against the odds.[14]

If the crusaders had been united in their travails, they were now divided in victory. For Bohemond insisted on having Antioch turned over to him, as per the promises exacted before the final assault. But other members of the force, most notably Raymond of Saint-Gilles – who may not have been party to the agreement – claimed that these were pre-empted by the earlier oaths to Alexios. For some time, the army remained at an impasse. Yet Bohemond refused to budge, so Raymond eventually accepted the inevitable and moved on with the rest of the princes.

As with Baldwin the previous year, we must be wary of interpreting Bohemond's actions as a betrayal of the crusade. From the start, the expedition had been a means of acquiring land and influence. And he may, like Baldwin, have felt that he'd done his bit for his fellow Christians. Asia Minor was safely back in Byzantine hands. Bohemond would now hold Antioch, ensuring that Jerusalem, should it be taken, would not be cut off from its Christian allies to the north and west. A significant portion of Bohemond's force remained with him, establishing new lordships. The resulting principality of Antioch would therefore be the most 'Norman' of the crusader states; and its rulers remained Bohemond's descendants right up until its conquest in 1268 by the Mamluks.[15]

We should not, however, exaggerate the Norman character of Bohemond's polity – nor should we underestimate that of the other crusader states. The crusading forces were extremely fluid, with men passing between lords and companies at many points during the campaign. By 1098, many of Bohemond's men wouldn't have hailed from southern Italy, while a significant number of those who'd made

Queen Emma and King Cnut give a cross to the New Minster in Winchester.

The anonymous author of the *Encommium Emmae* presents his work to Queen Emma. Her two sons, Harthacnut and Edward, are waiting in the wings.

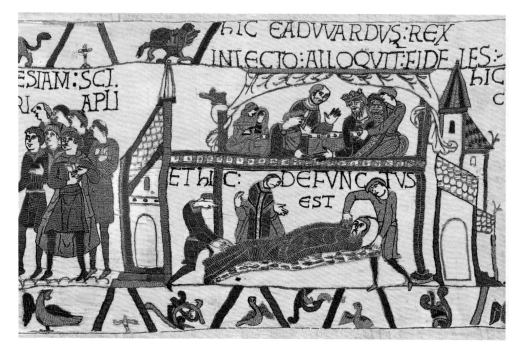

Edward the Confessor's death, as depicted in the Bayeux Tapestry.
Harold Godwinson and Queen Edith are among those at his bedside.

Edward's funeral cortège en route to the newly constructed
abbey church of Westminster.

The Tapestry's vivid portrayal of the Norman fleet crossing the Channel.

Harold's death scene. Is he the man with an arrow in his eye, or the one being hacked down by a Norman knight?

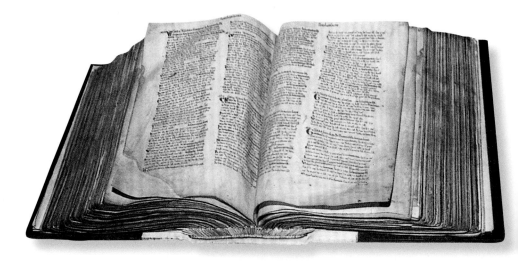

Great Domesday, the most impressive product of the
Conqueror's massive survey of 1086.

The Conqueror's charter for the bishopric of Exeter (1069). In appearance and
layout it looks every inch a pre-Conquest document, yet the names of the
senior witnesses are all Norman.

The interior of Durham Cathedral. Note the distinctive mouldings on the arches and the ribbed vaulting.

The walls of Dyrrachion (modern Durrës), which held out valiantly against Robert Guiscard and Bohemond.

Roger II being crowned by Christ. Mosaic panel in
Santa Maria dell'Ammiraglio, Palermo.

The apse of Santa Maria dell'Ammiraglio, the leading church of Roger II's
new Kingdom of Sicily.

David I of Scotland's charter granting Annandale to Robert I de Brus (1124).

Château Gaillard, Richard Lionheart's impregnable castle.

The tomb of King John, Worcester Cathedral. The lion at his feet bends the sword with his jaws in a possible play on John's nickname, 'softsword'.

Emperor Frederick II seated in majesty, from an early manuscript of his treatise on falconry.

their way east with him may have joined others. In fact, a considerable degree of Norman influence can be detected within the later crusader kingdom of Jerusalem to Bohemond's south. Much of this can be put down to the part played by Curthose and his men in the conquest and colonisation of the region. But some must be laid at the door of Tancred, Bohemond and their followers; and more still to later arrivals.[16] Beyond Antioch's name – it was the only crusader state to be named a principality, like the Lombard states Bohemond knew from southern Italy – the Italo-Norman contribution to the crusader states presents something of a paradox. It was clearly significant during the first generation or two of settlement. But thereafter the connection was severed, and the Sicilian realm is notably under-represented in later crusading expeditions. This ambivalence was the result of both accident and design.[17] As the movement evolved, crusading became a strongly familial affair, with generation after generation from the same dynasty often participating.[18] While in much of France and the Low Countries this encouraged involvement, in southern Italy it had the reverse effect. Here Bohemond had been the black sheep of the Hauteville family, so neither Roger Borsa nor Roger II (Borsa's successor) had any reason to exalt in his legacy. Moreover, most of Bohemond's men settled with him in the Middle East, leaving few Italian heirs to follow in their footsteps. The significant Muslim minority in Sicily further complicated matters. Roger II and his successors took a notably flexible and pragmatic approach when it came to relations with these groups and this may have served to dampen crusading zeal.

Political developments were equally important. In 1113, Baldwin of Jerusalem – the same Baldwin who'd begun his career as count of Edessa – would marry Adelaide del Vastro, the dowager-countess of Sicily (Roger I's wife, the mother of Roger II). Baldwin had long enjoyed good relations with the Normans. He was the son of Eustace of Boulogne, and his first wife, Godevere of Tosny, hailed from the duchy. The match promised to extend these contacts to the Normans of Italy. A condition of the marriage was that any children of Adelaide with Baldwin would succeed him as king; failing that, the throne would pass to Adelaide's adult son, Roger II of Sicily. The latter detail was crucial. Adelaide was not a young woman at the time – she must have been at least in her late thirties – and Baldwin did not have any children of his own, so there was a good chance that the throne of Jerusalem would soon be left vacant.

Yet Italian influence in the Holy Land would prove fleeting. Over the winter of 1116/17, Baldwin fell severely ill. Faced by the prospect of an absentee monarch, the local magnates rallied together to block Roger II's succession in preference for that of Baldwin's older brother, Eustace III of Boulogne (who was a sometime crusader himself). Baldwin himself seems to have been amenable to the plan (relations with Adelaide were strained). And soon after his recovery, Baldwin sent Adelaide rudely packing – without her rich dowry. William of Tyre reports that Roger II then 'conceived an undying hatred of the kingdom and its inhabitants', one which lived on among his heirs.[19] If in parts of Europe crusading zeal became a familial trait, in Sicily crusading cynicism proved similarly heritable.

Equally significant were developments in Antioch itself. Here the death of Bohemond's son and eventual heir, Bohemond II, in 1130 created considerable uncertainty. The young prince was in his early twenties and only left a two-year-old daughter, Constance, as heir. In order to stabilise the situation, Constance was married to Raymond of Poitiers – the great-nephew of Raymond of Saint-Gilles – changing the political orientation of the principality significantly. Symptomatic of the shift is the fact that Constance and Raymond gave up claims to Taranto, Bohemond's original Apulian patrimony, which he and his son had so carefully maintained. But just as we should not exaggerate early Norman influence, so we should not underestimate its longevity. Most of the early settlers remained in place, both in Antioch and Jerusalem; and there is little evidence for the wave of Poitevin newcomers sometimes associated with Raymond. Indeed, marriage made Raymond a Hauteville rather than Constance a Poitevin, and it's telling that their eldest son bore the distinctively Italo-Norman name Bohemond.[20]

The precise Norman contribution to the Holy Land remains hard to gauge. From at least the later tenth century, Norman and French identities were not hermetically sealed. Much like a modern inhabitant of Leeds can be a proud Yorkshireman and Englishman, so it was possible to be both Norman and French (or Frankish). Byzantine sources had always called the Normans Franks (much as English sources called them French); Arabic sources now did likewise. And it was as Franks that the crusaders themselves identified. Many hailed from France; and those who did not were mostly Romance speakers with claims to Frankish pedigree. In this context, there was little to distinguish Robert Curthose from Baldwin of Boulogne – or Norman from French (or even Italian) influence.

~

As we might expect, Bohemond's own career did not end with the conquest of Antioch. His machinations had won him a major prize, but they'd also earned him a bitter enemy. Antioch had been in Byzantine hands as recently as 1078, and Alexios was not about to roll over for the Norman turncoat. Bohemond, for his part, continued to have ambitions of his own concerning the eastern empire. The years immediately after 1098 were ones of consolidation. In August 1100, however, Bohemond was unexpectedly defeated and captured by the Danishmend Turks. There was much wrangling over his release, during which Tancred ably held the fort in Antioch. Upon Bohemond's return in 1103, he was able to make little headway with expanding his domains. And after being defeated by the Turks again in the summer of 1104, he decided to change tack.

Bohemond now set out for France, where he began to recruit forces for a 'crusade' against Alexios. This was in part a response to the challenge posed by the empire to his new principality. Alexios was Bohemond's immediate neighbour to the west and was angling for the restitution of Antioch, which he saw (not without reason) as rightfully his own. Bohemond's move also reflects his longer-term ambitions. In the early 1080s, he and his father had attempted to take Constantinople; and in 1096/7, he'd entertained another strike against Alexios. Now Bohemond made a final bid to topple the eastern emperor. Successful crusaders were treated with awe and reverence upon their return to Europe, and Bohemond was no exception. The crusade had done much to burnish his (already formidable) reputation, and his recruiting efforts met with considerable success. Bohemond was also able to win the hand of Constance, the daughter of the French king Phillip I.[21]

By 1107, Bohemond was ready to make his move. He had unfinished business with Alexios. And rather than returning to Antioch and striking at the neighbouring Byzantine territories to his north and west, he now attacked at the empire via the Adriatic – just as he had a quarter of a century earlier. As then, Bohemond claimed to be acting in the name of the true Byzantine emperor, this time a purported son of Romanos IV Diogenes. Bohemond's army was probably larger this time, but his luck was no better.[22] For unlike in 1082, Alexios was now in a position of strength. Bohemond launched his invasion from Brindisi in early October, landing at Aulon. After ravaging the countryside, he then prepared to besiege Dyrrachion. The late season, however, meant that siege operations could only begin in earnest the following spring. By this point, Alexios had had ample time to prepare his defence. The emperor now marched west with a large force from Thessaloniki. But rather than seek battle, Alexios blockaded the Normans between his army and the walls. The hunter now became the prey.

Alexios had evidently learned the lessons of previous encounters. It was hard to beat the Normans in battle, but easy enough to outmanoeuvre them. For Bohemond and his men, the situation soon became desperate. By late summer, he was forced to sue for peace. The resulting Treaty of Diabolis saw Bohemond accede to almost all of Alexios' demands, agreeing to acknowledge Byzantine overlordship of Antioch and restore disputed territories in Cilicia. For the proud Hauteville, this was humiliation. Rather than return to Antioch and see the city pass into Byzantine hands, he therefore headed back to southern Italy, where he died three years later. This was a final snub to Alexios, and it ensured that the terms of the treaty would never be implemented. In Antioch, Bohemond's nephew Tancred continued to rule in his stead; and eventually, his own son Bohemond II would take the reins. If Bohemond died a failure, his legacy thus lived on. Antioch was to prove one of the longest lived of the crusader states, influencing the politics and society of the Middle East into the late thirteenth century. And Bohemond's fellow Hautevilles remained a potent force in the central Mediterranean. The only question was, where would they strike next?

15

A Bridge Too Far?
North Africa, 1142–59

While Roger de Hauteville was completing the conquest of Sicily, messengers came from the maritime city-states of Genoa and Pisa, inviting him to join them in a strike against Mahdia. The populous city of Mahdia on the coast of modern Tunisia was the capital of the Zirid rulers of North Africa. And the attack was framed in religious terms, as a strike against the forces of Islam – a proto-crusade of sorts. Religious zeal was not the only motive, however. Pisa and Genoa were looking to muscle in on the lucrative trade between the western and eastern Mediterranean. Given Roger's growing prominence and developing maritime expertise, he was the obvious choice of ally.

Roger's advisers were keen to cash in on this opportunity. Or so the later Arab chronicler Ibn al-Athīr would have us believe. In his account, the canny Hauteville was unimpressed. He lifted a thigh and released a thunderous fart, before proceeding to explain why such flatulence was better counsel than that proffered by the wiser heads at court. For as Roger observed, if the Normans were to join the venture, they would soon find themselves in the worst of all possible worlds. If they succeeded, the profits would go to their northern allies, while in the case of failure, the Normans would bear the brunt of the repercussions. Moreover, they would end up footing much of the bill for supplying the expedition. Roger had recently concluded a peace with the Zirid ruler, Tamīm ib Mu'izz; he was not going to risk this on a speculative venture.

Ibn al-Athīr's account was written almost a century and a half after these events, and he confuses certain details. He has the second ruler of Jerusalem, Baldwin of Edessa, as the driving force behind the plan, not the city-states of Pisa and Genoa; and he seems to think that Roger was an independent ruler, not an agent (however nominal) of his elder brother Guiscard. By his description of Roger's behaviour he clearly means to underscore the barbarism of the new Norman lords of Sicily. Still, al-Athīr did not invent the tale from scratch. He draws on earlier sources, often of high quality. And the attack on Mahdia was very real, representing an important precursor to the First Crusade. We know from other sources that Roger declined an invitation to participate in the invasion. There is, therefore, every reason to believe the gist of his account.[1]

What al-Athīr's earthy portrait reveals is the degree to which Roger and Robert had been thrust into the complex political world of the Mediterranean, in which the rulers of North Africa were prominent players. Ibn al-Athīr sought to write a comprehensive history, which from his perspective meant including everything that touched on the world of Islam.[2] By the 1080s, this evidently included Roger. And in years to come, Roger and his son and successor, Roger II, would figure ever more prominently in the politics of North Africa.

Sicily and North Africa were of great strategic and commercial significance. Despite the dislocation caused by the fall of the Western Roman Empire in the fifth and sixth centuries, the Mediterranean continued to be an important conduit of trade (and information) between Europe, North Africa and the Middle East. By the eleventh century, the volume (and value) of this commerce was rapidly rising. Italian city-states such as Pisa and Genoa now sought – with considerable success – to control trade across the north-western Mediterranean, while the Byzantines, Venetians and Fatimids cornered the market in the east.[3] The importance of Sicily and the Islamic province of Ifrīqya (encompassing modern Tunisia, as well as parts of Algeria and Libya) lay in their position between these two spheres. Whoever could control them, stood to make a tidy profit.

Thanks in part to many years of Islamic rule, Sicily and North Africa were closely integrated. The Sicilian capital, Palermo, lay closer to Mahdia than Rome. And Sicily now supplied grain to North Africa, providing a vital lifeline to a province which suffered increasingly frequent droughts. When Roger began to tighten his grip on Sicily, the natural question became how this trade would be affected.[4] As with his response to the Genoese and Pisans, Roger approached the subject with his typical pragmatism. If there was profit to be made, he wasn't one to rock the boat. Indeed, both he and his son sought to come to terms with the Muslim and Greek communities within and beyond their domains. They favoured Christians over Muslims (and the Latin rite over the Greek one), but welcomed and maintained contacts with people of all backgrounds. One of the leading advisers of Roger II was the Syrian Christian George of Antioch, who'd previously served the Zirid rulers of Ifrīqya; another was Phillip of Mahdia, who succeeded George to the post of amir/admiral (Latin: *amiratus*).[5] Such men were known as Roger's 'palace saracens'. Conversion was formally a requirement for service, but this may often have been skin-deep. At Roger's court, loyalty trumped religious faith – and profit trumped nativism.

As Norman rule became more firmly established, the rulers of Sicily began to assert themselves in the Mediterranean. Roger I had already taken Malta in 1091. Norman control was soon ousted, but was reinstated by Roger II in 1127.[6] Malta's position between Sicily and Ifrīqya made it a natural staging post to these North African domains. But before Roger could build on such success, he was forced to turn his attention to affairs on the Italian mainland.

The fact that an independent Norman strike against North Africa was even conceivable reveals how much had changed over the past half-century. In the 1080s, Roger I was still busy securing Sicily. Any further Norman conquests looked likely to take place in the Adriatic, where Guiscard and Bohemond were now heavily invested. Roger had only countenanced attacking Mahdia as part of a powerful maritime coalition – and soon dismissed the idea. Since then, the balance of power within the Norman domains of southern Italy had changed decisively. Following Guiscard's death in 1085, Roger lent his support to his nephew Roger Borsa (Robert's designated heir). But the latter never commanded the same respect as his father. Guiscard had already faced a series of serious revolts in Apulia; and the succession of the young and relatively inexperienced Borsa simply fanned the flames.

Roger Borsa eventually secured his position, but he remained heavily dependent on his uncle. Roger I's death and the succession of his own young sons, Simon and then Roger II, did little to change this relationship. The mother of the latter two, Adelaide del Vastro – the future queen of Jerusalem – led a successful regency, ensuring that

Simon and Roger's domains survived intact. In 1111, Borsa died, leaving the young William II on the ducal throne. Roger II and William II were roughly the same age, but the former soon emerged as the more powerful political force. William enjoyed precedence as duke, but this was increasingly nominal. And when William died in 1127 without legitimate offspring, Roger was quick to secure direct control of Calabria and Apulia, pre-emptively declaring himself William's heir.[7]

The effect of these developments was that power within the Italo-Norman realm shifted south and west, from Bari, Brindisi and Venosa to Salerno and Palermo. If Guiscard had looked across the Adriatic to the Balkans, his nephew gazed south across the Mediterranean to North Africa. Yet the expansion of Roger's domains also brought considerable complications. His succession to the mainland duchy was hotly contested, not least by the pope, who since the accords of Melfi claimed the right to invest the duke. The situation was exacerbated by Roger's decision to claim royal status in 1130. If his seizure of ducal authority had been presumptuous, Roger's claim to kingship was seen as adding insult to injury.

Others outside Italy were also disquieted by these developments. The Byzantine emperors – who had a residual claim to southern Italy – had every reason to fear Roger's growing power, not least in the maritime sphere. And the German rulers shared their concerns. By dint of the imperial title, they too had an interest in the south. Moves were soon put in motion to secure an alliance between the pope and the two emperors – a resurrection of Leo IX's old alliance of the 1050s. This helped galvanise dissent within Apulia, where not all looked kindly on rule from Palermo.

As a result, Roger II spent much of the 1130s seeing off threats, both internal and external.[8] Still, he never lost sight of other interests. As count, Roger had quarrelled with the Zirid rulers of Ifrīqya over trading rights, ordering an abortive strike against Mahdia in 1123. In 1135, internal struggles within the province provided him with the pretext for further intervention. The local Zirid amir, al-Ḥassan, had appealed for Roger's help against the Hammadid ruler of neighbouring Bougie. Roger's fleet was able to provide the requisite cover. But they also took the opportunity to seize the strategic island of Djerba, just off the North African coast. This was a statement of intent, and its significance was not lost on Roger's northern counterparts. At an assembly held in Merseburg, Byzantine and Venetian emissaries reported – with a degree of exaggeration – that the Sicilian upstart had seized all Africa, the 'third part of the world'.[9]

Pressing affairs on the Italian mainland initially prevented Roger from building on this base. But by the early 1140s, the time was ripe. Divisions continued to wrack Ifrīqya, pitting the traditional Zirid amirs against the Hammadid Berbers to their west. Droughts also made al-Ḥassan increasingly dependent on Sicilian grain supplies. Roger was able to leverage this to secure the amir's submission in 1141/2. The following year, he initiated a series of naval attacks on the coastal towns of western and eastern Ifrīqya. These were framed as attempts to shore up al-Ḥassan's rule. But soon enough, Roger pivoted from supporting to replacing his Zirid allies. In June 1143, Sicilian forces struck at Tripoli, which had sought to remove itself from Zirid rule. And while the attack failed, greater success was achieved at Djidjelli (Jījiil), in modern Algeria, which was sacked. The following year saw similar successes, with Barasht (Bresk) falling in the west and the island of Kerkenna doing likewise in the east.

When Tripoli was taken in 1146, the foundations were laid for a North African kingdom in Roger's name. Hitherto, these expeditions had been little more than opportunistic acts of piracy. Now, Roger began to make the transition from intermittent raiding to permanent conquest.[10] His cause was assisted by continuing famines, which weakened his opponents at crucial junctures. And as his father had done in Sicily, Roger was careful to conciliate the local Islamic population. While they were forced to pay an additional tax, Muslims would be free to continue worshipping as they had before. Such treatment took the sting out of Christian rule. And soon enough, Roger started to be approached by dissident elements in other regions of Zirid rule.

For the Zirids, the final blow came in 1148, when a large Sicilian fleet appeared outside Mahdia. Realising that resistance was futile, al-Ḥassan now fled inland. Afraid of the prospect of Christian rule, many of the inhabitants followed suit. But once they heard of Roger's even-handed treatment of the local population, most returned. Momentum was now decisively with Roger, and his forces soon secured Sousse (Susa) and Sfax, strategic port cities to Mahdia's south. Elsewhere, Tunis was reduced to tributary status and Gabès (Qābis) acknowledged Roger's suzerainty. Impressed by this progress, Pope Eugenius III consecrated a new 'archbishop of Africa' (i.e. Ifrīqya). The domains of the radical Almohads – who in contrast with other Islamic powers, did not tolerate Christian minorities – had recently been expanding in north-western Africa. Roger's realm now promised a bulwark against them.

The Sicilian Normans seemed unstoppable, and Ibn al-Athīr asserts that Roger would have conquered all Africa had he not been distracted by conflicts with Byzantium.[11] This is an overstatement. At most, Roger might have added a few more coastal cities to his domains. Still, al-Athīr's report gives a sense of the feeling within Zirid circles. Roger's men had been making quick work of the region; and the Second Crusade, which saw Roger strike against Byzantium in 1147 and 1148, must have come as a welcome relief.

Roger's own pride in these conquests is clear. He had coinage issued in North Africa and seems to have experimented with the title 'king of Africa/Ifrīqya', particularly in Arabic documents in his name.[12] (In Roger's trilingual realm, documents were issued in Latin, Greek and Arabic.) Yet as with Guiscard's conquests in the Adriatic, Roger's gains in Africa were dangerously exposed. To the immediate west lay the Almohads, who were unlikely to tolerate a Christian neighbour for long. To the east lay the domains of the Fatimids, the nominal overlords of the Zirids. The latter enjoyed good relations with Roger, and it was with their tacit approval that he'd established his North African enclave. As Roger began to find his feet, however, cracks started to appear in this relationship. The weak Zirids had been of little use to the Fatimids, but the rapidly expanding Normans now presented a rather different problem.

In spring 1153, a large Arab coalition backed by Roger was decisively defeated by the Almohads at Sétif in modern Algeria. In response, Roger sent a fleet under the command of Philip of Mahdia to take the port of Bône (modern Annāba), in the hope of creating a buffer zone. The longer-term prospects for the new African province were now starting to look grim. What sealed its fate was Roger's death in early 1154. The ensuing years saw considerable instability, as

Roger's heir, William I, sought to establish himself. William's priority was to secure his core Sicilian and Italian domains. Only once this had been achieved, could he afford to direct his attention to the situation in North Africa.

By then, it was too late. The mid- to later 1150s had seen a set of major revolts against Sicilian-Norman rule, as native rulers sought to re-establish their independence. Their cause was assisted by the continuing Almohad threat. In the end, it was this which proved decisive. In 1159, a large Almohad force moved against the coastal cities which were the linchpins of Norman authority in the region. Tunis soon surrendered; it was followed by Tripoli, Sfax and Gafsa. Greater resistance was offered at Mahdia, where the Normans had holed up within the walled city. Informed of the situation, William re-directed his fleet – which had just returned from raiding Almoravid-held Ibiza – to break the siege. And though these efforts failed, the city itself held out for another six months.[13]

Some at the Sicilian court felt that William hadn't done enough, and there may be an element of truth to this.[14] But with Almohad pressure mounting, it simply wasn't worth the time, money and manpower to maintain this precarious toehold in North Africa. Roger's conquest had always been an opportunistic affair, assisted by Zirid weakness and Fatimid acquiescence. There was little sense in maintaining it in the face of a sustained resistance.

In this respect, Roger's conquest proved little different from the many regime changes North Africa had experienced since first falling to the Vandals in the early fifth century. The head of state may have been replaced, but the structures of rule – inherited ultimately from the Roman and Byzantine empires – remained intact. When the Almohads overwhelmed the region, they were able to rule it much as it had been for almost a millennium. How far Roger's African domains were meaningfully Norman (or even Sicilian) may therefore be questioned. Yet from the start a key feature of Norman rule – be it in North Africa or northern France – was its adaptability. The Normans were a product of settlement and acculturation, processes they continued to undergo within the widely dispersed diaspora. On the death of Roger II, their domains in Italy were as much Sicilian, Calabrian and Apulian as they were Norman. Still, a sense of shared culture was maintained with the homeland. Roger is said to have preferred French and Anglo-Norman courtiers, on account of their shared heritage.[15] And the names chosen by the Hautevilles for their sons are telling. Robert, Roger and William are not Italian designations. Even as they adopted local customs, the Normans didn't forget their roots.

The eclipse of Norman rule in Africa was by no means inevitable. The odds may always have been against a sustained presence in the region. But it was only the confluence of three factors – Almohad pressure, Fatimid opposition, and internal problems in Sicily and Italy (occasioned by Roger's death) – which proved decisive. Had Roger lived longer or the Fatimids proved more amenable, there's no way of knowing how much longer the Norman kingdom might have survived.

Had it done so, Norman influence on the region would doubtless have been far greater. Compare the fate of Islamic Sicily. The Hauteville rulers' recruiting of Muslim administrators here was pragmatic toleration rather than self-conscious multiculturalism. Christians were preferred for senior roles – and where possible, Latin Christians. The result was a slow but steady (and cumulatively significant) population shift away from Islam (and also, to a degree, from the Greek Orthodox rite). Lombard settlers from the mainland were encouraged, as was conversion. In the 1160s, toleration had already begun to give way to coercion, and these efforts were stepped up in the following century. As the Latin Christians established themselves more firmly, they begin to display the chauvinism so characteristic of the era. Pressure mounted on the remaining Muslim enclaves, and massacres and expulsions became common.[16]

In 1148, all this, potentially, lay in store for the inhabitants of Ifrīqya. Fortunately for them, Sicilian-Norman rule did indeed prove fleeting. And so it remains little more than an intriguing footnote in the long history of Norman conquest and colonisation. False starts are, however, every bit as interesting as successes. And Roger's short-lived kingdom of Africa is a salutary reminder that the Norman influence on Europe, Africa and Asia could have been greater still.

16

Northern Wales: A Wolf in
Wolf's Clothing, 1068–98

When Gruffudd ap Cynan set sail from Dublin for northern Wales in 1075, he was taking a calculated risk. Gruffudd only had a handful of men with him, generously supplied by his mother's relatives, the powerful Viking rulers of Dublin. With their support, he hoped to establish himself as ruler of Gwynedd. The hope was not entirely vain. For Gruffudd's father was a prince of the royal line, who'd been forced into Irish exile in 1039 when Gruffudd ap Llywelyn, a member of a rival dynasty, seized the throne. Now the younger Gruffudd ap Cynan was out to exact revenge for his father's mistreatment.

His chances were helped by the political situation in northern Wales. He'd begun preparations upon hearing of the death of Bleddyn ap Cynfyn, Gruffudd ap Llywelyn's half-brother and successor. Still, time and distance were not on Gruffudd ap Cynan's side. And while he moved fast, by the time he arrived off Anglesey a few months later, Gruffudd found that Trahaearn, the cousin of Bleddyn, had established himself as ruler in his stead. Gruffudd ap Cynan now made contact with a few local allies, before sailing east to the castle of Rhuddlan, in north-central Wales. Here he secured the support of the local lord, Robert. The cousin of Hugh, the new Norman earl of Chester, Robert of Rhuddlan had been extending his influence into northern Wales for some time. He and Hugh were only too happy to support Gruffudd ap Cynan and, with their assistance, Gruffudd was able to make quick work of his opponents. Finally, Gruffudd ap Cynan was able to sit on his ancestral throne.[1]

~

At a glance, these events may seem rather unspectacular. One provincial Welsh ruler replaced another, in one of those complex dynastic struggles that had long characterised the region. Yet when we look more closely, differences appear. Gruffudd ap Cynan was only able to secure the throne with Robert's support; and once established, he immediately moved against his Norman backers. The Normans were now an important new force in Welsh politics.

By this point, the Normans had been making incursions into Gwynedd and its southern neighbours for a number of years. The difference between these undertakings and the events of 1066 is that they were private ventures, taken at the initiative of the new lords of the march (as the English frontier with Wales was known). With a kingdom and duchy to his name, the Conqueror had little interest in extending his direct rule into the poorer regions to England's west and north. For his aristocrats, however, the situation was different. Conquest had whetted their appetite; and they were hardly going to stop at the frontier. For his part, William was happy to cheer on his men. If Norman influence could be extended without any cost to the Crown, William stood to gain as much as his men.

It was out of these processes that the marcher lordships of Wales slowly emerged.[2] The term 'march' refers to a border or frontier (much like the German *Mark*). In its Old English form, it had already given rise to the name of the Mercian people of the West Midlands (literally, 'the people of the frontier'). These regions had thus long possessed a frontier character, and the great eighth-century Mercian ruler Offa famously erected a dyke running north–south along the Welsh-English border. Low-level conflict between the groups was common, and the dyke may originally have been intended to prevent cattle rustling. At a political level, however, stability generally reigned. English kings often exerted a degree of overlordship over their Welsh neighbours, but made little effort to conquer them or rule directly.

The years before the Conquest had started to see this change. In the tenth and eleventh centuries, Wales was generally divided into two realms: Gwynedd in the north (also encompassing Powys in north-central Wales) and Deheubarth (literally meaning 'the southern part') in the south west. These were often ruled jointly and remained distinct from Morgannwg (Glamorgan) in the south east, which enjoyed closer connections with the neighbouring English.[3] In 1055, the northern ruler Gruffudd ap Llywelyn secured control over

Deheubarth and also over these south-eastern domains. He now presented a very different kind of threat, a threat exacerbated by ongoing factional conflicts at the English court. These years saw the ascendency of the Godwins, which was bitterly resented by the earls of Mercia, represented by Ælfgar. And Ælfgar soon became a firm friend and ally of Gruffudd ap Llywelyn, his immediate neighbour to the west. It was the Welsh king who offered Ælfgar a safe haven when he was exiled in 1055. In the following years, the two often made common cause. Gruffudd ap Llywelyn married Ælfgar's daughter Edith. And when Ælfgar was exiled a second time in 1058, it was with Gruffudd's assistance that he was restored.[4]

Ælfgar's death in 1062 left Gruffudd exposed, however, and the Godwins were quick to take advantage of the situation. Having obtained royal sanction for a pre-emptive strike, Harold marched along the northern coast of Wales in late December 1063, ravaging as he went. The plan was to catch Gruffudd unawares. This failed, although Harold took the opportunity to torch Gruffudd's residence at Rhuddlan. The following spring, he gathered forces in Bristol and began a joint land and naval assault with his younger brother Tostig. Gruffudd was now driven into Snowdonia, where his men turned on him. The Welsh king's decapitated head was then sent to Harold as a grim peace offering.

The result of Gruffudd's fall was turmoil, which Harold happily exploited. The regions between the Dee and Clwyd were now brought under English control (and integrated into an enlarged Cheshire). The main gains, however, were made in the south, where Gruffudd's power had always been weakest. In the early to mid-1050s, the earldom of Wessex had been expanded to incorporate the south-west Midlands, which bordered on the old kingdom of Gwent in eastern Morgannwg. Gruffudd's fall allowed Harold to extend his authority here, building a hunting lodge at Portskewett. He also married Gruffudd's widow (Ælfgar's daughter Edith). This was partly a move to forge an alliance with the earls of Mercia. But it was also an act which resonated in Wales. As in other parts of Europe, it was common here to wed the widow of a defeated foe; Harold was symbolically enacting victory.[5] Despite this interruption, the alliance between Gruffudd's and Ælfgar's families lived on. And when Ælfgar's sons Edwin and Morcar rebelled against the Conqueror in 1068, they were supported by Gruffudd ap Llywelyn's successors, his half-brothers Bleddyn and Rhiwallon.

The West Midlands had itself seen significant Norman influence before the Conquest. It was here that Ralph of Mantes' modest earldom was to be found, and it was here that the earliest Norman castles were constructed in the 1050s. Their numbers multiplied rapidly after 1066, as Norman aristocrats were introduced to the region in ever larger numbers; and the Welsh march soon boasted a higher density of fortifications than any other part of the British Isles.[6] The Anglo-Saxon dyke had given way to the Norman motte and bailey. Yet the new lords of the march had more than modernising the defences in mind. The castle was primarily an instrument of lordship, and it was this that was at stake: control over men and land.

The emerging march attracted (and bred) a particularly aggressive sort of lord – men accustomed to high risks and high gains. Few better exemplify this spirit than Hugh d'Avranches, the first earl of Chester.[7] Hugh's father had been a major contributor to William's invasion fleet in 1066. And though Hugh was too young to participate, he crossed the Channel soon thereafter to assist in consolidating Norman rule. Hugh was initially rewarded for his father's loyalty with command of the castle of Tutbury in Staffordshire. But Hugh was marked out for greater things, and was soon entrusted with the strategic town of Chester and the newly created earldom of this name.[8] Chester was one of the main English ports on the Irish Sea, facilitating trade between the Midlands, Wales, Ireland and Scotland. It was also located just on the English side of the frontier with Wales, controlling traffic up the Dee. From his seat, Hugh could keep tabs on the northern Welsh kings, who'd long been the most powerful (and dangerous) of the native dynasties. Edwin and Morcar had recently looked to Wales for support for their 1068 uprising; the Conqueror was now placing a trusted man on the frontier in response.

What drew Hugh and other like-minded lords to the region were the opportunities afforded by the frontier. The Norman conquest of England had been remarkably swift. Most new lords were in place within a decade of 1066; and by the time the Domesday Survey was compiled in 1086, the process was all but complete. This meant that ambitions would now have to be directed outward, towards the independent realms to England's west and north. It was only here that new lands and lordships were to be gained.

Hugh soon set about realising these prospects. Shortly after his appointment, Hugh's men secured the lowland areas to the west and south of Chester which Harold had won in 1064. Some of these went to new Norman lords, but most were earmarked for Hugh's cousin (and right-hand man) Robert of Rhuddlan. It was Robert who, under Hugh's aegis, would now drive Norman expansion in the region. He was following in Harold's footsteps; and by 1073, Robert had set himself up at Gruffudd ap Llywelyn's old residence at Rhuddlan. A formidable fortress was now erected on royal orders.

Hugh and Robert both participated in a raid on Llŷn, probably in the mid-1070s. And by 1078, they'd extended their authority to Degannwy, overlooking the Conwy. Most of these gains were made by Robert, but Hugh was present at crucial junctures, taking the lead in a foray of 1081 and returning again in the mid-1090s, upon Robert's death. When the Domesday inquisitors came to Cheshire, they included the entire region up to the Clwyd within the survey; in their eyes, this was effectively England. They also did not ignore the lordships established by Robert beyond this. North Wales – as they term Gwynedd – may not have been England proper, but it was evidently within the English orbit. From these territories, they record that Robert paid an annual tribute of £40 – the same sum owed by the Welsh ruler of Deheubarth in the south west.[9]

By the early 1090s, Hugh and Robert had erected castles at Aberlleiniog (on Anglesey), Caernarfon and Bangor; there may also have been similar structures in Tomen y Mur and Tomen y Bala in Meirionnydd. By 1092, they were in a position to appoint a Norman to the bishopric of Bangor, in the heartlands of the old kingdom of Gwynedd. As in England, claims to religious, political and cultural domination went hand-in-hand.[10] When the southern ruler Rhys ap Tewdwr fell in 1093, local chroniclers record that all Wales had fallen with him. It's easy to see why they thought this. The north had been in Hugh and Robert's hands for some time; now, it was joined by Deheubarth to the south. This was a view shared on the other side of the frontier. In the West Midlands, John of Worcester likewise reports that 'kings ceased to rule in Wales' at this point.[11] Norman influence was everywhere; it seemed but a matter of time till this was formalised.

This is not to say that Norman incursions went unresisted. One of the main opponents of Hugh and Robert was Gruffudd ap Cynan, with whom we began. Gruffudd is the only Welsh ruler of the Middle Ages for whom we have a contemporary biography, so we can follow his career in unusual detail.[12] Initially, Hugh and Robert were happy to support Gruffudd ap Cynan, doubtless in the hope of establishing a pliable client king. Yet once established, Gruffudd turned against his Norman allies. Fortune did not, however, favour the new king. Before 1075 was out, Gruffudd had been defeated and driven out by Trahaearn ap Caradog, whom he'd just replaced. Gruffudd did not, however, give up hope. In 1081, he returned in force, backed by the southern ruler Rhys ap Tewdwr. The two of them met Trahaearn at Mynydd Carn (a site somewhere north of St Davids), and there they defeated and slew him.

Gruffudd now marched into Gwynedd again, targeting the lands of his opponents along the way. Upon arrival, he secured the throne. Yet his second reign would prove to be not much longer than the first. This time, it was the Normans who brought Gruffudd down. Earl Hugh had been happy to use Gruffudd against other northern Welsh rulers in the mid-1070s, but he had little desire to let him establish an independent regime of his own. Hugh therefore enticed Gruffudd to a meeting at Rug in Edeirnion, just west of modern Corwen. Here the unsuspecting prince was captured by his old ally, Robert of Rhuddlan. Gruffudd now spent over a decade in an Anglo-Norman prison. During these years, Hugh's own attention was frequently drawn elsewhere, as the division of the Conqueror's massive cross-Channel realm between Robert Curthose and William Rufus (II) threatened his Norman patrimony.

Soon enough, however, the earl was forced to return to Chester. In 1093, Robert was killed by a Welsh raiding party, leaving Hugh's lands dangerously exposed. The following year, a full-blown rebellion was under way. After two decades of steady advance, the Normans now came to appreciate the difficulties presented by the fractious world of Welsh politics. Like southern Italy, Wales was a mountainous landscape in which rapid conquests and centralised states were the exception rather than the rule. Around this time, Gruffudd himself escaped – indeed, he may have been responsible for Robert's death (the later chronicler Orderic Vitalis mentions a 'Gruffudd king of the Welsh' in this connection). Certainly by 1097, Gruffudd was on the loose and looking to make good his claim to his north Walian patrimony.

The 1090s was a decade of contestation. Initially, the momentum lay with the Welsh. A rising against the Normans had begun in the north, where it was led by Cadwgan ap Bleddyn, the son of Gruffudd ap Llywelyn's half-brother and successor. But rebellion spread and 1094 saw castles fall across Gwynedd, Ceredigion and Dyfed. Hugh's authority was pushed back beyond the Conwy, never to be fully resuscitated. So serious was the situation that William Rufus appeared twice, in 1095 and 1097. But the Welsh refused to be drawn into battle and the gains were few.

In the end, the Normans did prevail. But it would be the marcher lords who secured the victory. In 1098, Hugh joined forces with Hugh de Montgomery, the earl of Shrewsbury. Together, they marched along the northern coast of Wales, driving back the men of Gwynedd and Powys, led by Cadwgan ap Bleddyn and Gruffudd ap Cynan. The latter two were not natural allies. But with Normans just across the Menai Strait, they were willing to co-operate. Even so, there was no stopping the advance, and both Cadwgan and Gruffudd were forced into exile across the Irish Sea.

Yet Norman success was to be partial and fleeting. For at this moment in 1098 the restless king of Norway, Magnus 'Barelegs', appeared off the coast of Anglesey. Magnus was following in the footsteps of his own Viking forebears, who'd long dominated the Irish Sea from bases at Dublin, Man and the Isles. Sailing over from Norway, he'd first established himself on Man. From there, northern Wales was a natural target, particularly in the light of recent political instability. But just as Magnus' ships approached land, a skirmish broke out with the Normans guarding the shoreline. Our sources give contradictory accounts of the conflict, but most agree that Magnus felled Hugh de Montgomery with a spear thrown from the deck of his ship. This threw the Normans into disarray, but the Norwegians were in no position to press their advantage. Magnus only had six ships at his command and may already have overextended himself. The

Norwegian king therefore retreated to Man, while Hugh de Montgomery's men returned to Shrewsbury, where they laid the earl to rest seventeen days later.

Hugh d'Avranches likewise retired to his base at Chester. Anglesey was simply too far from Chester (or Rhuddlan) to make outright conquest viable. The people here remained loyal to their native lords, and would do so well into the thirteenth century. Hugh therefore made contact with Gruffudd, offering to restore him in exchange for his submission. Similar agreements were made elsewhere, with Cadwgan being established in parts of Powys and Ceredigion under the oversight of the new earl of Shrewsbury, Robert de Bellême.

These arrangements were a significant step back from the ambitions of earlier years. But we should be wary of branding them failures. Men such as Hugh and Robert were out for fame and fortune, and willing to use any means to achieve them. The risings of 1093 had demonstrated the limits of Norman power and control. Provided a degree of overlordship could be maintained, Hugh was happy to cut his losses and leave matters at that.

Hugh was, in any case, not much longer for this world. In late 1100 or early 1101 he fell ill. And sensing the end was nigh, he took monastic vows. Writing at Saint-Evroult in Normandy in the 1130s and 1140s, Orderic Vitalis paints a vivid picture of Hugh. Orderic had grown up on the march, so was well acquainted with the earl's stomping grounds. He also had a more direct source of information, in the form of Robert of Rhuddlan's brother, who was a fellow monk at Saint-Evroult. According to Orderic, Hugh was the pre-eminent lord of the Conqueror's realm (a slight exaggeration) and a 'lover of this world and earthly pomp' (no exaggeration). The earl was a great warrior, who always fought from the front; and a man of prodigious generosity and lover of luxury. Here we see the ideal attributes of the Norman marcher aristocracy – bravery, generosity and *joie de vivre*.[13] These characteristics are reflected in the monikers Hugh earned. To many, he was 'Hugh the Fat'; to others, he was 'Hugh the Wolf'. Yet as his deathbed conversion reveals, Hugh was also possessed of piety. Hugh's ambition was rivalled only by that of his cousin Robert of Rhuddlan, who was driven by 'pride and greed' to 'unrestrained plunder and slaughter' (or so Orderic has it).[14]

What marks the conquests of Hugh and Robert out is their enterprising nature. It was they, not the Conqueror and Rufus, who drove Norman expansion into northern Wales. William I only came to Wales once (in 1081), and then to have his (nominal) overlordship acknowledged. William II was a more regular presence, but only in the crisis years of the later 1090s. Norman gains in Wales therefore took on a very different character to those in England. Here the king was at most a distant overlord. This was, of course, part of the appeal. Marcher lords were men of independent means, not simply agents of the Crown. As the later saying went, the king's writ did not run in the march. Sometimes, marcher lords interpreted this quite literally. When Walter Clifford received a royal missive which was not to his liking in the thirteenth century, he made the messenger eat his words – ink, parchment and all![15]

Over time, this independence came to be formalised. The result was the marcher lordships of the central Middle Ages – or the March proper (with a capital M).[16] What characterised this was independence from the Crown. As one contemporary noted, here each lord was 'like a king' (*quasi rex*) within his own domains.[17] This meant not only oversight of justice, but also control of what we might now call 'foreign affairs'. Marcher lords were free to make peace and wage war with each other and their neighbours. This was the 'Wild West' of medieval Britain, where lordship was asserted at the end of a spear point. It's no coincidence that the John de Warenne who produced a rusty sword as evidence for his tenure in England in the late thirteenth century was of marcher stock.

The marches were also hybrid in character: these were Anglo-Norman lordships erected on Welsh foundations. Elements of local practices and power structures were adopted, and marriages and alliances with Welsh rulers were common, particularly in earlier years. The March was thus a point of contact between England, Normandy and Wales, a culturally and politically dynamic region in which bi- and even trilingualism was common.[18] This is not to suggest that the March was some sort of modern multicultural paradise – quite the reverse. The flip side of cultural contact was cultural chauvinism, as the dismissive attitudes of Anglo-Norman writers to the Welsh reveal. The March was a place where identities blurred, but were also reasserted.

17

Southern Wales: Making
a Mark, 1068–98

In the summer months of 1081, William the Conqueror marched along the south coast of Wales. This was William's first (and only) visit to the region. The occasion was the death of Caradog ap Gruffudd, the ruler of Morgannwg in the south east. Caradog had fallen in battle against Rhys, the powerful ruler of neighbouring Deheubarth. What now beckoned was a power vacuum, into which William and his Normans happily rushed. William headed for Wales almost as soon as he heard of Caradog's demise. And he and his entourage progressed through Morgannwg to St Davids in the heartlands of Deheubarth. Welsh sources optimistically gloss this as a 'pilgrimage', but there can be no doubt as to the reality. William was here to assert authority, not simply to pray to the local patron saint. Important steps had also been taken to realise William's control, including the erection of a castle at Cardiff, just downstream from the important bishopric at Llandaff. In the coming years, the extension of Norman lordship into southern Wales stepped up apace. No worthy successor was found for Caradog. And while native power structures lived on in upland pockets for another eighty years, slowly but surely, Welsh Morgannwg was becoming Anglo-Norman Glamorgan.[1]

At the same time, Bernard de Neufmarché was making similar inroads into Brycheiniog, a minor kingdom to the immediate north of Caradog's Morgannwg. This lay under the nominal overlordship of Rhys. Bernard himself was a distant kinsman of the Conqueror, who made his way across the Channel either late in William's reign or early in that of Rufus. Bernard soon settled on the march, marrying a local noblewoman, Nest. As her name suggests, Nest was of mixed heritage. Her father was a Norman, the son of one of those who'd first settled in the West Midlands under the Confessor. Her mother, another Nest, was Welsh, the daughter of Gruffudd ap Llywelyn. A wealthy heiress capable of moving within both Norman and Welsh aristocratic worlds (she sometimes went by the Norman designation, Agnes), Nest was the ideal bride for an ambitious young baron like Bernard.

Thanks to these connections, Bernard swiftly established himself. By 1093, he and his men had occupied Talgarth, the traditional capital of Brycheiniog (now a small market town mid-way between Hay-on-Wye and Brecon). And when Rhys sought to expel Bernard, he was decisively defeated in April 1093. Rhys himself fell in the fray, leaving Brycheiniog in Norman hands – and Deheubarth itself undefended. It was this which inspired contemporary observers to comment that all Wales had fallen. Brycheiniog was now becoming the Norman marcher lordship of Brecon.[2]

The most significant advances into middle and southern Wales, however, were those made by the earls of Shrewsbury. The first of these, Roger de Montgomery, hailed from Upper Normandy and had been one of the Conqueror's closest companions since youth. During the Hastings campaign, Roger had been tasked (alongside Roger de Beaumont) with advising and supporting Matilda, who was acting as William's deputy. Soon he was rewarded for his efforts, receiving lands at Arundel and Chichester along with the new Shrewsbury-based earldom of Shropshire. The latter appointment probably came (like that of Hugh to Chester) in response to the rising of Edwin and Morcar in 1068. A reliable hand was now required in the central march – and William's old friend Roger was the obvious candidate.

Under Roger, Norman influence extended into neighbouring Powys, which had long been ruled from Gwynedd in the north. In 1072, Roger's son (and future heir) Hugh led a devastating raid up the Severn Valley. The following year, we hear of attacks on Ceredigion and Dyfed in the south west. Soon, Roger and his men began extending more direct control over their neighbours. Symbolic of the earl's desire to impose his will on Wales was the new castle erected at Hen Domen, within the old kingdom of Powys. This gave birth to the later town of Montgomery (named after the earls) two miles to the south, where the castle was relocated to in the early thirteenth century.

That Roger was seeking to extend (rather than simply defend) his territory is revealed by the castles he erected running up the Severn from this new base.[3] Roger's men looked set to expand beyond Powys into southern Ceredigion (where he now erected a castle at modern Cardigan) and even into Rhys's kingdom of Deheubarth. As in the north, there was an element of overreach here. During the rebellions of 1094 to 1098, Cardigan was lost, along with the most recent gains in Ceredigion and Dyfed. Welsh power and authority were also resurgent in the Severn valley; and even the symbolic castle of Montgomery was taken in 1095. Only those regions under secure Norman control in 1093 went on to form the basis of the later March. By contrast, those areas still largely free – Ceredigion, much of Gwynedd and parts of Powys – would come to constitute the Principality of Wales; 'pure Wales' (*pura Wallia*), as it was known.[4]

Roger died just as these risings were beginning to spread, so it fell to his son and heir, Hugh, to respond. Hugh was not Roger's eldest son. Like the Conqueror, Roger left his Norman estates to his first born, Robert de Bellême, letting Hugh take charge in the considerably richer (but much more precarious) lordships carved out in England and Wales. Hugh would have to work hard to maintain his position. The Normans were on the back foot when he became earl; and the situation was compounded by Hugh's own involvement in a rebellion against the king. We next catch sight of Hugh in 1098, when he and his northern namesake re-established Norman influence over much of Gwynedd and Powys. Hugh's death at the end of this expedition, however, effectively marked the end of the line for his family. Hugh's elder brother, Robert, succeeded to the earldom. But Robert was soon caught up in struggles between the Norman duke and English king, eventually forfeiting his Welsh and English lands.

The fate of the Montgomerys mirrors that of many other early marcher lords. William fitz Osbern's earldom of Hereford, established around the same time as those of Roger and Hugh of Chester, had already disappeared by 1075. And if that of Hugh d'Avranches fared better for a time, it too eventually fell to the vagaries of fortune. An initial challenge was posed by Hugh's death in 1101, which left his son, the young Richard, as heir. Richard had scarcely come of age when disaster struck again: he and his half-brother perished aboard the White Ship in 1120, bringing the dynasty to an abrupt end. Still, the achievements of these early marchers lived on. The most ambitious gains of the 1080s and 1090s may have proved abortive, but capillary expansion into the lowland regions of southern, central and north-eastern Wales changed the face of the region, laying the foundations for the March.

It is important not to present such expansion in terms of a clash of cultures. The Welsh and Normans may often have been at loggerheads; and, in the long run, there would be major socio-political fault lines between the March and Principality. But in practice, relations between the two were pragmatic, running the full gamut from hatred and hostility to friendship and alliance. The same Gruffudd ap Cynan who was ejected from Anglesey by Hugh d'Avranches and Hugh de Montgomery in 1098 returned with Hugh's support the following year. Indeed, as common as Cambro-Norman conflicts were those between the many independent and semi-independent Welsh rulers. It was these which often first drew the Normans into the region, as in the case of Gruffudd and Gwynedd. Nor were the Anglo-Norman ranks any more disciplined. Men such as Hugh d'Avranches and Roger de Montgomery were competitors as much as co-operators, and violent struggles between marcher lords were no rarity.

As in the Mediterranean, the Normans found a fragmented political world here, in which making inroads was easy but effecting lasting conquests difficult. The landscape also bore similarities, being marked by hills, mountains and valleys. This mitigated the technological advantage the Normans otherwise enjoyed. Only in the lowland areas of the south and north east could their mounted knights make a real impact – not coincidentally, the first regions to fall to them and the heart of the future March. Fortifications were also less effective in such terrain. Wales may boast more castles than any other part of the British Isles, but few of these are to be found on land higher than 600 ft (c.180 m) above sea level, an elevation exceeded by much of central and northern Wales. Geographical and political fragmentation went hand in hand here, and the Normans regularly found themselves facing a bewildering array of local princes.

In the early years, the Normans thus did little more than add an additional strand to the complex web of local Welsh politics. Soon, however, this began to change. In the 1080s, the most important political conflicts were ones between native princes; after 1093, they tended to be between Welsh and Normans. Local rulers continued to compete with one another, but there was now an increasing sense of the need to co-operate against a common foe. On both sides, this new hostility started to find ideological expression. The Welsh turned to the native tradition of history and prophecy – to tales of a time when they (in the guise of the ancient Britons) had dominated the island and to predictions that they would do so again. These found their most famous (if idiosyncratic) expression when refracted through the literary lens of Geoffrey of Monmouth, the ultimate source of the later Arthurian legends. Geoffrey was an Anglo-Norman, but hailed from the march. He happily plundered Welsh legends for his own purpose, introducing the rest of Europe to such figures as Arthur and Merlin. Reworking these materials, Geoffrey's English contemporaries were soon able to stake their own claims to Arthur's legacy.[5]

The most lasting effect of this estrangement is to be found in the cultural chauvinism of the Anglo-Norman marcher lords. In England, the Normans had found a society not dissimilar to that of their native Normandy. They might at times cast aspersions on the local population; but behind such statements lay an understanding of how society operated, and often a grudging respect for the cultural and military achievements of the English. Such common ground was harder to find in Wales. Here the Normans were confronted with a much less hierarchical society, in which power was distributed more equally; peasants were freer and lords more constrained. In absolute terms, Wales was also much poorer. Its hills and mountains did little to generate wealth in an economy heavily dependent on arable farming. Without large agrarian surpluses, there was little call for (and ability to support) the urban settlements which drove economic growth elsewhere. On account of these features, Welsh principalities tended to be smaller and weaker than their English or French counterparts; and when wider-ranging polities were formed (as under Gruffudd ap Llywelyn), they proved fleeting. The cumulative effect of these differences was to make Wales a far stranger place.

These were not the only differences. Welsh society was one in which self-help was the order of the day. Feuding and cattle rustling were common. To Norman eyes, it was a land beyond the rule of law. Later Anglo-Norman observers contrasted the Welsh 'land of war' with the English 'land of peace'. Even in the practice of war, the Welsh stood out. Norman aristocrats did not eschew violence, but they possessed a strong sense of *esprit de corps*. Fellow nobles might be killed in the heat of battle, but they were not to be butchered while fleeing – and every effort was made to keep casualties to a minimum. The same rules did not apply to Wales, where (as in pre-Conquest England) it was common to enslave, kill and mutilate hostages – and even rival members of the same family – well into the thirteenth century.

The natural response to these differences, particularly when emotions ran high, was condescension. The marcher lords thus became the original ex-pats. Their aim was to exploit or replace the natives, the result often being an uncomfortable apartheid. This served to discourage cultural exchange. The Welsh eventually adopted many of the trappings of western European elite culture, including castles, sealed charters and elements of the chivalric ethos. But they proved far less keen on doing so than their English or Scottish counterparts.[6]

Much as they did in the Holy Land, the Normans served a higher purpose in Wales (or so they liked to believe). This was a civilising mission, which presumed the inferiority of the local population. It was an effective, but deeply dehumanising calling. It was also one which ensured that such efforts were not restricted to Wales.

18

Iberia: 'The Race of the Normans Declines No Labour', 1147–8

In June 1147, the largely Muslim population of Lisbon found itself under attack from a considerable foreign force. Part of this was composed of their Christian neighbours to the north in the rapidly expanding kingdom of Portugal. Their leader, Afonso I – Afonso 'the Great' (*O Grande*) in Portuguese – had recently declared himself king, following victory over the Almoravid governor of Córdoba at Ourique in 1139. Since then, Afonso had steadily chipped away at the territories of al-Andalus (Islamic Iberia). Now his eyes were firmly set on the prize of Lisbon.[1] Yet the lion's share of his soldiers were not Iberian at all. They hailed from northern Europe – from Flanders, the Rhineland, and (above all) Anglo-Norman England.

This episode is therefore part of the wider story of Norman conquest and consolidation. The Norman complexion of the force is underlined by the anonymous Latin text known as 'On the Conquest of Lisbon' (*De expugnatione Lyxbonensi*), written by an Anglo-Norman cleric.[2] According to this, the unusually cosmopolitan army had first gathered that spring at Dartmouth in south-western Devon. The occasion of the muster was the Second Crusade, the first major expedition to the East since Bohemond's abortive strike against Byzantium in 1107 to 1108. The crusade had been called following the loss of the strategic city (and county) of Edessa in 1144. For the first time since 1099, the western presence in the Holy Land looked to be at risk. What was needed was a pre-emptive strike to regain Edessa and reinforce the Christian hold on the holy of holies.

The poster boy of the Second Crusade was Bernard, the charismatic abbot of Clairvaux in France, who was (after the pope) the most influential churchman in western Christendom. Bernard preached about the need for the crusade in his native land and in the German

Rhineland. Helped by memories of the First Crusade, his message met with great enthusiasm.[3] At Bernard's instruction, both Louis VII of France and Conrad III of Germany took the cross – and, with them, a large cross-section of the French and German aristocracy. Yet crusade fever was not limited to such elevated circles. Many others among the lower nobility and merchant communities of Europe's rapidly growing cities of the Rhineland and Low Countries were keen to do their bit for the cause. It was men such as these who composed the bulk of the force which gathered at Dartmouth. Here they chose to organise themselves along co-operative lines, much like a guild, commune or urban association, swearing mutual oaths to act in tandem and uphold certain common principles. According to these, the army would avoid costly dress (which leads to sin), not let women go out in public and maintain regular religious observances. They would also elect two representatives from every thousand men, who would oversee the settlement of disputes and distribution of booty.[4]

We know frustratingly little about the Anglo-Norman contingent. A significant element hailed from East Anglia, including Hervey de Glanvill, in whose service the author of *De expugnatione Lyxbonensi* stood. Others may have come from the home counties of the south east, and some probably joined from Devon and the south west, where the army gathered. The choice of Dartmouth as a point of assembly was, however, largely dictated by practical concerns. The deep-water harbour there stood on the natural sea routes from southern and eastern England to the Mediterranean, and it only required a short detour for the detachments joining from the Rhineland and Low Countries.

From here, the fleet set sail on 23 May 1147. According to our main account, this comprised some 164 ships, though other sources suggest the number may have approached 200. This was a considerable force of perhaps between 8,000 and 10,000 men. The Anglo-Normans were the largest element, probably constituting just shy of half the army. Three days after departing, they came within sight of Brittany. Here, they were becalmed for two days. As the wind picked up and they made their way across the Bay of Biscay, however, the crusaders ran into trouble. For favourable winds turned into a tempest and the fleet's ships were dispersed. Many of those aboard interpreted this as a sign of divine displeasure. And only once they'd confessed their sins and offered prayers of repentance, did the storm start to abate, allowing them to make for the harbour at the port of S. Salvador (then known as Gozzim, now Luanco just north of Oviedo). From here, they proceeded along the northern coast of Spain. Some of the party seem to have stopped off to visit the famous pilgrimage site of St James at Santiago de Compostela, before finally reaching Oporto on 16 June.[5]

It was here that Lisbon came into the picture. The crusaders were met at Oporto by the local bishop Peter Pitões, acting on behalf of King Afonso. Afonso himself was on campaign in the south, and it was Peter's task to win the crusaders over for the Portuguese cause. Afonso had probably been planning this for some time. He'd attempted to take Lisbon five years earlier, also with external help, so knew full well how pious pilgrims might be won over. He may have been further encouraged by the amorphous nature of the Second Crusade. This had always been envisaged as a set of loosely associated initiatives, focussed on the Holy Land, but encompassing strikes against Muslims and pagans elsewhere in Iberia and central to eastern Europe.

It's even been suggested that Lisbon was the fleet's destination from the start. This is unlikely. The siege may have offered a natural prelude to the following year's action in the Middle East, but the author of our account – who writes as an eye-witness – gives no indication of such plans. Quite the reverse, he makes it clear that the crusaders took much persuading. After receiving the king's initial invitation, they waited till the following morning to deliberate. At this point, Bishop Peter is reported to have preached to them, playing up the threat presented by Islamic al-Andalus to the Christian population of the Portuguese realm and underlining the importance of redeeming Lisbon. These lengthy justifications – invented though they probably are by our author – are a clear sign that the consent of the crusaders was not assured. It was only after Peter's impassioned plea that they agreed even to meet with Afonso.[6]

The crusaders now travelled south to Lisbon, in order to hear more from the king. Here, they were treated to another lengthy set-piece speech, this time by Afonso himself. The problem for the crusaders was that they'd sworn oaths to pursue the crusade, so any unsanctioned diversion – and Lisbon had not been formally identified as part of the crusading cause – was potentially a breach of faith. In response, Peter and Afonso both presented the attack on Lisbon in terms of the defence of Christendom. But without formal papal sanction, it was far from certain that this constituted a *bona fide* crusade. A second set of problems arose from the fact that some of the Anglo-Normans had been part of the earlier force which had sought to take Lisbon in 1142. This had been a similar undertaking, with Afonso redirecting a group of pilgrims on their way to the Holy Land.[7] We know little about the campaign, save that it ended in failure and recriminations. Those who'd been involved were now adamant that the king was a man of bad faith and encouraged their comrades to bypass Lisbon and head straight for the Holy Land.

Most of the fleet, however, was convinced by Afonso's words. It therefore fell to Hervey de Glanvill to win over the eight recalcitrant crews of Anglo-Normans with yet another speech. This is the most famous section of the whole account in *De expugnatione*. In it, Hervey appeals to a shared sense of Norman pride. Noting the variety of peoples brought together beneath the crusading banner, he emphasises how essential it is for the Normans to pull their weight:

> [R]ecalling the virtues of our ancestors, we ought to strive to increase the honour and glory of our race rather than cover tarnished glory with the rags of malice. For the remarkable feats of the elders kept in memory by the successors are signs of love and honour. If you are worthy emulators of the elders, honour and glory will follow you; but if [you are] unworthy, then the disgrace of reproach [will do so]. For who does not know that the race of the Normans declines no labour in the continual practice of valour?

Hervey then reproached them for their troublemaking, noting that there were no such divisions among the men of Cologne (the Rhinelanders) or Flanders. In a final plea, he returns to his theme, urging them not to bring shame on their fellow countrymen – and on Normandy itself, the 'mother of our race'.[8]

This moving entreaty had the desired effect, and the reluctant crews fell into line. As our account is written by an associate of

Hervey, we may doubt that they were won over by eloquence alone (or indeed that Hervey was alone in applying pressure). But embellished though the speech may be, it provides precious insights into how the expedition was understood by its participants. It reveals that, despite the communal ethos of their vows, the crusaders remained starkly divided along ethnic lines – divisions exacerbated by the refusal to participate of a small Anglo-Norman detachment. Afonso had been surprised to learn that there was no single leader of the force; and now the difficulties of the army's complex constitution were laid bare. Communal government worked well when there was consensus, but struggled in the face of dissent.

In the end, Afonso got the men he needed. He agreed generous terms, including paying the crusaders for their service and giving them the right to sack the city (and ransom its population). Lisbon was well defended, as Afonso had learned five years previously. Even with these additional forces, success was far from inevitable. The siege began on 1 July and would last the better part of four months.

The first move for Afonso and his men was to secure the suburbs. They met with success here and were fortunate to secure the lion's share of the city's stores, which (rather unwisely) had been kept outside the walls. Further progress was not immediately forthcoming, however, and both sides settled in for a lengthy siege. Efforts were made to bring siege engines to bear, but these had little effect. As the months passed, spirits began to flag within the crusader camp. What had been intended as a brief detour now risked becoming an all-encompassing affair. The cost of the siege is revealed by the cemeteries consecrated for the crusaders, one for the Anglo-Normans to the west and another for the Rhinelanders and Flemings in the east. Yet just when morale was starting to hit rock bottom, good fortune shone on the besiegers. They intercepted a boat trying to break the blockade, which bore letters pleading for help from the ruler of Evora to the east. Soon thereafter, they intercepted a message back from Evora, informing the citizens that no such help would be forthcoming. These tidings put wind in the crusaders' sails.

By late October, the writing was on the wall for the people of Lisbon. The Anglo-Normans had now managed to bring a siege tower to bear on the south-west corner of the walls. In response, the inhabitants asked for a night's truce to consider their options. The following morning, they offered terms of surrender: the city and all its gold would go to Afonso, provided the citizens were spared. As was probably the intention, this created fresh divisions among the crusaders. This time, it was the Flemings and Rhinelanders who were the problem. While the Anglo-Normans were apparently happy to accept the terms and move on, their comrades insisted that it was unfair for Afonso to profit from a victory they had won. Initially, they were forced to relent. But when the time came to occupy the city, the Flemings and men of Cologne proceeded to sack it anyway. Only with great difficulty was order re-established, so that the gains might be properly distributed.

Once Lisbon had fallen, the town of Sintra to the north and the castle of Palmela to the south west likewise submitted. A member of the crusading force, Gilbert of Hastings, was now chosen as the new bishop of the city. On All Saints' day (1 November), Lisbon's leading mosque – a church and seat of the local bishopric until the eighth century – was ritually purified and re-consecrated. Thereafter, the Muslims of the neighbouring regions suffered a severe pestilence, which our author interprets as a sign of divine disfavour. He includes an extended thanks to God, before concluding his account.

Our author is a well-informed observer; but by his own admission, he is far from neutral. He writes from the perspective of the Anglo-Norman camp – and from Hervey's section thereof. When other Anglo-Normans drag their feet, they're in the wrong; when the Flemings and Rhinelanders cause troubles, it's put down to greed and impiety. In reality, matters must have been more complicated. Many Anglo-Normans seem to have been put out by the terms of surrender, and it's unlikely that they refrained from the ensuing sacking of the city.

But whatever caveats we may raise, there's no reason to doubt the gist of the report. Our author may exaggerate, but invention would not have got him very far. Letters from the German contingents serve to complement his account. We also possess briefer notices of these events, which confirm the broad outline of his narrative. Indeed, precisely because of the many groups involved, the sack of Lisbon is reported in histories and chronicles from across the Low Countries,

Saxony, England, Scotland and France.[9] These other reports help trace the crusaders' movements after the siege, at which point the anonymous chronicler goes silent. Many of these have the army proceed straight to the Holy Land, where it joined the main crusading force. But there is reason to doubt this was so. For the Flemish *Annals of Elmar* – which are well-informed on this score – report that the army departed in February 1148 (a detail confirmed in other sources), then sacked Faro in southern Portugal.[10] Evidently the crusaders continued to do their bit for the Christian cause while circumnavigating the peninsula.

Nor did they leave matters at that. An aside in the Genoese statesman and historian Caffaro's account of the siege of the Catalonian city Tortosa (1147–8), for which Genoa provided crucial naval support, reveals that there were Anglo-Norman troops involved here. And while Caffaro gives no explanation as to how they got there, this was almost certainly the same army (or a portion thereof). In fact, this is precisely what a Cologne chronicler reports: after taking Lisbon, the army helped storm Tortosa, before proceeding to the Holy Land. The latter chronicler writes within living memory of these events, in the city which had supplied the army's Rhineland contingent.[11]

Later charters from the region reveal significant Anglo-Norman settlement in and around Tortosa. This indicates that while most of the army made its way to the Holy Land (as the Cologne chronicler has it), elements stayed on to help settle the newly Christianised city.[12] There is an interesting contrast here with Lisbon. With the exception of Bishop Gilbert, we have no evidence of any settlement there. This may in part be because the charter record is richer for Catalonia than it is for Portugal. Yet it also reflects the different nature of the two undertakings. There was some uncertainty as to whether the siege of Lisbon was part of the crusade, but there could be no such doubt at Tortosa. Here Pope Eugenius III had indeed called for crusade. Having seen the siege through to its end, the crusaders had therefore fulfilled their vows. And with Count Ramon Berenguer IV of Catalonia keen on settlers, it must have been tempting to serve the Christian cause there. To this day, 'Angles' survives as a distinctive regional surname in Catalonia.

The Second Crusade was not the only Norman involvement in Iberia. While his countrymen were making initial advances into southern Italy, Roger of Tosny had carved out a fearsome reputation for himself in early eleventh-century Catalonia. In many respects, the situation within the two regions was analogous. Political authority was fragmented and there were gains to be made at the expense of Islamic neighbours – as well as other Christian potentates. And much like his Italian counterparts, Roger soon married into the local noble family. But just as Roger looked set to put down roots, he was driven from the region by an ambush (perhaps sprung by jealous Catalan magnates). Still, involvement in the peninsula seems to have become something of a familial tradition, and Roger's son is also reported to have spent time in the region.[13]

Connections between Normandy and Iberia never became especially strong, but there are ample signs of continuing interest in the peninsula in later years, particularly in the context of conflicts with al-Andalus and its Christian neighbours.[14] Robert Crispin is said to have taken part in the siege of Barbastro in 1064, before finding further employment in Italy and then Byzantium. More lasting was the contribution made by two other Normans, Rotrou de la Perche and Robert Burdet, in the early twelfth century. The former had joined the First Crusade among the forces of Robert Curthose and may have joined in early campaigns led by Alfonso I ('the Battler') of Aragon (c.1104/5). Certainly by the 1120s, Rotrou was at Alfonso's side. He was rewarded with some sectors of Saragossa and is named count of Tuleda (which fell in 1119) by 1123. Rotrou would return to Normandy in 1125 with much of his entourage, but reappeared in Aragon in the early 1130s, still in the role of count of Tuleda.[15] It was, however, one of Rotrou's followers, Robert Burdet, who would leave the more lasting mark. Robert had been Rotrou's second-in-command at Tuleda. In 1129, he was invited to take over the newly created frontier lordship of Tarragona. Robert went on to rule this with great success, attempting to found an independent polity much like that of the Hautevilles. However, opposition from the local archbishops, as well as the counts of Barcelona and kings of Aragon, eventually brought these dreams to an end. Still, a Norman presence was maintained in the region until 1177.[16]

Norman involvement in Iberia was thus by no means negligible, and bears comparison with what we've seen in the Balkans and Asia

Minor. As in the latter regions, the Normans were involved at a number of key junctures, leaving a lasting mark on the political landscape (Lisbon would go on to be the capital of Portugal, while Tortosa became an important Catalan holding on the Christian–Muslim frontier). Yet they were never fully integrated into local power structures and attempts at independent state-building did not meet with success. In part, this was a matter of luck. In Italy, it was only a combination of good fortune and political nous which ensured that the early Norman presence would endure; in Iberia, the misfortunes of Roger of Tosny and Robert Burdet had the reverse effect. It also reflects the smaller numbers involved. Many northern magnates participated in the conquest and colonisation of al-Andalus, and the Norman presence, while not insignificant, rarely stood out.

19

Scotland: Honoured
Guests, 1072–1153

When the great abbot-historian Aelred of Rievaulx came to set down the achievements of his close friend King David I of Scotland, he naturally waxed lyrical. David had been holy and devout – gentle, just, chaste and humble. He was the best of men and best of kings. His greatest achievement, however, lay in the reform of the Scottish realm. David had softened the barbarity of his nation, subduing its natural ferocity for the greater good. It was David who'd bowed the Scots' necks to the rule of law, establishing peace and punishing the unrighteous. He had found the kingdom with no more than three or four bishops, but left it with nine. He also transformed the landscape, turning Scotland from a land of famine to a land of plenty, boasting ports, castles and cities. Just as importantly, David had calmed the savagery of his people with Christian religion. It was he who introduced chastity in marriage and clerical celibacy.[1]

These may sound like clichés, and to a large extent they are. But Aelred was a well-informed observer, who'd served at David's court. And his remarks convey something of the essence of David's reign, at least as David understood it. For these years saw Scotland open up to cultural and political influences from England and mainland Europe. This was achieved by the large numbers of Anglo-Norman magnates who flocked to David's court. In many respects, these processes look like what we see in Wales and Ireland in these years. However, there is a crucial difference. The Normans came to Scotland to bolster, not to overthrow, the local political order. This was Normanisation by choice.

~

The years following 1066 saw a new Norman ruling elite established along the Scottish frontier. As in Wales, the danger was that it would not stop its conquering ways at the border. There were, however, important differences, which ensured that Norman influence north of the Solway Firth took different forms. The most obvious was in the nature of royal power and authority in England. The kingdom conquered by William had been forged by the rulers of Wessex in the south. The royal writ ran most firmly south of the Thames, and became weaker the further one travelled north. The Midlands and East Anglia were under close oversight; north of the Humber, however, the king's influence was heavily mediated.[2] A further distinction can be drawn in the north between the old earldom of York (modern Yorkshire and parts of Lancashire) and that of Bamburgh to its north. The former was still a core part of the English realm, overseen by an earl who answered to the king. The latter, however, was ruled in hereditary succession by local dynasts. Here the English monarch was more of an overlord than a king.[3]

These differences are reflected in the Domesday Survey, which covers Yorkshire and parts of Lancashire, but stops at the Tees. The modern counties of Northumberland and Durham were evidently considered to be more like Wales and Scotland than England proper. This also emerges from a charter of William Rufus for the church of Tynemouth, which confirms its possessions 'north of the Tyne, south of the Tyne and in England (*Anglia*)'. While the document itself is a later forgery, it provides a valuable local perspective on political geography.[4] The former were areas of English overlordship and influence, not direct rule.

Because royal power and authority faded out as one travelled north, direct intervention in these regions was rare, and there are few signs of English intrusion into Scotland such as we see in Wales before the Conquest. Conflict was still common, but generally localised. The northernmost parts of England were also much less urbanised and saw less use of coinage than the south and east (or even Yorkshire, for that matter); in social and economic terms too, England blended into Scotland, rather than facing it cheek by jowl. For its part, Lothian in south-eastern Scotland had seen considerable English settlement in the early Anglo-Saxon period and remained more plugged in to the socio-economic world of the south than much of Wales or the northern Highlands. Indeed, one of the first recorded uses of the term 'England' (Old English: *engla lond*) is for Lothian, not for the modern country.

Since the late ninth century, Scotland had been dominated by the kingdom of Alba in the north and east, which in the course of the eleventh century came to encompass the old British kingdom of Strathclyde/Cumbria.[5] The resulting realm was a composite one. Well into the twelfth century, 'Scotland' in the strict sense only designated the region north of the Firth of Forth, and was but one of the lands under the control of the king of Alba. Moray in the north and Galloway in the south west remained largely independent.[6] Still, Alba was a powerful kingdom. And though its resources were no match for those of the English kings, its rulers – the kings of Scots, as they are increasingly known – were considerably wealthier than their Welsh counterparts. The risks of conflict for the new Norman lords of the frontier was therefore considerably less favourable here.

For their part, William and his successors were no more interested in Scotland than they were in Wales. The region was too poor and too far from Normandy to warrant the expense of permanent conquest. As in Wales, however, the Anglo-Norman monarchs were keen to maintain a degree of hegemony over these regions.[7] And in the years following 1068, their interest was piqued by the presence of Edgar the Ætheling, the last remaining scion of the native English dynasty.

Malcolm (Máel Coluim) III, the king at the time, was more than happy to welcome Edgar. If Edgar were to re-establish himself in England, he would owe his Scottish allies a good turn; if not, his presence could be used to destabilise the new Norman power to the south. In fact, Malcolm soon strengthened this alliance by marrying Edgar's sister, Margaret. This not only connected him to one of Europe's most venerable dynasties, it also gave Malcolm and his heirs a claim to the English throne. He and Margaret underlined this in their choice of names for their offspring: Edward, Edmund, Æthelred, Edgar, Alexander and David for their sons, and Edith and Mary for their daughters. Of these, all save Alexander, David and Mary – the names given to the youngest siblings – are names of earlier English kings and queens.[8] These interests naturally placed Malcolm on the side of native English resistance. In the upheavals of the later 1060s, he repeatedly backed the rebel factions in the North. And following the Harrying of the North, he took the opportunity to strike at northern England himself.

Still, there could be no question of directly challenging the Conqueror. When the latter came to Scotland with a large army in 1072, Malcolm was quick to come to terms. He submitted, doing homage to William at Abernethy, a strategic site within the Scottish royal heartlands. This was a pragmatic arrangement which suited both parties. William's superiority was acknowledged, while Malcolm's independence of action was left undiminished. With the Scottish court continuing to support Edgar, however, relations remained frosty. When tempers next flared in 1081, William sent his eldest son, Robert Curthose, north. The result was much the same – a pragmatic peace, but little more. Malcolm now did homage to Robert in William's place, much as he had at Abernethy.[9] But tensions remained high, and Malcolm would meet his death while on a raid into English territory in 1093.

A series of regime changes eventually helped bring rapprochement. Malcolm was initially succeeded by his brother Donald (Domnall) III. One of Donald's first recorded actions was to drive out 'all the English' who'd come north with Edgar and Margaret – a pointed break with his brother's Anglophile politics. While this may look like a conciliatory gesture to the Norman court, it was largely a move to dissociate Donald from his nephews (Malcolm's sons), many of whom were well placed at the Anglo-Norman court and had their own ambitions regarding the Scottish throne. In fact, within a year William Rufus had installed one of these, Duncan (Donnachad) II, as king in Donald's stead. Duncan was Malcolm's son from his first marriage; and as such, as much a rival as an ally to the many sons of Margaret still waiting in the wings. Donald was, in any case, able to reassert himself in 1094. But three years later Rufus succeeded in imposing another of Malcolm's offspring. This was Edgar, Malcolm's eldest son with Margaret, who'd been named after Margaret's brother, the exiled Ætheling. The Ætheling himself – now reconciled to Anglo-Norman rule in England – played a key part in establishing his nephew's new regime. For William Rufus, this killed two birds with one stone. It secured his northern frontier, while removing the threat of Malcolm's many sons to his own rule. Henceforth, their energies would be directed to securing their position within the Scottish realm.

Following Rufus' death and the accession of Henry I, relations warmed further. Keen to defuse further any potential threat from the old West Saxon line, Henry married Edgar's sister Edith (who now took the suitably Norman name Matilda). This meant that the king of Scots was the brother-in-law of the Anglo-Norman monarch, as were his brothers and successors, Alexander I and David I. The Scottish kings were thus moving in the same circles as their Norman counterparts, and Alexander went on to marry Sybilla, one of Henry I's illegitimate progeny (of which there were more than twenty).[10] Alexander's younger brother, David, married a great-niece of the Conqueror, Matilda of Huntingdon (Sybilla's second cousin). The latter was a particularly good match, as Matilda was the heiress of Waltheof, bringing to the marriage the rich earldom of Huntingdon.

The result of these unions was to integrate the Scottish royal family firmly into the Anglo-Norman aristocratic world. Yet they did more than this. As Matilda's husband, David became a significant landholder south of the border. And when he succeeded Alexander I as king in 1124, he did so not only as a Scottish prince (David had been entrusted with overseeing Cumbria), but also as an Anglo-Norman earl. Not surprisingly, David's reign saw Norman influence on the Scottish court grow, as Aelred's epitaph attests. David was a man of Norman tastes, whose eldest son was named Henry (after the reigning English king). Henry himself would go on to wed Ada de Warenne, a leading Anglo-Norman noblewoman and great-great-aunt of the later Earl John, who would so proudly wield her grandfather's rusty sword in the late thirteenth century.

In Scotland, David's reign was characterised by an influx of Anglo-Norman aristocrats. Most of these came via the English court, where they'd often first met David. The result was the formation of something of a shared Anglo-Scoto-Norman elite. At David's court, the most favoured magnates were all of Norman (or at least French) descent, and their numbers grew steadily across the twelfth and thirteenth centuries. The result was not a complete displacement of the native aristocracy, but rather a mixing (and at times jostling) between this and the Anglo-Norman incomers. Such shifts were not welcomed by all, however, and signs of tension can be seen across much of the twelfth century. Indeed, malcontents rallied around rival branches of the royal family, backing Alexander's illegitimate son Malcolm (named after his grandfather) in David's early years. And such oppositional forces would return in force following David's death.

Still, this was not armed conquest. It was (largely) peaceful settlement, encouraged by the Scottish kings – and also elements of the native aristocracy. The twelfth and thirteenth centuries were an important period of change within the Scottish realm, which saw the first formal structures of bureaucratic rule erected. The importation of Norman aristocrats was part of these shifts, the main effect of which was to entrench the powers of the king and aristocracy (particularly its upper echelons).[11]

From the perspective of our (largely English) sources, these changes are looked upon with favour. We have seen how Aelred wrote approvingly of King David taming his nation's barbarous ways. Here we see similar tropes to those invoked on the Welsh March: the Anglo-Normans are the forces of order, out to tame Scotland's native barbarism. Yet there is an important difference. Aelred speaks of the Scots embracing this world.[12] Similar sentiments had already been expressed by William of Malmesbury in the mid-1120s. William dedicated his monumental *History of the Kings of England* to Empress Matilda (the daughter of Henry I and Edith/Matilda – and thus David's niece), in which he, also, describes how David had cast off the barbarism of his land and had raised standards of living, dress and diet.[13]

Of course, not all Englishmen were as sympathetic as Aelred and William (and even they were capable of stern criticism upon occasion). Still, there are signs that genuine change was afoot. We can see this most clearly in the practice of war. Scottish custom was much like that of the Welsh and pre-Conquest English, which was to kill or enslave those defeated in battle (and their civilian populations). This was still the case in the late eleventh century, when Malcolm III's raids on northern England are reported with horror by Symeon of Durham. To a Norman audience accustomed to mercy among aristocrats in war, the large-scale enslaving of defeated enemies by the Scottish was

beyond the pale.[14] David's invasion of 1138 was in many respects similar, with substantial numbers of those captured sold off into slavery.
Yet there are hints of change. Many accounts draw a distinction
between the Norman, lowland English, Scottish and Galwegian (or
'Pictish') elements within David's army, with the worst of the atrocities ascribed to the latter groups. It would seem that David's forces
were only half-barbarous. Moreover, David himself is said to have
returned his share of the slaves as a pious gesture. Evidently he was
keen to play by the Norman rules of engagement.[15]

By 1173 to 1174, when David's grandson William the Lion next
invaded northern England, these distinctions had blurred further.
The only difference between William's personal retinue and their
English foes lay in their loyalties – or at least so Jordan Fantosme, the
Anglo-Norman poet, would have us believe. Of course, not everything had changed. Jordan remarks that the local inhabitants of the
regions ravaged by William's men (in fact, Flemish mercenaries) were
fortunate that the Scots (their 'mortal enemies') were not present, for
they would have shown no mercy. And William of Newburgh, writing in Latin, still describes the force as a 'horde of barbarians' and
'more savage than beasts'. (Though even William lets slip that the
Scottish king mistook the English attackers for his own men – a clear
indication that the Anglo-Norman elite at both courts was largely
indistinguishable.)[16]

The line between chivalry and barbarism had always been a fluid
one. To the Norman invaders of 1066, the native English were uncivilised. By the time Symeon of Durham wrote in the 1120s, they'd
begun to join the Normans in their 'sweet civility'. With growing
numbers of Normans (and English) making their way to the Scottish
court, Scotland was now moving in a similar direction. These changes
did not, however, embrace all of Scotland in equal measure. Norman
settlement was heaviest in the largely English-speaking regions of
Lothian, as well as the northern Lowlands of Fife, Gowrie, Angus
and the Mearns.[17] And already in the accounts of the Battle of the
Standard (1138), we see hints of the distinction between Highlanders
and Lowlanders, with only the latter readily adopting the norms of
the Anglo-Norman court. This dichotomy, which would become
the major cultural cleavage in later Scottish society, was taken up with

gusto by clerical writers of the Lowlands, who underline the barbarism of the Highlanders, much as earlier English writers had that of the Scots.[18]

One of the clearest signs that the Scottish court was entering the European mainstream is that its kings and princes were knighted at the hands of continental dukes and monarchs. Duncan had already received his arms from the Conqueror's son Curthose in 1087, while David I went on to be knighted by Henry I of France. Malcolm IV was then dubbed by Henry II in 1159, as was his brother David somewhat later, while the future Alexander II was knighted by the infamous 'bad King John' in London in 1212. The ritual of knighting, one of the archetypal symbols of chivalric culture, was well-suited to the relationship between the Scottish and the English monarch. It symbolised a degree of hierarchy, but like homage constituted an honourable form of submission. That the Scottish were in some sense the equals of their Anglo-Norman counterparts is revealed by the fact that they could return the favour, as when David I knighted the young pretender to the English throne, Henry Plantagenet (the future Henry II).[19]

Of the Norman families to make their way north under David, few were more famous (and influential) than that of Robert de Brus. Robert was already a prominent figure in England and Normandy in the 1120s. He'd been a supporter of Henry I, whose reign had seen relations with the Scottish court improve so markedly. And he was rewarded for his loyalty with a series of manors in Yorkshire.[20] It was through the Anglo-Norman court that Robert first met David, then earl of Huntingdon. David himself first appears in the documentary record in a charter of King Henry confirming the rights of Robert in 1103, and it may be that the two served together in the Cotentin.[21] Certainly when David established himself on the Scottish throne, Robert was one of the first (of many) Norman associates to appear beside him.

Robert's arrival in Scotland is recorded in a charter of 1124, issued at Scone, the traditional site of royal inauguration. This is the first document David issued as king and is in many respects symbolic of his reign. In it, David grants Robert Annandale a large swathe of land in exchange for loosely defined service. The aim was clearly to win the loyalty of an up-and-coming Anglo-Norman baron (and long-time associate), whose know-how and connections would be sorely needed if Scotland were to survive and thrive as an independent nation. David had probably given Robert these lands some time earlier, while deputising for his elder brother in Cumbria. The purpose of the charter is to formalise the arrangement. The witness list shows David in his element, enjoying the company of the new crop of Anglo-Norman magnates he'd brought north (all eight of the charter's witnesses are newcomers). And the text itself is only addressed to David's French and English subjects – i.e. the Norman incomers and the inhabitants of Lothian – leaving out their Scottish and Galwegian counterparts to the north and west. This is an indication of the original audience for the grant. This act was for the benefit of the small cadre of new favourites at court. The grant itself is equally noteworthy. This not only secured the services of a useful ally, but created a new lordship overlooking Galloway, a largely autonomous region in which the king of Scots often struggled to assert himself.[22]

From Robert came the de Brus (or Bruce) line, one of the great noble families of medieval Scotland. Another was founded by Bernard de Balliol, the scion of an Anglo-Picard noble family. Both Robert and Bernard remained first and foremost Anglo-Norman barons. And when conflict erupted in 1138 and again in 1173 to 1174, they and their heirs backed the English Crown against their new Scottish lords (indeed, it was Bernard's youngest son who's reported to have captured William the Lion in 1174). Still, this did not stop the Bruces and Balliols climbing the ranks at the Scottish court, and both families would eventually find themselves on the throne itself: the Balliols in the person of John (II) de Balliol (John I of Scotland) in the late thirteenth century, the son of the founder of Balliol College, Oxford; and the Bruces in Robert (VII) the Bruce (Robert I of Scotland) and his son and heir, David II, shortly thereafter. When the Bruce line failed after the second generation in 1371, the kingship passed to another Scoto-Norman lineage first established under David I: the Stewarts.[23] Under their more genteel later designation (the Stuarts), this family would come to sit upon the English throne too, in 1603. Through the twists and turns of dynastic fortune, Norman settlement in Scotland thus lay the foundations for the union of Scottish and English crowns – for Great Britain. And this would not be its only manifestation.

20

The Power Behind the Throne: Scotland Under Ada de Warenne, 1153–78

When Ada de Warenne presented her pious son Malcolm with a pretty young maid, she knew exactly what she was doing. Malcolm had recently come to the throne and desperately needed an heir. His mother was just helping him along the way. Unfortunately for Ada, Malcolm's mind was on higher things. He accepted the lady into his quarters out of courtesy. But Malcolm insisted on giving up his bed for her – in order to maintain his chastity. The next morning, the king was found on the floor by his attendants, wrapped in a cloak. Where most would have been unable to resist temptation, Malcolm resolutely refused to be corrupted.

Or so the English chronicler William of Newburgh reports.[1] The account is shot through with saintly motifs and cannot be taken entirely at face value. Nevertheless, William's remarks neatly encapsulate the political difficulties of the 1150s and 1160s in Scotland. For Malcolm came to the throne at the tender age of twelve in 1153, at a moment of considerable uncertainty. Malcolm's father Henry had originally been intended to succeed David; but he'd died the previous year, leaving Malcolm next in line. Little more than a boy, Malcolm could scarcely be expected to step into his grandfather's shoes. That was not all. There may already have been signs that Malcolm was ailing, and this may have inspired his deep piety. Yet while chastity may have helped Malcolm's cause in the Eternal Kingdom, it only compounded his problems in the earthly one. A weak king without an heir was a double liability.

Keenly aware of these dangers, Malcolm's mother stuck close by his side. By all accounts, Ada de Warenne was a force of nature. She repeatedly prevailed upon Malcolm to marry, reminding him that he was a king not a monk. Eventually, Malcolm had to ask her to desist.

But still Ada kept the interests of her lineage in mind, ensuring that her younger son William was ready and waiting to succeed his brother when the time came.

~

David I had initiated the settlement of Norman magnates in Scotland, but it was under his grandsons Malcolm and William that these efforts bore fruit. David's own Francophilia can be traced back to his youth. As a younger son, there was no guarantee that David would accede to the Scottish throne. And so, like a growing number of men of the era, David had set out to make his own fortune. As a prince, his marriage prospects were good. And his subsequent marriage to the wealthy Anglo-Norman heiress Matilda of Huntingdon had brought with it a place at the court of King Henry I of England.

It was in Henry's interests to encourage David's ambitions. As prince of Cumbria, David provided a point of contact with the Scottish court; and if David could be made king, Henry would have one of his own leading barons as his neighbour. When David's brother Alexander died in 1124, Henry was therefore quick to support David's bid for the throne, against the rival claims of Alexander I's son. With such exalted backing, David was soon able to establish himself. In Scotland, his position now resembled that of the Confessor in England in the previous century. David had spent much of his adult life among Norman aristocrats and had come to the throne with their assistance. In the coming years, he would look to them to help him rule.

Yet if David was as Norman as he was Scottish, his son Henry was even more so. Born in England shortly after David's marriage to Matilda (c.1114), Henry entered the world not as a Scottish prince, but as the heir of a leading Anglo-Norman earl. He had had some acquaintance with Scottish affairs from an early age, since David remained prince of Cumbria. Nevertheless, Henry's future seemed to lie at the Anglo-Norman court, as his distinctively Franco-Norman name reveals.

These connections were maintained following David's elevation to the Scottish kingship. The death of Henry I in 1135 and ensuing succession dispute in England (the so-called 'Anarchy'), however, served to sour relations between the English and Scottish courts. As befitted an old friend of Henry I, David favoured the claims of Matilda

(Henry's daughter and preferred heir) over those of Stephen (Henry's nephew). Nevertheless, this did not preclude a degree of pragmatism. David initially submitted to Stephen, securing his familial interests in England. When revolt broke out in Matilda's favour, however, David was quick to join this. His forces were roundly defeated by Stephen's at the Battle of the Standard (1138), forcing David to come to terms once more. The continuing threat of Matilda's claim meant that Stephen was in no position to press his advantage, and David's son Henry was able not only to retain the earldom of Huntingdon, but also to add that of Northumberland. David and Henry may have lost the war, but they'd won the peace.

The strength of David and Henry's position is reflected by the latter's marriage to Ada de Warenne the following year (1139). As the granddaughter of William (I) de Warenne, one of the Conqueror's close associates, Ada was an excellent match. Her family lands lay in Surrey, a region which supported Stephen; and her half-brothers, the Beaumont twins (the grandsons of Roger de Beaumont), were among Stephen's most prominent backers. The union was intended to tie Henry (and thus David) to Stephen's cause. In this respect, it was only partially effective. For by 1141, Henry and David were back to their old ways, supporting Matilda. Nevertheless, the union would have long-reaching consequences for the Scottish realm.[2]

With Henry, Ada went on to have three sons and three daughters. Of the former, Malcolm was the eldest, born in the spring of 1141. The choice of a Scottish name is significant: Malcolm was named after his great-grandfather, Malcolm III, and, unlike Henry, he was clearly intended for the Scottish throne from the start. The couple reverted to form for the name of their second son – William – who was born in 1143. William was a Warenne name, and the young prince was named after Ada's father, William (II) de Warenne, who had himself been named after his father. Their third (and final) son was David, named after Henry's father. The couple's daughters bore similarly cosmopolitan names: one was named Ada, after her mother; another Margaret, after her great-grandmother (Malcolm III's wife); and the third, Matilda, after her grandmother.

After the upheavals of the late 1130s, relations between England and Scotland stabilised over the following decade. David (and Henry) continued to favour Matilda's claim to the English throne when they could; but the focus of Stephen and Matilda's warring factions was the south, and the Scottish court was spared the worst ravages of the Anarchy. Of more lasting consequence was the continuing influx of Anglo-Norman magnates to the north. Many of these came from northern England, regions with which the Scottish monarchs and their magnates maintained regular contact. It's from here that both the Balliols and Bruces hailed. Yet not all the incomers came from the North. A large number hailed from Huntingdon, King David's southern earldom, and its environs. Rather less self-evident is the connection between Scotland and the West Country, which (for reasons which remain obscure) formed a third major area of recruitment for magnates seeking to settle in Scotland. In most of these cases, the Normans continued to hold lands south of the border; and in many cases, in Normandy too. And while the families soon started to put down roots, the importance of these ties should not be underestimated.[3]

Much has been made of the 'Davidian revolution' in Scottish politics in this connection. By importing Norman magnates and know-how, David I is thought to have dragged the backward Scottish realm kicking and screaming into the twelfth century. David and his Normans certainly stand at the start of a process, but one in which David's daughter-in-law and grandsons were to have far more important parts to play – not to mention Scotland's own native magnates. For his part, David ended up being a victim of his success. His longevity meant that he outlived his only son, Henry, by a year. David had already designated Henry his heir, on the Franco-Norman model. With Henry dead, he now did likewise with young Malcolm, Henry's eldest. When David died peacefully in 1153, the throne therefore passed directly to his twelve-year-old grandson.

The accession of a child was always a test for a medieval kingdom. It produced a power vacuum at the top of the political hierarchy, and success of the child's reign rested on the ability of friends and associates to steady the ship – and the willingness of the realm's great and good to support them. That the kingdom of Scots survived its first brush with boy kingship is a testament to the foundations laid by David. It also speaks of the political nous of Malcolm's guardians, foremost amongst these his mother Ada de Warenne.

Ada's prominence in these years requires explanation. As the most tangible link to the previous regime, the queen mother frequently played a part in medieval regencies. Nevertheless, this was not a role which could be taken for granted. When King John of England died in late 1216, his wife Isabella was accorded no place in the regency for the nine-year-old Henry III (her son). And even in the case of Malcolm, Duncan I, earl of Fife, was initially foreseen as chief guardian, perhaps on account of the role played by the earl of Fife in Scottish royal inauguration traditions.[4] But scarcely had Duncan overseen Malcolm's accession – itself rushed through shortly after David's death – than he died. Into this gap stepped the able Ada. Over the coming years, a close-knit group around the queen mother called the shots at court, composed largely of David's (and Ada's) Norman favourites – men such as Walter fitz Alan, Hugh and Richard de Moreville, and David Olifard. There was no sharp break when Malcolm came of age, as his earlier guardians stayed on as trusted advisers.[5]

Ada's decision to remain with Malcolm was probably informed by the king's frailty. Certainly by the 1160s, he was suffering from symptoms of a serious illness. And if, as modern historians suspect, this was a case of Paget's disease (a disease of the bone, which can lead to abnormal growths and even death), then the initial onset may have been much earlier. Malcolm's insistence on remaining chaste was probably a response to this. With an unwed and ailing son on the throne, Ada's legacy was far from secure. And while her attempts to encourage Malcolm to produce an heir failed, she continued to do everything in her power to ensure the continuance of her line.

Ada was right to be wary. Soon after Malcolm's inauguration, a major rebellion started brewing in the northern reaches of the realm. This was led by Somerled, the powerful lord of the Argyll. Northern and western Scotland were regions with a long history of independence, both *de facto* and *de iure*. This was, however, not so much a bid for freedom as an attempt to place a rival line on the throne. For Somerled is said (rather cryptically) to have rebelled with 'the sons of Malcolm'. The Malcolm in question has sometimes been identified as the later earl of Ross; however, he was almost certainly the illegitimate nephew of King David, who'd rebelled before, early in his uncle's reign. This was thus a continuation of earlier opposition to David and his Franco-Norman rule.[6]

We know less about the rising than we'd like – detailed sources for internal Scottish politics being slender in these years – but it serves as a reminder of how fragile the grasp of David's lineage was on the throne. If Malcolm IV failed, there were plenty of others waiting in the wings. Luckily for Ada, first among these was Malcolm's younger brother, William. And when Malcolm finally succumbed to his illness in 1165, William stepped swiftly into his shoes, ruling the Scottish realm for the best part of the next five decades.

Ada is far less prominent in these years. An adult man in his early twenties, William did not need his hand held in the same fashion as his brother. Ada also had her own reasons for keeping her distance. It was in these years that she began to suffer a series of severe illnesses, which would plague her till her death. She now focused her remaining energies on religious patronage, as was customary for a dowager queen. Still, Ada continued to be the only prominent woman at court – and as such, to command considerable influence. For like Malcolm, William was unmarried in 1165 and would remain so for over two decades. (Unlike his brother, however, William was certainly not chaste, for we know of at least one illegitimate child from these years.) It would seem that Ada fulfilled the role of *de facto* queen so well that neither of her sons was in a rush to replace her.

It was under William, known to posterity as 'the Lion', that many of the processes initiated by David came to fruition. Part of the story here is one of continued Anglo-Norman settlement and influence. For there was not a single influx of immigrants in the 1120s and 1130s, but rather a slow but steady stream under David, Malcolm and William. Three of William's four grandparents were Anglo-Norman; now the court and kingdom started to take on an ever more Francophone character. The address clauses of royal charters reflect this. And as we've seen, when William marched south against Henry II in 1173 and 1174, there was little to distinguish his personal entourage from his southern foes. These were not the only changes. By the time of the reign of William's son, Alexander II, Scottish kings began to extend mercy to rebels, in much the same manner as their Anglo-Norman counterparts.[7]

However, the Norman element in Scotland remained small in absolute numbers, even among the nobility. And while William and his household troops might pass for (or indeed be) Anglo-Normans, the bulk of the Scottish army continued to be composed of the native light infantry which so terrified English observers. Indeed, a number of southern commentators present William's defeat in 1174 as divine punishment for his inability (or unwillingness) to restrain the rapacity of the more barbarous elements within his army.

The most enduring changes were the adoption of new forms of government and documentation. In neither case can these be laid at the feet of the Norman incomers alone, but, in both, they played a part. Before the eleventh century, we have almost no documentary records from Scotland. Over the course of the reigns of David and his grandsons, this changed swiftly. We must be wary here of equating new evidence with new social and political structures. To a considerable extent, these documents allow us to see better patterns which had long existed. Still, there can be no doubt that Scottish government and society was shifting decisively away 'from memory to written record'.

It's the form which these records take which is of particular interest. The earliest Scottish charters – in the names of kings and leading magnates – from the early twelfth century are closely modelled on their Anglo-Norman counterparts. The address clauses which first alert us to the growing Francophone element at and beyond court take the form of those in the Anglo-Norman writ-charter (itself the heir of the Anglo-Saxon sealed writ). It is, therefore, entirely appropriate that the earliest surviving document of this type should be David I's grant of Annandale in 1124 to Robert (I) de Brus.[8] Yet these developments were not limited to the small (but growing) cadre of Francophone aristocrats at court. Address clauses speak more frequently of the 'Scots' and 'English' (Latin: *Scotti* and *Angli*) than they do of the French/Normans (*Franci*). And soon enough, Gaelic-speaking lords were also receiving and issuing such documents. A partial contrast emerges with Wales here, where, despite a significant Norman settlement and influence, local princely charters remained more eclectic in form and nature.[9]

Closely tied to the adoption of new types of documentation was the patronage of new forms of religious life. As in Wales and Ireland, the native Scottish Church was perceived as backward and corrupt by reform-minded prelates in the south. But while in the former regions religious reform was often the frontline of English imperialism, in Scotland it was the Francophile ruling dynasty which took the lead. Already Margaret is reported to have brought new religious ways to Scotland. And David went on to found a number of houses belonging to new religious orders, including the Tironensians, Cistercians and Augustinians. Many of the earliest royal charters are for these abbeys.[10]

This growing body of evidence allows us to observe other important shifts in state and society. Far more than David or Malcolm, William the Lion was an innovator in government. It's in his reign that moves can be discerned to centralise power and authority in the hands of the king and his local representatives (above all, sheriffs and earls). From 1184, there are signs of sheriffs regularly holding local courts; it's also in these years that steps towards the territorialisation of the office of earl can be seen. William's own son and heir, Alexander II, was to go even further. As a result, the Scottish kings and their magnates emerged much empowered. It was in these years, too, that the first native coinage was struck, starting under David I and picking up steam under Malcolm and William.[11]

As part of these processes, we start to see new practices of land tenure and lordship emerge – what historians would once have called feudalism. The 'f-word' is now generally avoided by specialists, and rightly so. It's unclear whether there was ever a coherent 'feudal system' in the Middle Ages, with well-defined rules of tenure and service. What is clear, however, is that in Scotland we start seeing grants of land made by kings and lords in the form of fiefs (or feus, to use the Scots term). The fief was a form of dependent holding, granted out in exchange for service (typically of a military nature). While the granting of land for service was hardly itself a novelty, the vocabulary used was – as were the detailed provisions for service.

We can see these processes at work in the granting of Annandale to the Bruces. Though older textbooks have it that David I granted these lands to Robert as a fief, this is not strictly true. The original document simply states that de Brus is to hold Annandale according to 'those customs which Ranulf Meschin ever had in Carlisle' (whatever they may have been!). When Robert's son, Robert II, had these rights confirmed by William the Lion fifty years later, however, it was a different story. Now Annandale is indeed termed a fief (Latin: *feudum*), and Robert receives this in exchange for the service of ten knights; he is also granted various judicial rights over the lands. Similar terms are used for such arrangements in England and Normandy; and the resulting practices also approximate (without fully replicating) what we see there.[12] In this more limited sense, we can indeed speak of Scotland becoming a feudal society. Yet these practices were not imposed from outside, but rather adapted to local circumstances. The classic forms of feudalism were still developing in England and Normandy in the twelfth century; Scottish monarchs were simply treading a parallel path.

Norman influence on Scotland presents us with a paradox. Because the Normans arrived at royal behest and in royal service, they had a far greater impact on government and society than they did in Wales and Ireland.[13] Yet the Normans are as much a symptom of change as they are its cause, reflecting the new cultural and political orientation of the native kings. Here we glimpse what might have been in England, had the Confessor had an uncontested heir: considerable Norman settlement and influence, leading to a symbiosis of native and continental forms. In objective terms, Scotland became more Norman than Wales or Ireland ever did. But it did so very much on its own terms. And when it came to relations with the Anglo-Norman and Angevin kings to their south, Scotland always gave as good as it got.

21

Strongbow in Leinster: Stealing a March, 1167–71

When Gerald of Wales came to speak of Henry II's conquest of Ireland, it was in panegyric terms. Addressing the king, Gerald spoke of how his victories were known throughout the globe. 'Our western Alexander', Henry had established domains which spanned the known world. This is the language of courtly sycophancy. And as the remarks about Alexander reveal, Gerald was not so much describing Henry's achievements as setting up a flattering (and suitably learned) comparison between the English monarch and his Classical forebears.[1]

Gerald's aims are all too familiar: personal advancement. He was an ambitious churchman, keen to curry favour with the king. Yet precisely on this account, Gerald provides privileged access to feelings at and around the English court in Henry II's reign. For in taking Ireland, the new Angevin (or Plantagenet) monarch had indeed exceeded the achievements of his predecessors. Almost from the moment of victory at Hastings, the Normans had begun their claim to wider dominion within the British Isles. William had been swift to secure the submission of the neighbouring Welsh and Scottish kings. And such ambitions sometimes extended further to Ireland. In its epitaph for the Conqueror, the E version of the *Anglo-Saxon Chronicle* reports that William would have taken the island, had he but lived two years longer. This is an exaggeration. But it points to a deeper truth. For in conquering England, William found he had inherited political interests spanning the Isles.[2]

In practice, royal interest in Ireland was intermittent, much as it was in Wales and Scotland. The Conqueror and his sons typically had bigger fish to fry, not least in mainland Europe, where their French and Angevin neighbours were a constant threat. Nevertheless, when circumstances allowed, the Anglo-Norman kings certainly indulged in dreams of a wider dominion. Upon sighting Ireland from the Welsh coast, Rufus is reported to have wanted to build a pontoon bridge to storm it. And though Henry I cut an altogether more down-to-earth figure, he too is said to have been feared by the king of Munster in the south.[3]

If royal interest in Ireland proved fleeting and quixotic, the demands of the Church were a different matter. A central justification for William's conquest of England had been the need to reform the English Church. And similar pretexts were soon given for the introduction of Francophone churchmen to Wales and Scotland. Norman settlement was often conceived as part of a civilising mission; and in Ireland, this was doubly true. Here Anglo-Norman settlement came later, but was followed by more sustained reforming efforts within the Church.

Signs of interest in Ireland can already be seen during the pontificate of Lanfranc, the Conqueror's chosen archbishop of Canterbury. Lanfranc was a reformer in the continental vein. The sins of the English, in his view, were bad enough, but as nothing compared to those of the Welsh, Scottish and Irish. The archbishop's central interest here lay in asserting his see's primacy – that is, Canterbury's right to ecclesiastical authority over the entire British Isles. And his immediate focus was control of northern England, where the archbishopric of York threatened to diminish Canterbury's powers. But Lanfranc was well aware of the wider implications of his claims, particularly at a time when Norman influence was starting to extend beyond the traditional English frontiers.

The Church hierarchy we take for granted – with archbishoprics overseeing bishoprics – was a product of developments during the Middle Ages. The office of archbishop had only emerged slowly in England and mainland Europe, over the course of the eighth and ninth centuries. Wales, Ireland and Scotland harked back to an earlier age here. Church structures remained fluid, without the kind of stable and defined hierarchy characteristic of other regions. Only occasionally are archbishops attested for these regions (mostly in Wales and Ireland).[4] For the new archbishop of Canterbury, this presented a unique opportunity.

A central plank of Lanfranc's claims was that Canterbury had been founded as primate – a super archbishop, if you will – of the entire British Isles in 597. As archbishop, Lanfranc was the rightful ecclesiastical lord not only of the province of York, but also of the neighbouring churches of Wales, Scotland and Ireland. When the opportunity arose for the primate to flex his muscles, Lanfranc and his successors were therefore only too happy to oblige.[5]

Circumstances in Ireland played into his hands. Here the eleventh century had seen the foundation of a new bishopric at Dublin, the most important Viking settlement on the island's eastern coast. Little is known about the first bishop, Dúnán. But in 1074 his successor, Gilla Pátraic (Patrick), was consecrated by Lanfranc at St Paul's, swearing an oath of obedience. An Irishman, Gilla Pátraic had apparently been trained at Worcester under the saintly bishop Wulfstan. And when Gilla Pátraic returned to Dublin, it was with letters from Lanfranc to his secular overlords, urging them to reform the wayward ways of their people.[6] After Gilla Pátriac's death, his successor Donngus sought consecration from the archbishop of Canterbury. And when Donngus died in late 1096, Lanfranc's successor Anselm went on to consecrate the next bishop of Dublin, Samuel. Anselm had also just consecrated the first bishop of Waterford in 1095. The common denominator here is that, like Gilla Pátriac, these bishops were all English educated.

Subsequent years saw Canterbury's influence ebb, as York challenged its claims to primacy in England and the political instability of Stephen's reign distracted attention from wider ambitions. There were also increasingly successful efforts in Wales, Ireland and Scotland to establish (or re-establish) independent national churches – efforts which took direct aim at Canterbury. On their own, Canterbury's ambitions were never likely to gain much traction. But they ensured that earlier claims to secular dominion were kept alive. And when the English rulers started to prove more amenable in the later twelfth century, the archbishops were waiting in the wings.

～

In 1154, Empress Matilda's son Henry had succeeded Stephen as Henry II, laying the foundations for a cross-Channel empire even larger than that of the Conqueror. Henry's first priority was to re-establish royal power in southern England. But a sense of bustle and ambition is clear from the start; and earlier claims to imperial dominion over the Isles were now back on the agenda, with an eye firmly trained on Ireland. The Norman chronicler Robert of Torigny reports that in 1155 Henry considered conquering Ireland, in order to grant it to his younger brother William (whose own ambitions had hitherto been stymied). And while modern historians have often doubted how serious such plans were, a contemporary Flemish chronicler states that an army was raised and readied, but then used to face down a more immediate threat from the French king.[7]

It's in this context that an extraordinary document was solicited from Pope Hadrian IV, the only Englishman to occupy the throne of St Peter. This is the text known as *Laudabiliter*, after the first word of the Latin original (meaning 'commendably'). The document survives embedded within Gerald of Wales' account of the English conquest of Ireland, a particularly jingoistic (and tendentious) narrative intended to justify the incursion and amplify the contribution of Gerald's own relatives. There is good reason to believe that, in the form it takes there, *Laudabiliter* has been tampered with by Gerald, in order to make it a blueprint for the later invasion. The document, in its original form, issued at some point between late 1155 and 1159, was striking enough, however. It granted Henry the right to intervention in Ireland only if he could secure local support for the venture. This was an attempt to *discourage* an English invasion, since an open invitation hardly seemed likely.[8]

Laudabiliter demonstrates that royal intervention in Ireland was on the cards early in Henry's reign. It also reveals that the reformist ideals which had underpinned Canterbury's claims to primacy were central to this – the hypothetical conquest was to be another civilising mission, endorsed by the pope. Yet like Canterbury's earlier claims, little came of these efforts, presumably because of the pope's hesitancy. Henry was, in any case, soon distracted by more pressing concerns elsewhere. It would take over a decade before the king was in a position to turn his attention back to the Emerald Isle. And then, it was not by choice.

The crucial developments here came not in Canterbury, Rome or Anjou, but in those parts of eastern Ireland which had long been in contact with the Anglo-Norman world. For it was not an act of political aggrandisement which launched the English invasion, but an invitation from the native Irish rulers, much as in Scotland, Byzantium and (to an extent) Italy. The key figure was Diarmait Mac Murchada. Diarmait was the king of Leinster in the east, who'd extended his control over the nearby city of Dublin. Thanks in part to their proximity to this burgeoning metropolis, the rulers of Leinster had long enjoyed ties to Wales, the West Country and the West Midlands. It had been to Leinster that Harold Godwinson had fled in 1051, when his family was exiled; it may also be from here that Ælfgar of Mercia drew support in 1058, during a similar episode.

It is therefore unsurprising that Diarmait turned to his Welsh and English allies, when in 1166 he was driven from his domains by Ruaidrí Ua Conchobair, the ruler of Connacht to his west. Ruaidrí had long been a powerful presence on the Irish political scene. Shortly before ejecting Diarmait, Ruaidrí had secured the high kingship of Ireland. This was not so much a formal office as an honorary title, accorded to those who managed to achieve hegemony over their neighbours. Still, it indicated a significant degree of power and influence. The high kingship was sometimes passed from father to son or brother to brother, but was also frequently contested between dynasties. In Ruaidrí's case, he'd violently succeeded his old rival Muircheartach Mac Lochlainn of Tír Eoghain (Tyrone) earlier in the year, thanks in part to support from Tigernán Ua Ruairc, the ruler of Breifne. Diarmait himself was a long-time ally of Muircheartach, who'd previously abducted the wife of Tigernán. Not surprisingly, he was now first on Ruaidrí's hit list.

Unable to rally friends and allies in Ireland, Diarmait looked across the sea for succour. He first turned to the court of King Henry, whose interest in Ireland had not passed unnoticed. Diarmait had every reason to expect a warm reception. Not only had Henry been looking for an excuse for intervention in Ireland for some time, but just the previous year Diarmait had provided naval support for the king's (abortive) Welsh campaign. Yet Henry was now occupied with pressing matters on his continental frontiers and could ill afford the distraction of an Irish expedition. He therefore granted Diarmait permission to recruit men from within his domains, but otherwise left the Irish king to his own devices.

The only assistance Henry offered was a base in Bristol.[9] Bristol was the natural place from which to launch a bid for restitution. The city lay directly across the Irish Sea from Dublin and had long been the most important English port for Irish trade. Bristol was also well-placed from the perspective of recruitment. It lay just across the Bristol Channel from the southern Welsh marches, whose lords were known for their violence, bravery and acquisitiveness.

Diarmait's search for supporters soon proved a success. A group of Pembrokeshire Flemings entered his employ; and with their assistance, he was able to re-establish himself in his ancestral domains in southern Leinster the following year (1167). The Flemings were an important feature of Norman conquest and colonisation in Britain and Ireland. They were to be found in large numbers in parts of England and southern Wales, and were also a growing presence in Scotland. Now they began to make their mark on Ireland.[10]

Of more lasting consequence was a second (larger) group of recruits, which started to arrive two years later. These consisted of marcher lords and their men, drawn by the prospects of conquest and settlement. The leader of this contingent was Richard de Clare (Richard of Strigoil), better known to posterity as Strong-bow. Richard came from a prominent marcher family. His father had been the first earl of Pembroke in south-western Wales, and it's no coincidence that Diarmait's Flemish recruits hailed from his domains: these were largely Richard's men, intended to lay the groundwork for his later invasion. Yet though a great lord by inheritance, Richard had struggled for advancement. His father had been made earl by Stephen, Henry II's old rival. And Henry treated Richard with suspicion, denying him his father's title and referring to Richard as the 'son of Earl Gilbert' in official documents – a pointed snub.[11] Local political considerations also made a foreign venture appealing to Richard at this juncture. Stephen's reign had seen Norman enchroachment into Wales falter; and while Henry had managed to stabilise the ship, there was little prospect of further gain. For men first lured to Wales by the hope of riches, Diarmait's invitation was most welcome. In Richard's case, the earl may also have hoped to leverage such prospects for his own benefit. When Diarmait wrote to Richard in 1170, requesting his assistance, Richard is said to have gone first to King Henry, asking that he restore him to his father's domains. Only when this request went unanswered did Richard commit fully to the Irish venture.

The plan had always been that Diarmait's restitution would proceed in stages. Richard and the greater marcher lords needed time to prepare. And by returning with a small force in 1167, Diarmait was able to establish a base of operations in his old Uí Chennselaig home-lands of southern Leinster. The first larger contingent joined him here in May 1169, swiftly establishing Diarmait's authority over the rest of Leinster. More men came under Raymond 'le Gros' ('the fat') the following year. They captured Waterford, another foundation with longstanding political (and ecclesiastical) ties to England and Wales. It was only once these foundations had been laid that Richard himself arrived in August 1170. All was going to plan. And soon after his arrival, Richard married Diarmait's daughter Aífe, as per prior arrangement.

While the Anglo-Norman arrival in 1169 has come to take on an iconic quality in Irish history, there was little indication at the time that this would mark a sea change in the island's politics. Diarmait's first group of recruits was small. And even once reinforced, they hardly comprised an invincible force. Irish annalists note the presence of the incomers, but do not accord them any particular significance. At this stage, they were just another group of mercenaries on an island which had seen their likes before. There was every reason to believe that they would soon return home or settle down, much as the Vikings of previous years had done.

It was Diarmait's death in early May 1171 which ensured that the Anglo-Norman presence would become permanent. In 1167, he's already reported to have promised Strongbow succession to the king-dom of Leinster. And while we may doubt how seriously Diarmait meant this – exiled men may promise many things, and Diarmait had three sons of his own – Richard clearly understood the offer to have been made in earnest. The timing of Diarmait's death played into Richard's hands. In spring 1171, Richard stood at the head of a large and well-trained force; he'd also just married Diarmait's daughter. Succession to the throne in Ireland normally passed through the male line, but practices were fluid and open to manipulation.[12] In Strongbow's case, it was less that marriage to Aífe gave him formal rights of inheritance than that it sweetened what might otherwise have been a bitter pill.[13] As with Guiscard's union with Sichelgaita (and Cnut's with Emma), this was an olive branch to the native aristocracy.

That many of the local Leinster magnates chose to work with Strongbow should not come as a surprise. Even more than Wales, Ireland was politically divided, with local rivalries running deep.[14] Any leader who offered the prospect of victory over old foes was welcome, even if he was – as Irish sources put it – a *Saxanach* ('an Englishman'). For Diarmait's kin, the best prospects now lay in supporting the newcomers. Richard was family by marriage; but if he failed, they'd be on hand to reassert themselves. This is not to say that everyone was happy with the arrangement. Diarmait's son Domnall threw in his lot with Strongbow, but his brother Murchad now claimed the Uí Chennselaig lands for himself, joining forces with the same Ruaidrí who'd expelled Diarmait back in 1166. This sort of dispute was common in Ireland, and as Murchad's alliance with Ruaidrí reveals, should be seen in dynastic terms. This was not an Irish nationalist stand against foreign influence, but a conflict between competing branches of the Leinster royal family.

By involving Ruaidrí, Murchad put Richard in a corner. A large Irish force soon had Richard and his men penned up in Dublin, in a siege which would last two months. Ruaidrí offered to accept Richard's submission, but only if the earl and his men would settle for control of the coastal towns of Dublin, Wexford and Waterford, leaving Leinster to Murchad. Richard refused. Shortly thereafter, his men dealt Ruaidrí a major blow. A sudden sortie caught the Irish off guard, driving them from their camp. Realising that Richard's bite could match his bark, Ruaidrí now withdrew, leaving the Normans in control of Leinster.

Richard looked well on course to create a march on the Welsh model – or possibly even an independent realm of his own. Much like Bernard de Neufmarché, he'd used a combination of military force and local alliance-building to establish himself as the ruler of one of the island's traditional kingdoms. Yet with success came scrutiny, above all that of the English king. Henry had much to gain from the restoration of his old ally Diarmait; he had less interest in one of his own men setting up shop across the Irish Sea. This threatened the territorial integrity of Henry's domains and the king would not wait long to react.

22

Hugh de Lacy:
Lord of Meath, 1171–7

After a hard-won victory over the men of Waterford at Dún Domnaill (modern Baginbun, Co. Wexford), the newly arrived Anglo-Normans were presented with a quandary. What should become of the seventy or so men they'd captured? Traditional rules of engagement held that they should be treated with mercy. And this is precisely what Raymond le Gros, one of the Norman leaders, proposed. As Raymond noted, the Irish were not the Normans' implacable foes, but fellow humans, who'd done no more than defend their lands and livelihoods. Their cause was an honourable one, so it would be dishonourable to slay them in cold blood. Mercy was the better part of valour here; and since it was only fortune which had granted the Normans victory, it behoved them to show restraint. Slaying the captives would only bring infamy on the newcomers, sullying their good name. Ferocity was all well and good in the heat of battle, but should be set aside once the fray was over.

Raymond's impassioned plea was met with murmurs of approval. But just then Hervey de Montmorency, another of the leading Anglo-Norman barons, began to speak. By contrast, he asserted that Julius Caesar and Alexander of Macedon had not achieved greatness by showing mercy, but through armed might and terror. Until the will to resist had been broken, there was no place for clemency. If spared, the Irish captives would just return to their old ways, swelling the ranks of the Normans' (already considerable) foes. Moreover, had the roles been reversed, the Irish would have shown the Normans no such mercy. As far as Hervey was concerned, the choice was simple: the invaders could either stay the course and kill the captives, or show mercy and sail back home. In the end, Hervey prevailed, as hawks have a tendency to do in times of war, and the Irish were summarily executed – the first in a long line of English atrocities on the island.[1]

In many respects, this episode, recorded by Gerald of Wales, encapsulates the Anglo-Norman conquest of Ireland. A smaller band prevails against superior numbers, then metes out terrible vengeance. Of particular interest is the clash of cultures illustrated here: were the Norman incomers to stick to their traditional cultural practices, or adapt to local customs? Equally important are the divisions among the invaders. Raymond and Hervey were vying for power and influence within the expeditionary force; and such rivalry would be one of the most important spurs to conquest and settlement in years to come.

~

For Henry II, Strongbow's actions presented an opportunity as well as a challenge. Now that his men had begun to carve out domains in Ireland, Henry had the ideal grounds for intervention. The bull he had received from Hadrian IV specified that he was only to attempt conquest at the invitation of the local Irish lords. With Richard and his men running amok, it took little to convince them that Henry was the lesser of two evils. The clause once designed to prevent English interference, now actively invited it.

The conditions were thus met for a papally sanctioned incursion, and Henry was not a man to think twice. He may already have been making plans early in the summer of 1171. Certainly once Strongbow prevailed at Dublin, it was clear that a royal presence was necessary. In September, Henry therefore assembled an army at Pembroke in southern Wales – Strongbow's old stomping grounds. The king now demanded the absentee earl's presence. For Richard, survival depended on presenting himself as a loyal vassal, happy to hold his new domains from the king. Gerald of Wales reports that Henry was livid about the conquests made without his consent. And while we must treat such testimony with care – Gerald thought little of Strongbow and places these events (perhaps erroneously) in Gloucestershire – there is almost certainly an element of truth to the tale.[2]

Despite these tensions, ruffled feathers were soon smoothed and the expedition was able to proceed. In mid-October, the English army landed in Waterford, where Strongbow and his men formally submitted to Henry. In exchange for the crucial port cities of Dublin, Wexford and Waterford, Richard was permitted to retain his position in Leinster, which he now received from the king as a fief. Such arrangements were in the interests of both parties. Strongbow could not hold out against Henry, while the king's best bet for asserting his authority was to work with those of his men who'd already established themselves in Ireland. A clear sign of rapprochement is offered by Henry's charters, which from this point on refer to Strongbow as 'Earl Richard' (sometimes 'of Strigoil') – not quite his father's title, but an acknowledgement of his status nonetheless.[3]

Shortly thereafter, Henry received the submission of the local Irish king of Desmond (in south Munster), Diarmait mac Carthaig, before proceeding on to Dublin for a Christmas court.[4] En route, Henry and his men passed through Cashel. It was here, just outside the royal complex on the Suir, that Henry received the submission of the king of Thomond, Domnall Mór Ó Briain – the other main player in Munster.

From Cashel, Henry headed to Dublin. The twelfth-century city was already well on its way to becoming the political centre of Ireland. It was the most important of the many Ostmen (i.e. Viking) towns founded on the eastern coast, controlling access to the Irish Sea. Anyone who wished to claim dominance over the island had to make his (or her) influence felt here.[5] Since the late eleventh century, Dublin had also been an important point of contact with the Anglo-Norman Church. In a carefully choreographed event, Henry now received the submission of the remaining Irish rulers (save Ruaidrí Ua Conchobair), in a special wooden structure built outside the city walls. The form of submission combined Anglo–Norman and Irish traditions, involving ritual homage, communal feasting and the exchange of hostages. From the perspective of the Irish, this was largely a matter of exchanging one overlord for another (Ruaidrí for Henry), with the possible advantage that Henry was likely to be an absentee high king.

As important as Henry's political manoeuvres were his ecclesiastical interventions. Since his arrival, the king had been in contact with the local papal legate, Gilla Crist (Christian) of Lismore. Gilla Crist had been a staunch supporter of Diarmait in 1166; he was also a proponent of the reforming ideals popular within the Anglo-Norman Church. For a king keen to justify his invasion in religious terms, the bishop was a natural ally. Henry passed through Lismore on his way to Cashel, ordering the construction of a castle there – a type of fortification as new to Ireland as it had been to Wales and England a century earlier. And while at Cashel, he met with the local archbishop, laying plans for a major Church council. Invitations were sent out throughout Ireland; and a few months later – probably in early 1172 – a council was convened. Like Dublin, Cashel was a deeply symbolic setting. It was the traditional ceremonial centre of the kingdom of Munster in the south west, from which the legendary king Brian Boru and his heirs had ruled their domains.[6]

We know of the council almost exclusively from English sources. And the silence of the local Irish annals – which typically record such events – is significant. It was in the interests of Henry and his apologists (who in this context may have included Gilla Críst) to emphasise the pan-Irish nature of the gathering: here was Ireland's new high king, taking essential steps to reform the island's Church. Yet it seems unlikely that all the bishops of Ireland attended, particularly since Ruaidrí continued to resist Henry in the west. Indeed, later in the year we hear of another council, at Tuam. The province of Tuam, which had recently been created at the synod of Kells (1152), precisely comprised Ruaidrí's domains. This was clearly a counterpart to the council of Cashel, and Ruaidrí himself attended. And just as Henry's council is only mentioned in English sources, so Ruaidrí's is uniquely recorded in the *Annals of Tigernach*, a work with close ties to the local rulers of Connacht.[7]

Henry's actions must therefore be viewed through the prism of local Irish politics. He was supporting those dynasts who'd fallen foul of Ruaidrí and was warmly welcomed by those elements of the Church closely aligned with them. What we are observing is therefore not a case of Anglophile reform at loggerheads with Irish recalcitrance, but competing versions for how politics and reform should play out – and which churches and rulers would benefit.[8] Independent of Canterbury's efforts, large elements of the Irish ecclesiastical establishment (including Gilla Críst) had now embraced calls for change, attempting (with varying degrees of success) to bring local custom more closely in line with continental norms. At Cashel, Henry was piggybacking on these efforts.[9] With local bishops berating their flocks in increasingly strident tones, Henry could present himself – how cynically, we may never know – as an agent of reform. This lent his expedition, like that of the Conqueror to England, the air of a holy war, conducted in the name of the faith.[10]

Provided Gerald's version of events can be trusted (and at least in this regard, it probably can), the council concerned itself largely with matters already raised by local Irish reformers over the course of the previous century: the institution of formal diocesan structures; the payment of tithes and Church dues; and the observance of Church teachings on marriage and incest. What was new were not the measures, but the alliance between reformers and the Angevin court – a court which could bring much greater influence to bear.[11]

For Henry, there was a further significance to these events. In late December 1170, only just over a year before the council, six of his men had been responsible for the violent death of Thomas Becket, the archbishop of Canterbury. News of this spread rapidly, earning Henry and his dynasty infamy across Europe. It was partly to avoid meeting with the legates of Pope Alexander III that Henry had embarked for Ireland in the autumn of 1171. Anything he could do to burnish his (considerably tarnished) reputation would therefore be welcome. And what better way to win over the pope, than to work with his local agent towards the reform of the Irish Church? This was not the only effort Henry made to reconcile himself with the ecclesiastical establishment. It was soon after his return from Ireland that the king adopted the formula 'by the grace of God' (*Dei gratia*) in his royal style, underlining more strongly the God-given (and God-fearing) nature of his authority.[12]

In early 1172, Henry was at the height of his powers and may well have contemplated an expedition against Ruaidrí. In the end, however, he was drawn away by affairs in his English and continental domains. Henry could not ignore Alexander III forever; and his eldest son, Henry the Young King, was now threatening rebellion. Before departing, however, Henry set his Irish affairs in order. He formally granted the kingdom of Meath (Mide) to one of his leading barons, Hugh de Lacy, on the same terms that he'd conceded Leinster to

Strongbow.[13] Hugh had come over with Henry and been employed in castle-building up to this point. Hugh's new domains bordered on Richard's to the north, and he was clearly intended to keep the latter in check. Henry had learned the lessons of the Welsh March: aristocratic ambition would be encouraged (and rewarded) in Ireland, but aristocratic state-building would not.

Yet if Hugh and Richard were in some sense rivals, they were also allies.[14] Anglo-Norman control was only well-established in Dublin and Leinster, and might easily be challenged, with Ruaidrí Ua Conchobair still angling to recreate his old dominance. By establishing another Anglo-Norman lordship, in an area where Ruaidrí had longstanding influence, Henry was creating a buffer zone for the new colony. Hugh was an excellent choice for the job. Like Strongbow, he was a marcher lord, who was well acquainted with the complex dynamics of conquest and colonisation. Hugh was also related to Richard, having wed the earl's cousin, Rose of Monmouth.

English and Irish sources vary considerably in their presentation of Henry's expedition. The former see this as a transformative event, the moment Ireland was finally brought within the Anglo-Norman fold. The latter see Henry simply as the most recent in a long line of high kings. Both perspectives are justified. In the long run, English conquest did indeed prove lasting and transformative. But in the short term, very little changed. When Henry departed in 1172, effective Anglo-Norman influence was limited to Leinster and the old Ostmen ports on the east coast. And there was every chance that their presence would prove fleeting. For the grants made to Hugh de Lacy were largely speculative. In early 1172, Henry did not have Meath to give. The kingdom was largely under the control of Tigernán Ua Ruairc, Ruaidrí's old friend and ally (who'd submitted to Henry at Christmas). Hugh would now have to win the kingdom for himself. All Henry's grant provided was the assurance that any gains would be duly approved by the king.

Tigernán was thus the main obstacle to Hugh's ambitions. Tigernán had been an enemy of Diarmait. And these factional lines continued to inform Irish politics for years to come, pitting the more recent arrivals against Ruaidrí and his associates. Strongbow and his men had dealt with the high king in 1171; now it was Hugh's turn to do likewise with Tigernán. He advanced as far as Fore in modern Westmeath, before agreeing to meet Tigernán at Tlachtga Hill (the Hill of Ward), just east of modern Athboy. This was the site of an Iron Age hillfort, which was closely associated with the kingdom of Meath. Five years previously, Ruaidrí Ua Conchobair had held an assembly here; now it was to be a place of parley. What precisely happened at the gathering remains unclear. Anglo-Norman sources say that Tigernán sought to ambush Hugh and his men, who saw through the ruse and struck down the Irish king. Irish sources, by contrast, claim treachery on Hugh's part. Either way, the result was the same: Tigernán was beheaded. His body was then hung upside-down north of Dublin, while his head was displayed above the gate of Dublin Castle, before being sent on to Henry II.[15]

Once again, the normal Anglo-Norman conventions of war had not been extended to the Irish. Indeed, Hugh was not alone in this behaviour, and these acts echo the earlier actions of Strongbow and his men, who'd publicly beheaded Áskell Ragavalsson and Murchad Ua Brain, two other of Ua Conchobair's leading allies.[16] That some Anglo-Normans were troubled by such violence is revealed by Gerald of Wales's report of the executions at Baginbun, with which we began this chapter. It's doubtful whether the events there played out precisely as Gerald reports. Raymond was Gerald's cousin, while Hervey was a nephew of Strongbow. And as elsewhere, Gerald is seeking to undermine the fitz Gilberts to the advantage of his own kin. In fact, the dramatic exchange of speeches is closely modelled on Sallust's *War of Catiline* (*Bellum Catilinae*), with Raymond's calls for clemency echoing those of Caesar, and Hervey's insistence on vengeance drawing on Cato's response. Still, the underlying tensions were real enough. And it's instructive that even Gerald, one of the most vociferously anti-Irish commentators of the era, should express such implicit sympathy for the Irish.[17]

Within ecclesiastical circles, there was likewise disquiet about the nature of the conquest of Ireland; and alongside stereotyped images of barbarism, we can also see signs of sympathy.[18] In French vernacular literature, which probably takes us closer to the attitudes of the Anglo-Norman barons responsible for the conquest, such shades of grey are clearer still. The *Song of Dermot and the Earl*, one of our most detailed accounts of the invasion, glories in bloodshed in a manner we would not expect elsewhere in the British Isles (save perhaps in parts of Wales and Scotland). Yet the attitude shown to the native Irish is one of clear, if at times grudging, respect. They are not uncivilised barbarians, but honourable (if culturally distinctive) foes. Their fault is not cultural or religious, but political: in ejecting their rightful lord, Diarmait, the Irish had proven themselves traitors and rebels.[19]

If warfare in Ireland was more violent than in England or Normandy, it was because the incomers adapted to local custom, as Gerald's report suggests. As children of the March, both Hugh and Richard were acquainted with straddling cultural worlds in this fashion. Still, adaptation presumes a degree of knowledge and understanding. And Hugh seems to have been particularly successful at winning over the Irish inhabitants of Meath. It was one thing to kill off a few political rivals; it was quite another to establish a stable regime. For this, hearts and minds had to be won. The process had begun in Leinster with the family and friends of Mac Murchada; now Hugh extended it to the local peasants and aristocrats of Meath.

In referring to Strongbow, de Lacy and their men as 'Anglo-Norman' so far, we have dodged the question of their identity. As we've seen, Norman immigrants to southern Italy soon put down roots; and by the time Roger extended his domains to North Africa, they can only be considered Norman in the second or third degree. In England, similar processes were afoot. By the mid-twelfth century, large sections of the ruling elite had started to identify as English, even though they were of Norman descent and spoke French. By the time Richard and Hugh set foot in Ireland, these processes were all but complete.[20]

Richard's and Hugh's conquests were undertaken under an English banner, as contemporaries knew full well.[21] The Irish annals typically speak of the incomers as 'foreigners' (Middle Irish: *Gaill*). But when they specify further, they write of them as 'English' (*Sagsannaich*). In doing so, they reflect the conquerors' perceptions of themselves, as the *Song of Dermot and the Earl* reveals: throughout the poem's 3,000-plus lines, it's always the English (Old French: *Engleis*) whom fitz Gilbert and his men are said to lead. But if the invaders saw themselves primarily as English, in cultural terms they remained firmly Franco-Norman.

They spoke the distinctive Anglo-Norman dialect of French, as the *Song* attests; they conducted warfare Norman fashion, introducing castles and knight service to Ireland; and at the highest levels, they maintained landed interests within the duchy, as revealed by the substantial de Lacy and, later, Marshal holdings across the Channel (William Marshal having eventually succeeded Strongbow to Leinster).

With Tigernán removed, Hugh was now able to secure his position. Warfare often caused displacement in the Middle Ages (as in the modern world), and the invasion of Ireland had been no exception. The conflicts saw many smallholders seek safety and security in neighbouring regions. Now Hugh was keen to lure them back. He offered conciliatory terms, restoring lands and rights to their prior holders. At the same time, he made sure to install his own cadets within a series of local lordships. The key to success lay in balancing the interests of local smallholders with those of the incoming Anglo-Norman elite.

But just as Henry's speculative grant of Meath was starting to resemble reality, Hugh was recalled (alongside Richard) to help the king face down a rebellion by the Young King. In their absence, the Irish went on the offensive, putting much of Meath to the torch. It would be 1175 before Hugh was in a position to return. He now found himself almost back to square one. After a year of active campaigning, Hugh had made good the losses, re-establishing himself in central Meath and extending his authority to the south and west. It remained to be seen how committed Hugh was to his new domains, however. He continued to have landed interests in Normandy and the Welsh March; and, by the end of 1175, he was back at the royal court in England, albeit in part to deal with Irish affairs. For Hugh's future in Ireland, the death of Richard fitz Gilbert in April 1176 proved decisive. This opened up new vistas in Ireland, where Richard had been the *de facto* leader of the Anglo-Norman party since 1172. In the following years, Hugh would dedicate his full resources to achieving a similar position. He went on to marry the daughter of Ua Conchobair, and was soon the leading figure in Irish politics.[22]

For his part, King Henry had originally foreseen Ireland as a domain he might entrust to his brother William. Younger sons and brothers were a perennial problem for medieval monarchs. By the time Henry went to Ireland in 1172, he'd accommodated William elsewhere. But with four sons of his own, he must have been aware that these new lands would soon come in handy. In 1175, Henry came to terms with Ruaidrí Ua Conchobair, agreeing to limit direct Anglo-Norman control in those parts of Meath, Leinster and Munster that were already in the hands of Richard, Hugh and their men. In exchange, Henry received formal (if largely nominal) acknowledgement of his overlordship over Connacht. Soon thereafter, at an important assembly at Oxford in 1177, Henry conferred Ireland on his youngest son John. The 1170s had seen much strife between Henry and his elder sons, who jostled for power and influence. As a result, the obsequious John was fast emerging as the king's favourite. Yet, as the youngest of four, John's prospects were poor. Henry now hoped that Ireland would offer John a kingdom of his own. It provided a base for future claims to the English throne; and if these failed, it might serve as a worthy consolation prize.[23]

Though it would be another eight years till John stepped foot in Ireland, the country was rarely far from his mind. And while the island never became a regular stop on the royal itinerary, Ireland figures much more prominently in the politics of John's mature years than it did in those of his father or brother.[24] For better or worse (often worse), Ireland's and England's fates were now firmly intertwined.

Yet just as Norman influence was being extended in Britain and Ireland, it was starting to be contested in mainland Europe. Would John's empire survive the test?

23

The End of Empire?
John and Normandy, 1204

In early March 1204, Roger de Lacy readied his men for the inevitable. The previous summer, he'd been charged with the defence of Château Gaillard, the prize castle built by Richard Lionheart in the late 1190s. The fortress overlooked a strategic stretch of the Seine, just 70 km (43 miles) upstream from the Norman ducal capital at Rouen. It was designed to protect the duchy's heartlands from French encroachment while providing a forward base for future forays into the Vexin, a territory long disputed between the Norman duke and French king. The castle's defences were state of the art, and its site on the top of a rocky outcrop overlooking the Seine afforded much natural defence. Richard is said to have boasted that it could hold firm even if its walls were made of butter. Yet the Lionheart's impregnable fortress was about to be taken.

The setting for these events is the early years of the reign of Richard's younger brother and successor, John. The French king, Philip Augustus, had declared the duchy of Normandy forfeit to the Crown in 1202, and, ever since, Philip had been working to wrest control of it from John. Like his recent forebears, John was both king of England and duke of Normandy (not to mention count of Anjou and duke of Aquitaine). For an increasingly assertive French monarchy, this presented an unacceptable challenge. As duke of Normandy, John ought to be beholden to Philip; yet as king of England, he was anything but. Rouen itself lay just 145 km (90 miles) from Paris as the crow flies, making it all too easy for John to strike at Philip's domains. By contrast, the French king would have to fight his way through Normandy then raise a fleet before he could even threaten John in England.

If Philip's proximity to John's continental possessions sometimes left him exposed, the reverse was equally true: these were potentially easy pickings. Indeed, John's sprawling domains, which stretched from Carlisle to Bayonne and Cork to the Vexin, were impossible to defend on all fronts. (By contrast, Philip was rarely more than a few days' forced march away from the Norman frontier, in the case of any trouble from his neighbour.) Despite these challenges, John's initial defensive efforts met with success. He won a stunning victory at Mirebeau in southern Anjou in early August 1202, at which his forces captured John's nephew Arthur, whom Philip had invested with John's continental domains (save Normandy). With his only dynastic competitor seized, John may have hoped that peace was round the corner. But by the end of the year, he'd squandered the advantage. John's main fault lay in his treatment of Arthur, who disappeared within eight months of the victory, under circumstances which were most suspicious. To make matters worse, John disregarded the advice of his counsellors and treated the other captives poorly, including starving twenty-two to death at Corfe Castle.[1] To the French aristocracy, firmly wedded to chivalric ideals, these were crimes of the highest order.

Shocked by John's behaviour, and increasingly aware of his failings as a king and military commander (Mirebeau would be John's only major victory), large swathes of the Angevin and Breton aristocracy began to turn to Philip, who welcomed them with open arms. And as John failed to react, they were followed by others from Normandy. Buoyed by these successes, Philip now decided it was time to invest Château Gaillard – the key to Normandy. The castle had been entrusted by John to Roger de Lacy, a member of the main branch of the same Lacy family we met in the last chapter. Unlike his more famous Cambro-Irish relations, Roger's lands lay exclusively in northern England, ensuring his loyalty to the mercurial John.

John was well aware of the strategic significance of the castle and soon attempted a relief. And while his overly elaborate plans for a combined land and naval assault on Philip's forces failed, French victory was still far from assured. The castle walls held firm through the winter months, and it increasingly looked as though John would get a second chance at relief in the spring. In response, Philip now took up command of the siege in person. Initially, he attempted an assault on the castle's south-easterly outlying fortifications – the only direction from which the castle could be directly approached. And though the French siege tower never made it to the walls, Philip's sappers were able to bring down the tower. Over the following days, the middle and then inner wards fell.[2]

Philip had achieved the unthinkable. Château Gaillard was his – and Normandy free for the taking. In the coming months, French troops took Falaise, Caen and Cherbourg. And once it became clear that no relief was coming from England, the biggest prize of all followed: Rouen.[3] Soon similar losses were being recorded in Anjou, Maine and Poitou, as Philip and his men rode the crest of the wave. For his part, John was left shocked by how quickly things had unravelled. In the space of less than two years, he'd gone from being victor at Mirebeau to watching powerlessly as his continental domains were dismembered. Even England was no longer secure, and he braced himself for a possible incursion there. John's childhood nickname, Lackland (i.e. 'the landless'), was starting to prove all too apt. It was increasingly joined by a second mocking moniker, 'softsword'.[4] For when decisive action was most required, John's response was to dither and delay.

The loss of Normandy weighed heavily on John and the English. As important as the financial and strategic losses (which were considerable) was the psychological and ideological blow this represented. Good kings were meant to defend and expand their domains; a loss on this scale could not be countenanced. In an era in which divine providence was believed to guide current events, there could be no clearer sign of God's wrath. The cause did not take long for contemporaries to identify: John's treatment of Arthur and the other captives of Mirebeau. Having sown the wind, John was reaping the whirlwind.

This was not the first time since 1066 that Normandy and England had gone separate ways. The Conqueror had placed the duchy in the hands of his eldest son, Robert Curthose, leaving England to his second, William Rufus. And though the two were reunited by Henry I in 1106, the duchy remained distinct from the English crown and repeatedly backed rival members of the royal family, including William Clito (the son of Curthose) and Henry fitz Empress (as Henry II was initially known). Still, it was not a rival member of the Anglo-Norman royal family who'd set up shop in Rouen now, but the king of France.

The likelihood of England and Normandy falling conveniently back into the hands of the same ruler was slim at best. Further complicating matters were the responses to these developments on both sides of the Channel. Both John and Philip now insisted on absolute loyalty. The latter dispossessed barons loyal to John of their holdings in Normandy, while John did the same to the English lands of those who plumped for Philip. Only the powerful William Marshal managed to avoid such a fate, and he paid the price for compromise with many years in the political wilderness.[5]

Language and culture also had a part to play in this estrangement. Though settlement after 1066 had ensured that the English ruling elite had much in common with its Norman counterpart, as families put down roots, differences started to emerge. Those on the northern side of the Channel came to identify as English, even when they remained for the most part culturally and linguistically Norman. And by the later years of the twelfth century, we start to see national stereotypes re-emerging. In French (and Norman) eyes, men such as the Marshal or Roger de Lacy had long since gone native. They were not expatriate Normans, but Englishmen, with all the cultural baggage this entailed. Language served to divide as well as unite here. For though the English barons continued to speak French, their increasingly distinctive Anglo-Norman dialect earned derision in France. (The long history of Parisian linguistic haughtiness starts here.) Normandy and England were increasingly two nations divided by a shared tongue.

Political circumstances also conspired to make the estrangement much greater following 1204 than it had been in 1087 or 1150, when the duchy was temporarily separated from the English crown by the succession disputes occasioned by the Conqueror's death and the Anarchy. In the years after 1066, most leading aristocrats held estates on both sides of the Channel. It was in their interest that amicable relations between the regions prevailed. Over time, however, there was a tendency for families to consolidate their holdings, passing Norman and English lands to different branches of the family, or selling off lands in one region to invest in the other. These trends were especially strong among the middle and lower aristocracy. By the time of John's reign, it was only the greatest barons, such as William

Marshal and Hugh de Lacy, who continued to have interests spanning the Channel.[6] There were now few with a vested interest in maintaining the Conqueror's cross-Channel empire; and for many, it was an unwelcome distraction.

So while John's problems were of his own making, they uncovered deeper fault lines within the Angevin empire. Detangling English interests from mainland Europe proved no simpler in the early thirteenth century than at any other time in history. Political interests pulled John's government in opposite directions. Honour demanded that he seek restitution of his lost domains; yet such efforts were bound to prove unpopular, particularly if (as was the case) they were unsuccessful. In response to these travails, John came to rely ever more on a small cadre of continental associates, comprised of men who'd lost out through Philip's annexations – men such as Gerard d'Athée, Engelard de Cigogne, Philip Mark and Peter des Roches. These men owed John complete loyalty and were fully committed to the restoration of his (and their) lands. But if this neatly got around problems of allegiance, it only exacerbated domestic tensions. Most of these figures came from the Touraine, south of Normandy, and their primary interest lay in the restoration of these domains rather than the duchy itself, where the interests of the rest of the Anglo-Norman aristocracy lay. The influence of these 'aliens', as they were known, was therefore deeply resented, reinforcing particularist sentiment within the English aristocracy.[7]

It was with the support of these new favourites that John launched a first attempt to regain his lost lands in 1205, but opposition in England prevented him from sending a large force. A more substantial expedition directly under royal command followed in 1206. This succeeded in regaining Poitou, before turning south to Gascony – the only continental holding John had retained intact. Here he was able to see off the threat from Castile to the south. Buoyed by these successes, John now struck at Anjou. But when Philip raised a large French force, John retreated back south, and the result was a stalemate.[8] During the following years John was largely occupied with affairs in the British Isles, as baronial unrest in Ireland and ongoing disputes with the pope and the archbishop of Canterbury kept him from campaigns on the continent. When he finally returned in force in early 1214, it was as part of a grand alliance with the German emperor, Otto IV. Otto was John's nephew and had his own reasons for wishing to curtail French political ascendancy, which threatened his (far from secure) grasp on the imperial throne. The plan was for a two-pronged attack, with John marching north and east from Poitou to meet Otto, supported by the earl of Salisbury, William Longespée.

The campaign started off well, with John retaking much of Anjou in late spring. But progress stalled when he invested the castle of Roche-au-Moine, ten miles south west of Angers. By early July, he and his army were back at La Rochelle, chased by a French force under the command of Louis, the eldest son of Philip Augustus. All hope was then lost when Otto's forces (including the battalion led by Earl William) were decisively defeated by Philip and the main French army at a close-fought battle at Bouvines in south Flanders. The days of Angevin ascendancy in northern France were over.[9] For John, this was the last in a long line of foreign policy failures. Domestically, it was a total disaster. As one modern historian has put it, 'the road from Bouvines to Runnymede was direct, short and unavoidable.'[10]

~

John's English barons had been plotting against him for years. After the humiliating defeat at Bouvines, this tipped over into open rebellion. By autumn, plans were being laid. The following year, civil war erupted, spearheaded by a group of northern magnates, who now found support across wide swathes of the south. When the rebels took London in late spring, John's hand was forced. On 15 June, he famously came to Runnymede, where he acceded to most of the baronial demands in the document which came to be known as Magna Carta (Latin for 'the great charter').[11] For John, this was humiliation. Yet what he may have lacked in military prowess, he more than made up for in cunning. By agreeing to the rebels' demands, he was able to retake the initiative. And within weeks of the charter having been issued, John had had it annulled. Scarcely had the ink dried on the copies than it became a dead letter. John would not, however, have long to enjoy his victory. The rebels now found support from Alexander II of Scotland and Philip Augustus. By spring 1216, the latter's son Louis had landed in England and joined the rebels. The flames of revolt were spreading fast when John himself died that October – an act which may, paradoxically, have saved his realm from foreign conquest once more, for the young Henry III, John's heir, and his regents proved much more popular (and ready to compromise) than his father.

It is, in any case, an enduring irony that England's most iconic constitutional document should owe its existence to such continental entanglements. As befits the context, Magna Carta itself is a thoroughly European (and Norman) document. It reveals similarities with the Statutes of Pamiers, a similarly programmatic set of customs issued by Simon V de Montfort for his domains in southern France in December 1212. Simon's family hailed from the Franco-Norman frontier and he'd (briefly) been earl of Leicester, so many in the baronial party would have known of this precedent.[12]

In the longer term, the loss of John's continental domains did not so much dismantle the Angevin empire as reconfigure it. With Normandy, Anjou, Maine and Poitou gone, the political ambitions of his successors were now directed towards control of their immediate neighbours within the British Isles. It was in Wales, Scotland and (in particular) Ireland that they were able to make good losses elsewhere.[13] The effect of these gains, however, was further to entrench the divide between England and Normandy. Till 1204, it had been possible to be both Norman and English; this was no longer so.

There were implications for Normandy as well as England here. In the tenth, eleventh and twelfth centuries, the Normans had claimed – with some justification – to be unique among the peoples of northern France. They alone were the descendants of Viking Northmen, an identity proudly announced by their ethnic designation. They remained politically distinct and tended to identify as French only in linguistic and cultural contexts – in the address clauses of royal charters or in major overseas expeditions, such as the crusades. With Philip's conquest, this all changed. Now the Normans were little different from the Angevins and Poitevins. Norman identity was slowly submerging into French identity.

The loss of Normandy in 1204 may not, therefore, have caused the political and cultural rift between the duchy and the English realm, but it did ensure that this would be permanent. For some time, the

Anglo-Norman aristocracy had been identifying as English; now, there was no going back. New conquests would come, but the resulting empire would be an emphatically English one.[14] There would be no more empires of the Normans. Or would there?

24

'Wonder of the World': Emperor Frederick II, 1198–1250

If Norman influence in the British Isles was starting to wane in the early thirteenth century, it was just getting started in Germany. Eight years after John's humiliating loss of Normandy (1204), the young Frederick II was establishing himself here. He was crowned king at Mainz by Archbishop Siegfried, Germany's leading church-man, in early December 1212, and soon began extending his control over other parts of the realm.

Frederick is often seen as an archetypally 'German' ruler. He was a member of the Staufer (or Hohenstaufen) dynasty, which had ruled Germany on and off since 1138. And he was named after the most famous German emperor of the Middle Ages, Frederick Barbarossa (his paternal grandfather). Yet such signs of continuity are misleading. By blood, Frederick was only half-German; and culturally, he was a Sicilian Norman through and through.[1] His mother Constance was the youngest daughter of Roger II, born shortly after the latter's death in 1154. And Frederick himself was born on Italian soil at Jesi, over-looking the Adriatic, in late December 1194. Even his baptismal name was not entirely German. For this was not simply Frederick, but Roger Frederick, reflecting his dual German and Sicilo-Norman pedigree.[2]

At the time of his birth, Frederick's father, the German emperor Henry VI, had just been crowned king of Sicily in Palermo. This honour had been a long time coming. When Henry had first been engaged to Constance in 1184, it was agreed that he would succeed to the Sicilian throne were William II (her nephew) to die without heir. Yet when this transpired five years later, William's nephew Tancred of Lecce – an illegitimate son of Roger III, Roger II's eldest – was able to secure the throne. Despite his illegitimacy, Tancred was a *bona fide*

Hauteville and enjoyed considerable support from the local aristocracy. He was therefore able to weather attempts by Henry and Constance to contest the throne in 1190 to 1191. For Henry, the situation was complicated by factional politics north of the Alps. His own father, Frederick Barbarossa, had just died (Henry probably got wind of this while marching south), and his grasp on the kingship was far from secure. This meant that Tancred was soon left to his own devices.

By the time Henry had secured his position in Germany, things were starting to look up. Tancred died in early 1194. And while the local aristocrats had elected Tancred's son, William (III), his heir, the latter was only a child and little obstacle to Henry's ambitions. Henry and Constance therefore marched south in the spring, their coffers filled with the ransom recently paid for the release of the English king Richard Lionheart (who'd fallen into the hands of the duke of Austria while on his way home from the Third Crusade). By August, Henry had taken Naples; Salerno followed in September. Finally, in late November he established himself at Palermo, the traditional Sicilian capital. On Christmas day, he was formally crowned.[3]

As in 1190, Constance had accompanied Henry south. In Milan, however, she parted ways with him. Henry then headed straight to Naples with the main army, while Constance followed at a more leisurely pace down the Adriatic coast. By now, it must have been clear that the empress was pregnant. And since she'd been captured by a group of Salernitans during their previous bid for the Sicilian crown, the couple weren't taking any risks. Constance had been thirty-two at the time of her marriage (1186) and seems to have had considerable difficulties conceiving (this is her only recorded pregnancy). Much therefore hinged on the fate of the empress and her unborn child. This long wait for an heir also helps explain later rumours that Frederick was illegitimate, rumours happily encouraged by the many enemies of the Staufer dynasty.[4]

By March 1195, however, Henry and Constance were reunited at Bari, the latter now with their son in tow. They must have been delighted. After years of uncertainty, they'd managed both to secure the Sicilian throne and line up a male heir. Yet the union of the Sicilian and imperial crowns was not universally popular. It had already ruffled feathers in the south, where some continued to hold out for the succession of William III. More importantly, it presented a direct threat to the pope, whose domains were now surrounded on both sides by Henry's.[5] No longer would it be possible to play German and Sicilian rulers off against each other, as many popes had done before. Celestine III therefore refused to consecrate Frederick as Henry's heir in 1196; and the dispute over Henry's succession plans was still rumbling on when the emperor himself fell severely ill in Messina in late summer 1197. By the end of September, Henry was dead.

The result was an extended period of political instability, especially north of the Alps. By this point, succession to the German realm had become elective. The son of the previous ruler often had an advantage, but he still required the formal endorsement of the leading princes in order to become king (and emperor-in-waiting). This was bad news for Frederick. For it was most unlikely that the princes would back a child – particularly one they barely knew. Most of Henry's allies now threw their weight behind the candidacy of his brother Philip of Swabia (Frederick's uncle); others, backed by the pope, preferred Otto of Brunswick, the son of Duke Henry the Lion and the English princess Matilda. A long and bitter succession dispute would follow.

Much now hinged on how Constance would react. She must have known that the chances of securing both the German and Sicilian crowns for Frederick were slim – and that of the two, the safer bet was the latter. In Sicily, dynastic succession remained the norm and the prospect of a child monarch held fewer fears: William II had come to the throne in his early teens in 1166, while in 1197 a faction had sought to install the infant William III. More to the point, here Constance could make the most of her own clout as a Hauteville. Conveniently, she was at the important port city of Messina when Henry died. From there, it was only a short march to Palermo, where Constance set about establishing a regency for her son. In late December, Frederick already starts appearing as 'king of the Romans and of Sicily' in the witness lists of her charters; the following Pentecost (17 May 1198), he was formally consecrated king.[6]

Even at the best of times, royal minorities could prove tricky. And given Sicily's turbulent past, there was every reason to expect the worst. Constance's first priority was, therefore, to shore up her son's position. The obvious ally was the pope. It had been with papal sanction that the Hautevilles had first established themselves in the south. And while relations had been strained in recent years, Celestine's successor Innocent III had much to gain by supporting Constance and Frederick. Like Celestine, Innocent's priority was to prevent Sicily and the German Empire falling into the same hands. And the best way to stop Philip or Otto from claiming Sicily was to support Frederick. The price of papal backing, however, was that Constance and Frederick abandon their claims to the north. Given the situation in Germany – with two grown men already competing for the throne, there was little space for the three-year-old Frederick – this was a price well worth paying. From the moment of his coronation, Frederick therefore ceases to bear the title 'king of the Romans [i.e. of the Germans] and of Sicily', settling for the simpler (and more accurate) 'king of Sicily, duke of Apulia and prince of Capua'.

Constance's urgency was increased by her own ill health. By autumn 1198, it was clear that the empress was ailing; and by late November, she too was dead. Negotiations with the pope were still ongoing, so Constance had little option but to entrust her son and his regime to Innocent III, in the hope that he would see them through the troubles to come. This meant that Henry's original hopes for Frederick were now well and truly dashed. Frederick would be king of Sicily, but not emperor – at least, not on Innocent's watch. Innocent's strength should not, however, be exaggerated. Frederick's regency may have been in need of support, but Innocent himself was in need of allies. Like earlier popes, Innocent held considerable authority but little real power. He could request, command and (at times) cajole, but had few means of imposing his will.[7] Stalin's alleged dictum, 'how many divisions has the pope?', rang as true in 1198 as it did in 1943.

For Frederick, Innocent's guardianship was a mixed blessing. It helped ward off rival claims, but did little to assist in the day-to-day governance of Sicily. Indeed, the pope proved an absentee regent – it would be 1208 till he even set foot in Sicily – who depended heavily on his legates to exert what influence they could.[8] As a result, the local Sicilian magnates were left to battle for real power and influence.

Foremost among these were the imperial chancellor, Walter of Paglia, and the marquis (or margrave) of Annweiler, Markward. The latter had been a favourite of Henry VI, but had fallen foul of Constance. He now claimed the right to run the regency, on the basis of the terms of Henry VI's will. By contrast, Walter and his associates called on Constance's testament and the tradition of papal oversight of the Sicilian realm to justify their position.

The result of this extended infighting was that Frederick's regency was even more paralysed than most. Under these circumstances, there was no opportunity to press claims to Germany, even had Frederick wanted to. In 1208, Innocent's guardianship was formally brought to a close. But Frederick was just fourteen and only gradually took the reins of power. By now, he had spent almost his entire life in southern Italy. His native tongue was the Sicilian dialect of Italian, in which he composed verses; he also had some command of Greek and (probably) Arabic, the other great languages of the Mediterranean. Germany (and German), by contrast, he only knew second hand, from the few northern magnates at the Sicilian court.

Frederick's background was, however, no obstacle to his political ambitions north of the Alps. Just as his father had been a German on the Sicilian throne, so Frederick would become a 'Sicilian on the imperial throne', as his most recent biographer puts it.[9] The foundations were laid by the violent death of Frederick's uncle Philip in 1208, just as Frederick was coming of age. By leaving Otto of Brunswick unchallenged in Germany (and northern Italy), this served to bring the question of Frederick's own claims to a head. Otto soon headed south to secure imperial consecration from the pope. In this connection, Otto also sought to bring old imperial claims to bear on Apulia and Calabria.

Otto IV, to use his imperial designation, was doing more than upholding traditional rights, however. As the son of Henry VI and nephew of Philip, Frederick was now the emperor's main rival; anything that could be done to destabilise Frederick's regime was therefore welcome. Yet Otto's old opponents north of the Alps re-grouped in his absence. They elected Frederick as king *in absentia*, forcing the emperor's return. For lasting peace, it was now clear that Frederick would have to establish himself in Germany. And so it was that in 1212 he made his way north at the invitation of his electors, securing the support of a number of key Lombard cities along the way. Frederick then made his way through what is modern Switzerland, stopping off at Constance en route for the old imperial city of Frankfurt. Here he was elected king of the Romans (i.e. ruler of Germany) a second time, before being crowned at nearby Mainz on 9 December.

Over the next year, Frederick steadily drew followers to his cause. It was, however, the defeat of Otto's army and their English allies at Bouvines which sealed the latter's fate. For while Otto escaped from battle alive, he was a spent force. His effective power and influence were limited to the traditional Welf heartlands in and around Brunswick, and by 1218 he was dead.[10] In response, Frederick was crowned king of Germany a second time at Aachen in July 1215, the traditional site of royal consecration north of the Alps. In 1212, the city had been in the hands of Otto's supporters, hence the recourse to Mainz; now it opened its doors to the new emperor-in-waiting.

If Frederick came to the German throne as a Sicilian, he soon adapted to local circumstances. In Germany, the king (or emperor) was first among equals. He was chosen by the princes and had to rule with them. In practice, the royal writ only ran unfettered in the (rapidly dwindling) crown lands and the ruler's personal lands; elsewhere he was heavily dependent on the consent and cooperation of the territorial princes. This stood in stark contrast with Sicily, where the king oversaw one of the most centralised states of Europe. These differences find their clearest expression in the manner in which rebels and political enemies were treated. In Germany, they could expect pardon, provided they submitted; in Sicily, they were lucky if they escaped with their lives.[11]

Frederick couldn't have changed the fundamentals of German politics if he'd wanted to. Nor is there any reason to believe that is what he did want. Frederick's aim was to assert his authority in something approximating the manner of his father and grandfather. Beyond that, he was happy to live and let live. His primary interest lay in the south; in Germany, he therefore went with, rather than against, the grain. Indeed, Frederick cast himself consciously in the mould of his forebears, supporting old allies and punishing old enemies. A key moment came at Christmas 1213, when he transferred the remains of his uncle Philip from Bamberg to the traditional imperial mausoleum at Speyer on the Rhine. Yet if Frederick was keen to present himself as an archetypal Staufer, he remained very much the 'boy from Apulia' (*puer Apuliae*), as contemporaries called him. For scarcely had Frederick seen his uncle buried with due pomp, than he was making plans for his own future interment in Palermo – the city of his youth.

From the start, Frederick intended to be an absentee ruler in Germany. Elected in his own absence in 1211, he spent eight years establishing himself between 1212 and 1220, then left the region to its own devices. Of the next thirty years, Frederick spent just two in Germany – and then to quell a rebellion. The circumstances here are highly revealing. In order to accommodate his extended absence, Frederick had established his nine-year-old son, Henry (VII), as king of Germany in April 1220. Henry and his regents were to rule in Frederick's stead, providing a point of contact for the local elite. This was also a sop to Innocent III, who looked on with dismay as Frederick re-established his father's old Sicilo-German empire. Innocent had been happy to back Frederick against Otto, when it looked as though the latter might establish himself in the south; now that the tables were turned, he began to regard Frederick with caution. By making his son king of Germany, Frederick could claim that the old distinction between the Sicilian *Regno* and the German Empire was being maintained: he only ruled the former, while his son ruled the latter.

In the coming years, direct contact between Frederick and Henry was rare, and this may explain the tensions we start to see. By the early 1230s, Henry was an adult and keen to make his own mark on German politics. Yet Frederick saw his son as a subordinate rather than an independent monarch in his own right. In part, this was a straightforward clash of political interests. Henry wanted to achieve as much power as possible, while it was in Frederick's interest to limit this. But it also speaks of the different political cultures in which the two moved. Frederick demanded absolute service from his son, as he did from his Sicilian followers; Henry expected room for manoeuvre, like that he allowed the German princes.[12]

In the end, these differences proved too great to reconcile. Henry was happy to acknowledge his father's overlordship, provided he was given independence of action – yet it was precisely this that Frederick was unwilling to brook. When, in late 1234, Henry began to move against an old ally of the emperor, Margrave Hermann V of Baden, Frederick responded by undoing his son's acts and restoring the margrave. This was a public affront, which Henry could not leave unchallenged. In the coming months, he therefore began to mobilise his allies. This was in keeping with aristocratic conventions north of the Alps, where rebellion was a show of strength, intended to bring about compromise and reconciliation. Frederick, however, interpreted this as treason and proceeded to bring the full force of the law against his son. He marched north in the spring and Henry submitted at Worms in July, clearly hoping that pardon would follow. Yet in keeping with Sicilian practices, Frederick showed no such clemency. Henry was imprisoned for the rest of his life. In his place, Frederick had his younger son, Conrad, elected ruler. Unlike Henry, Conrad was never formally crowned and consecrated. From the start, he was to be a sub-king, dependent on his father's will.

As we've seen in the case of the Conqueror, Norman rulers were not averse to harsh penalties, when they wanted to make a point – and certainly they had a meaner streak than their German counterparts. The process of settlement in southern Italy seems to have exacerbated these tendencies, creating a uniquely violent political culture. The first few generations of settlers still largely operated according to the traditional Norman rules of engagement (which conveniently approximated those of the local Apulians and Calabrians); but in Roger I's Sicily political violence came to be instrumentalised in altogether new fashions.[13] In part, this was a product of political instability. Roger's position was even more precarious than that of his elder brother Robert, leading him and his heirs to rule with the stick rather than the carrot. Yet this was not purely a matter of expediency. Execution, mutilation and imprisonment were all common punishments for rebels in Constantinople. Here, too, Roger and his heirs were taking lessons from the Byzantines.

If in life Frederick II was a Sicilian Norman, in his historical afterlife he would indeed become German. The key figure here is a young German Jew, Ernst Kantorowicz, who turned his attention to the study of Frederick II in the interwar period. Kantorowicz was part of the ultra-nationalist circles around the poet Stefan George (the so-called *George-Kreis* or 'George Circle'). His path-breaking biography of Frederick (first published in German in 1927) was inspired by George's ideas about a 'secret Germany' (German: *geheheimes Deutschland*) – a mythic view of Germany's past and present.[14] Kantorowicz sought to reclaim Frederick II for this, suggesting that despite his southern upbringing he was first and foremost a German – indeed, one of the greatest Germans to have graced this earth. Kantorowicz' own Jewish background led him to fall foul of the National Socialist regime which took power in Germany in the 1930s. Nevertheless, his book was taken up with gusto by the Nazis, who revelled in its unabashed nationalism. It was reportedly a favourite of Goebbels and may even have been read by the Führer. When German troops were retreating from Sicily in 1943, one of the last orders to come from Herman Göring was to remove the tomb of Emperor Frederick from Palermo. The great German emperor was coming home.

Thankfully, Göring's orders were never acted upon. Frederick therefore remains a proud Sicilian to this day.

Afterlives of the Normans:
A Europe Transformed

Frederick II's reign marks the end of Norman empire-building. The Normans had now transformed politics and society across France, Italy, the British Isles, the Middle East, Iberia and (increasingly) Germany. There was scarcely a region of Europe and the Mediterranean where the descendants of Rollo were not to be found. And even where they were no longer present, their legacy could be seen.

By accident and intention, the Normans had completely redrawn the map of western Eurasia. They'd integrated England into a sprawling (if now shrinking) continental empire and extended its frontiers deep into Wales and Ireland. Further north, they'd established the noble lines that would rule Scotland up to the Act of Union in 1707 – and in so doing, laid the foundations of the later United Kingdom. In France, by contrast, the Normans had forged one of the kingdom's most powerful duchies, which at first hindered, then later helped, the ascent of the Capetian kings of the era. And finally, under Frederick II, the Normans had brought new attitudes to law and justice to large parts of Germany.

Further south, the Norman impact was no less pronounced. In Iberia, the Normans had played an important part in the early expansion of the Portuguese realm; and in assisting at the siege of Tortosa (1148), they'd strengthened the union of Catalonia with the crown of Aragon. (When combined with that of Castile in 1469, this would go on to form Spain as we know it.) The Norman influence on Italy was even greater. Here, the northern settlers had unified the southern half of the peninsula, bringing Apulia, Calabria, Campania and Sicily under a single banner. The resulting Kingdom of Sicily would survive until Italian political unification (the *Risorgimento*) in the late nineteenth century. As importantly, Italo-Norman freebooters had helped undermine Byzantine rule in western and central Anatolia at a crucial moment, putting in train developments which would culminate in the First Crusade – a movement to which they also contributed directly. It's no exaggeration to say that the modern world would be unrecognisable had it not been for the Normans.

Yet if the Normans were everywhere, they were also nowhere. In each of these regions, they'd settled and put down roots. Norman influence was ubiquitous, but it was also increasingly hard to pin down. Frederick would not have identified as Norman, nor did most of the Norman diaspora elsewhere. Those who'd settled England, Wales and Ireland were now English, while their counterparts north of the Firth of Forth increasingly identified as Scots. In Iberia and the Holy Land, these processes had been even quicker: here the Normans had long since become Catalans, Spaniards and Franks/French. By the mid-thirteenth century, there were scarcely any Normans left outside the duchy. Robert the Bruce may have been of Norman blood, but it's as the 'Flower of Scotland' that he's celebrated in modern song.

Normandy itself was not spared these changes. Following the duchy's conquest in 1204, it was integrated – reintegrated, from a French perspective – into Philip Augustus' rapidly expanding realm. Norman distinctiveness did not die overnight. But there was now little to distinguish the duchy from the many other principalities over which Philip and his heirs asserted their authority. Like the Poitevins and Angevins to their south, the Normans were simply garden-variety Frenchmen. In the coming years, they were frequently on the opposite sides of political conflicts to their sometime countrymen in Britain and Ireland. The diaspora had decisively split.

Dramatic though these developments were, they are unsurprising. From the start, Norman identity had been a moving target. The earliest Normans were simply Viking Northmen – a Scandinavian intrusion into northern France, whose presence continued to arouse comment a century later. By the mid-eleventh century, conflict had given way to accommodation. The Normans now became culturally and linguistically French; and the ethnic designation might be applied to all inhabitants of the duchy, including those peasants and lower aristocrats of largely Frankish/French stock. The fiction was sometimes maintained that they were all descendants of Rollo's original pirates. But in practice, it was appreciated that the Normans had been a disparate group from the start. Dudo's account of the foundation of the duchy emphasises precisely this. It is only at the moment of Rollo's conversion and settlement that his motley crew of raiders become a unified people – no longer Northmen but Normans.[1]

As their descendants made careers outside the duchy, a diaspora emerged, defined by ties to a shared homeland and claims to descent (real or imagined) from the Scandinavian north. Yet just as Norman identity had been evolving in and around Rouen, so it also evolved as Norman aristocrats settled abroad. They not only came and conquered; they settled and put down roots. Sometimes these connections were very personal, such as when the Normans took native wives in Italy (Sichelgaita), Wales (Nest) and Ireland (Aífe).[2] At others, they were less tangible, but no less significant, such as when the earls of Hereford named their new castle Montgomery, after their original Norman home, or when Guiscard gave his eldest son the Greek name Mark. Slowly but surely, the Normans were becoming English, Scottish and Sicilian.

This was partly a matter of numbers. In none of the regions they settled were the Normans a majority; and integration was quickest in places such as Catalonia and Italy, where they were considerably outnumbered by the locals. As important, however, was their very ubiquity. Because the Normans were everywhere, Norman identity itself meant relatively little. More important became local affinities – to Sicily, the March and (above all) England and Scotland.

The historical Normans are, therefore, remarkably slippery subjects. It's partly for this reason that modern historians have sometimes spoken of a 'Norman myth': the idea, actively propagated by historians of the Middle Ages, that the Norman conquests were part of a unified process, the expression of an innate will to dominate. For such scholars, Norman unity is largely illusory, a figment of the fertile Norman imagination.[3] Yet if the Normans were a product of their own mythmaking, they were far from unique in this regard. The same is true of the English, Welsh and French – indeed all national identities of the Middle Ages.[4] What distinguished Norman identity, however, is that it was tied to a region in which most Normans no longer lived. It's this that made it so influential and ultimately so short-lived.

The most lasting legacy of the Normans lies in connecting and integrating large parts of Europe and the Mediterranean. Thanks to the Normans, this was a world in which members of the same family could be found in Wales, Italy and the Holy Land. To England, Ireland, Wales and Scotland the Normans brought castles, knight service and chivalric culture, immersing these regions in the political and cultural practices of mainland Europe. To Sicily and southern Italy, they brought closer ties to the pope and Rome, ensuring that these regions would form part of Catholic western Europe, rather than of the Islamic and Orthodox worlds of the southern and eastern Mediterranean.[5]

In the end, the Normans were victims of their own success. They became so much a part of the fabric of European society that they scarcely occasioned note. They were gone – and soon, forgotten.

Acknowledgements

While a book may bear the name of a single author, writing is inevitably something of a team effort, and I have been exceptionally fortunate in my team. Thanks must go first to my sometime agent Tessa David, who first encouraged me to try my hand at popular writing and whose input helped shape the project in its crucial early months. I hope the finished product lives up to her lofty expectations. I am similarly grateful to Laurie Robertson, who took over from Tessa, first as a maternity cover and then on a permanent basis. My editor at John Murray, Joe Zigmond, showed early enthusiasm for the project and has done much to assist in the process of writing and revision. My copy-editor, Candida Brazil, likewise worked wonders with a rather rough manuscript, while Joe's colleague Caroline Westmore stepped in valiantly to see the text into production. I am likewise thankful to the many academic colleagues who have shared thoughts, comments and work in progress. Particular thanks go to those who read and commented on individual chapters: Marc Morris, Graham Loud, Gregory Lippiatt, Lizzie Boyle, Colin Veach, Ben Guy, Alice Taylor, Matthew Hammond, Andrew Buc, Mike Humphreys and Lucas Villegas-Aristizábal.

As ever, my greatest debt is to my family. My wife, Catherine Flavelle, has advised me every step of the way, including helping with urgent last-minute revisions. The tolerance she has shown to a husband undertaking *yet another* book project has been nothing short of remarkable. I am equally grateful to our daughters, Clara and Lettie, whose smiles and laughter (and occasional shrieks and howls) have accompanied the writing process from the start. I dedicate the book to them, in the hope that someday they may read it.

Picture Credits

Notes

Abbreviations

ASC Anglo-Saxon Chronicle (cited by manuscript and year)
BL   London, British Library
PL   *Patrologia Cursus Completus, Series (Latina) Prima*, ed. J.-P.
     Migne, 221 vols (Paris, 1844–64)
TNA London, The National Archives

Preface

1. R. Bartlett, *The Making of Europe: Conquest, Colonization and Cultural Change, 950–1350* (London: Penguin, 1994); R. R. Davies, *First English Empire: Power and Identities in the British Isles 1093–1343* (Oxford: Oxford University Press, 2000).

Chapter 1: Beginnings: Strange Men from a Strange Land, Normandy, c.911–42

1. Dudo of St-Quentin, *Historia Normannorum*, II.25–9, ed. J. Lair (Caen, 1865).
2. On Dudo: B. Pohl, *Dudo of St Quentin's Historia Normannorum: History, Tradition and Memory* (Woodbridge: Boydell Press, 2015); on his reports: J. L. Nelson, 'Normandy's Early History since *Normandy before 1066*', in *Normandy and its Neighbours, 900–1250: Essays for David Bates*, ed. D. Crouch and K. Thompson (Turnhout: Brepols, 2011), 3–15, at 9–12; and on the site: *Dudo of*

St Quentin: History of the Normans, trans. E. Christiansen (Woodbridge: Boydell Press, 1998), 195 n. 201.

3. For excellent introductions to the Vikings: N. Price, *The Children of Ash and Elm: A History of the Vikings* (London: Allen Lane, 2020); C. Jarman, *River Kings: The Vikings from Scandinavia to the Silk Road* (London: William Collins, 2021).

4. S. Coupland, 'From Poachers to Gamekeepers: Scandinavian Warlords and Carolingian Kings', *Early Medieval Europe* 7 (1998), 85–114.

5. See J. Le Maho, 'Rouen à l'époque des incursions Vikings (841– 911)', *Bulletin de la Commission des Antiquités de la Seine Maritime* 43 (1995), 143–202, followed by F. Neveux, *The Normans: The Conquests that Changed the Face of Europe*, trans. H. Curtis (London: Robinson, 2008), 55–63. For words of caution: P. Bauduin, *La Première Normandie (X^e–XIe siècles)* (Caen: Presses Universitaires de Caen, 2nd edn, 2004), 110–12; Nelson, 'Normandy's Early History', 12–15. On Viking activity in West Francia (France) and Brittany: J. L. Nelson, 'The Frankish Empire', in *The Oxford Illustrated History of the Vikings*, ed. P. H. Sawyer (Oxford: Oxford University Press, 1997), 19–47; N. S. Price, *The Vikings in Brittany* (London: Viking Society for Northern Research, 1989).

6. *Recueil des actes de Charles III le Simple, roi de France (893–923)*, ed. P. Lauer (Paris: Imprimerie Nationale, 1940–9), nos 51, 53, 92. The former and latter charters are preserved as Paris, Archives nationales, K 16/5, and Paris, Archives nationales, K 16/9. On the latter in context, see G. Koziol, *The Politics of Memory and Identity in Carolingian Royal Diplomas: The West Frankish Kingdom (840–987)* (Turnhout: Brepols, 2012), 436–9. See also F. Lifshitz, 'The Migration of Neustrian Relics in the Viking Age: The Myth of Voluntary Exodus, the Reality of Coercion and Theft', *Early Medieval Europe* 4 (1995), 175–92.

7. Flodoard, *Annales*, s.a. 923–4, ed. P. Lauer (Paris, 1906). On Charles' politics: F. McNair, 'After Soissons: The Last Years of Charles the Simple (923–9)', *Reti Medievali Rivista* 18.ii (2017), 29–48, esp. 38–40.

8. Flodoard, *Historia Remensis ecclesiae*, IV.14, ed. M. Stratmann, Monumenta Germaniae Historica: Scriptores 36 (Hanover: Hahnsche Buchhandlung, 1998).

9. L. Abrams, 'Early Normandy', *Anglo-Norman Studies* 35 (2013), 45–64.

10. Cf. M. Townend, *Language and History in Viking Age England: Linguistic Relations between Speakers of Old Norse and Old English* (Turnhout: Brepols, 2002), esp. 181–211.

11. Richer of Saint-Rémi, *Historiae*, I.4, ed. H. Hoffmann, Monumenta Germaniae Historica: Scriptores 38 (Hanover: Hahnsche Buchhandlung, 2000). See further, D. Bates, *Normandy Before 1066* (London: Pearson, 1982); F. Lifshitz, 'La Normandie carolingienne, essai sur la continuité, avec utilisation de sources négligées', *Annales de Normandie* 48 (1998), 505–52; R. Allen, 'The Norman Episcopate 989–1110' (PhD thesis, University of Glasgow, 2009), 6–28.

12. Flodoard, *Annales, s.a.* 923.

13. Flodoard, *Historia Remensis ecclesiae*, IV.14.

14. *PL*, cxxxii, cols 661–74, with Nelson, 'Normandy's Early History', 4–9; M.-C. Isaïa, 'Hagiographie et pastorale: la collection canonique d'Hervé archevêque de Rheims (m. 922)', *Mélanges de Science Religieuse* 67 (2010), 27–48.

15. E. van Houts, 'Exogamy and Miscegenation in the Norman Worlds', in *The Normans and the 'Norman Edge': Peoples, Polities and Identities on the Frontiers of Medieval Europe*, ed. K. J. Stringer and A. Jotischky (London: Routledge, 2019), 129–47.

16. E. van Houts, 'The *Planctus* on the Death of William Longsword (943) as a Source for Tenth-Century Culture in Normandy and Aquitaine', *Anglo-Norman Studies* 36 (2014), 1–22, with an edition of the text at 18–20. The *Planctus* – our only strictly contemporary source – describes William being born 'across the sea' (*transmarino*), but that he had a French rather than Welsh or Irish mother (as per van Houts) may be the case in the light of William's name. Indeed, the *Plactus* merely says that he was born abroad, not that his mother was foreign. That said, it is possible that William was a baptismal name (Rollo had taken the name Robert upon conversion).

17. F. McNair, 'The Politics of Being Norman in the Reign of Richard the Fearless, Duke of Normandy (r. 942–96)', *Early Medieval Europe* 23 (2015), 308–28. See also Bates, *Normandy*, 13–15.

Chapter 2: Consolidating a Colony:
Rollo's Heirs, Normandy, 942–1026

1. Dudo of St-Quentin, *Historia Normannorum*, III.61–3. See also Flodoard, *Annales*, *s.a.* 943.
2. McNair, 'Politics of Being Norman'.
3. M. Hagger, 'How the West Was Won: The Norman Dukes and the Cotentin, *c.*987–1087', *Journal of Medieval History* 28 (2002), 20–55, esp. 20–3.
4. Pohl, *Dudo*, 109–24.
5. M. Fauroux, 'Deux Autographes de Dudon de Saint-Quentin (1011, 1015)', *Bibliothèque de l'Ecole des Chartes* III (1953), 229–34. For two further possibilities, see *Recueil des actes des ducs de Normandie de 911 à 1066*, ed. M. Fauroux (Caron, 1961), nos 11, 58, with E. Z. Tabuteau, *Transfers of Property in Eleventh-Century Normandy* (Chapel Hill, NC: University of North Carolina Press, 1988), 7–8.
6. Bauduin, *La Première Normandie*, 75–83.
7. M. Hagger, *Norman Rule in Normandy, 911–1144* (Woodbridge: Boydell Press, 2017), 266–88.
8. B. Pohl, 'Poetry, Punctuation and Performance: Was There an Aural Context for Dudo of Saint-Quentin's *Historia Normannorum?*' *Tabularia* 15 (2016), 177–216. More generally: A. Plassmann, '*Tellus Normannica* und *dux Dacorum* bei Dudo von St-Quentin: Land und Herrscher als Integrationsfaktor für die Normandie', in *Die Suche nach den Ursprüngen: Von der Bedeutung des frühen Mittelalters*, ed. W. Pohl (Vienna: Verlag der Österreichischen Akademie der Wissenschaften, 2004), 233–51; R. Canosa, *Etnogenesi normanne e identità variabili: il retroterra culturale dei Normanni d'Italia fra Scandinavia e Normandia* (Turin: Silvio Zamorani, 2009), 41–64.
9. *Recueil des actes des ducs*, ed. Fauroux, nos 15, 18. The latter survives as Rouen, Archives départmentales de la Seine-Maritime, 14 H 917 B. See further K. Cross, *Heirs of the Vikings : History and Identity in Normandy and England, c.950–c.1015* (Woodbridge: Boydell Press, 2018), 165–8.

10. J. Benham, 'The Earliest Arbitration Treaty? A Re-Assessment of the Anglo-Norman Treaty of 991', *Historical Research* 93 (2020), 189–204.

11. *ASC* CDE 1001 <*ASC* CDE 1001>, ed. C. Plummer, *Two of the Saxon Chronicles Parallel,* 2 vols (Oxford: Clarendon Press, 1892–9); William of Jumièges, *Gesta Normannorum ducum,* V.4, ed. E. M. C. van Houts (Oxford: Oxford University Press, 1992–5).

12. Dudo, *Historia Normannorum,* I.68.

13. Richer of Saint-Rémi, *Historiae,* IV.108. See similarly ibid., II.20, 28, 30.

14. P. Bauduin, 'Richard II de Normandie: figure princière et transferts culturels (fin dixième–début onzième siècle)', *Anglo-Norman Studies* 37 (2015), 53–82. See also Pohl, *Dudo,* 156–223; Cross, *Heirs of the Vikings,* 61–84.

Chapter 3: Queen Emma, Jewel of the Normans: England, 1002–42

1. P. Stafford, 'The King's Wife in Wessex 800–1066', *Past and Present* 91 (1981), 3–27.

2. For the date: S. Keynes, *The Diplomas of King Æthelred 'the Unready': A Study in Their Use as Historical Evidence* (Cambridge: Cambridge University Press, 1980), 210 n. 203; L. Roach, 'Ælfthryth – England's First Queen', *BBC History Magazine* May 2017, 38–41.

3. The best accounts of Emma's life and reign are P. Stafford, *Queen Emma and Queen Edith: Queenship and Women's Power in Eleventh-Century England* (Oxford: Blackwell, 1997), 209–54; S. Keynes, 'Introduction to the 1998 Reprint', in *Encomium Emmae reginae,* ed. A. Campbell (Cambridge: Cambridge University Press, 1998), [xxxiii]–[xxxiv].

4. *ASC* CDE 1003.

5. Ibid., 1002. See L. Roach, *Æthelred the Unready* (New Haven, CT: Yale University Press, 2016), 191–200.

6. *ASC* CDE 1013.

7. S. Keynes, 'The Æthelings in Normandy', *Anglo-Norman Studies* 13 (1991), 173–205, at 176–7, 181–3.

8. Keynes, 'Introduction', in *Encomium Emmae reginae*, ed. Campbell, [xxii]–[xxix]. On Cnut's reign, see T. Bolton, *Cnut the Great* (New Haven, CT: Yale University Press, 2017).

9. BL Stowe 944, fol. 6r., with C. E. Karkov, *Ruler Portraits of Anglo-Saxon England* (Woodbridge: Boydell Press, 2004), 121–45.

10. Henry of Huntingdon, *Historia Anglorum*, VI.2, ed. D. Greenaway (Oxford: Clarendon Press, 1996).

11. E. Treharne, *Living Through Conquest: The Politics of Early English, 1020–1220* (Oxford: Oxford University Press, 2012), 9–90; Bolton, *Cnut the Great*, 92–128.

12. A. Kennedy, 'Cnut's Law Code of 1018', *Anglo-Saxon England* 11 (1983), 57–81.

13. T. Bolton, 'Ælfgifu of Northampton: Cnut the Great's "Other Woman"', *Nottingham Medieval Studies* 51 (2007), 247–69. On marriage regulations: D. d'Avray, *Papacy, Monarchy and Marriage 860–1600* (Cambridge: Cambridge University Press, 2015); S. McDougall, *Royal Bastards: The Birth of Illegitimacy, 800–1230* (Oxford: Oxford University Press, 2016).

14. On Godwin and Leofric: S. Keynes, 'Cnut's Earls', in *The Reign of Cnut: King of England, Denmark and Norway*, ed. A. R. Rumble (London: Leicester University Press, 1994), 43–88, esp. 84–7.

15. P. Sawyer, 'Scandinavia in the Eleventh and Twelfth Centuries', in *The New Cambridge Medieval History*, iv, *c.1024–c.1198*, ed. D. Luscombe and J. Riley-Smith, (Cambridge: Cambridge University Press, 2004), vol. ii, 290–303, at 296–7.

16. *Encomium Emmae reginae*, III.2–6, with Stafford *Queen Emma*, 241–2, 245; Keynes, 'Introduction', [xxxiii]–[xxxiv], [lxii]–[lxv].

17. P. Grierson, 'The Relations between England and Flanders before the Norman Conquest', *Transactions of the Royal Historical Society*, 4th ser. 23 (1941), 71–112; E. Oksanen, *Flanders and the Anglo-Norman World, 1066–1216* (Cambridge: Cambridge University Press, 2012), 7–18.

18. *Encomium Emmae reginae*, III.8–9.

19. BL Add. 33241, fol. 1v. See Karkov, *Ruler Portraits*, 146–55.

Chapter 4: Edward the Confessor: A King
Across the Sea, England 1041–66

1. J. R. Maddicott, 'Edward the Confessor's Return to England in 1041', *English History Review* 119 (2004), 650–66.
2. M. K. Lawson, 'Harthacnut [Hardecanute] (*c*.1018–1042)', *Oxford Dictionary of National Biography*, xxv, 602–3. See also S. Keynes and R. Love, 'Earl Godwin's Ship', *Anglo-Saxon England* 38 (2009), 185–223.
3. *Recueil des actes des ducs*, ed. Fauroux, nos 69–70, 76, 85, with Keynes, 'Æthelings in Normandy'; E. van Houts, 'Edward and Normandy', in *Edward the Confessor: The Man and the Legend*, ed. R. Mortimer (Woodbridge: Boydell Press, 2009), 63–76, at 68–70.
4. T. Licence, *Edward the Confessor* (New Haven, CT: Yale University Press, 2020), 80–118; D. Woodman, *Edward the Confessor: The Sainted King* (London: Allen Lane, 2020), 21–36.
5. On Ralph and Godgifu: A. Williams, 'The King's Nephew: The Family and Career of Ralph, Earl of Hereford', in *Studies in Medieval History Presented to R. Allen Brown*, ed. C. Harper-Bill, C. Holdsworth and J. L. Nelson (Woodbridge: Boydell Press, 1991), 327–43; van Houts, 'Edward and Normandy', 63–8.
6. T. Licence, 'Robert of Jumièges, Archbishop in Exile (1052–5)', *Anglo-Saxon England* 42 (2013), 311–29.
7. William of Poitiers, *Gesta Guillelmi*, I.14, ed. and trans. R. H. C. Davis and M. Chibnall (Oxford: Oxford University Press, 1998); William of Jumièges, *Gesta Normannorum ducum*, VII.13(31); Eadmer, *Historia novorum in Anglia*, I, ed. M. Rule, Rolls Series (London, 1884), 5–7. Cf. G. Garnett, *Conquered England: Kingship, Succession, and Tenure 1066–1166* (Oxford: Oxford University Press, 2007), 1–44.
8. *ASC* C 1051, D 1052 (= 1051), E 1048 (= 1051).
9. *Vita Ædwardi regis*, I.3, ed. and trans. F. Barlow, *The Life of Edward Who Rests at Westminster* (Oxford and New York: Oxford University Press, rev. edn, 1992). On which: T. Licence, 'The Date and Authorship of the *Vita Ædwardi regis*', *Anglo-Saxon England* 44 (2016), 259–85.

10. *ASC* E 1048 (= 1051), D 1052 (= 1052); *Vita Ædwardi regis*, I.3, with Stafford, *Queen Emma*, 262–6. Cf. S. Foot, *Veiled Women* (Aldershot: Ashgate, 2000), ii, 215–31.

11. S. Baxter, *The Earls of Mercia: Lordship and Power in Late Anglo-Saxon England* (Oxford: Oxford University Press, 2007), esp. 17–60; Licence, *Edward the Confessor*, 160–248.

12. J. Blair, *Building Anglo-Saxon England* (Princeton, NJ: Princeton University Press, 2018), 399–400. For the wider context: ibid., 387–400.

13. S. Keynes, 'Giso, Bishop of Wells (1062–88)', *Anglo-Norman Studies* 19 (1997), 203–70, at 205–13; B. Savill, 'Prelude to Forgery: Baldwin of Bury meets Pope Alexander II', *English Historical Review* 132 (2017), 795–822, at 814–15.

14. C. P. Lewis, 'The French in England before the Conquest', *Anglo-Norman Studies* 17 (1995), 123–44.

15. *Vita Ædwardi regis*, I.11.

16. BL Stowe 944, fol. 29r., with T. Licence, 'Edward the Confessor and the Succession Question: A Fresh Look at the Sources', *Anglo-Norman Studies* 39 (2017), 113–27. See also S. Baxter, 'Edward the Confessor and the Succession Question', in *Edward the Confessor*, ed. Mortimer, 77–118.

17. K. Ubl, 'Der kinderlose König. Ein Testfall für die Ausdifferenzierung des Politischen im 11. Jahrhundert', *Historische Zeitung* 292 (2011), 323–63.

18. William of Malmesbury, *Gesta pontificum Anglorum*, I.73, ed. and trans. M. Winterbottom (Oxford and New York: Oxford University Press, 2007). Cf. William of Malmesbury, *Gesta regum Anglorum*, I.228, ed. and trans. R. A. B. Mynors with R. M. Thomson and M. Winterbottom (Oxford and New York: Oxford University Press, 1998).

19. E. Fernie, 'Edward the Confessor's Westminster Abbey', in *Edward the Confessor*, ed. Mortimer, 139–50. See further E. Fernie, *The Architecture of Norman England* (Oxford: Oxford University Press, 2002); Blair, *Building Anglo-Saxon England*, 402–4.

Chapter 5: William I: A Conquering King, Normandy and England, 1035–66

1. Orderic Vitalis, *Historia ecclesiastica*, VII.16, ed. and trans. M. Chibnall (Oxford: Oxford University Press, 1969–80); William of Malmesbury, *Gesta regum Anglorum*, III.283. For discussion: D. Bates, *William the Conqueror* (New Haven, CT: Yale University Press, 2016), 483–512.

2. E. M. C. van Houts, 'The Origins of Herleva, Mother of William the Conqueror', *English Historical Review* 101 (1986), 399–404.

3. S. McDougall, *Royal Bastards: The Birth of Illegitimacy, 800–1230* (Oxford: Oxford University Press, 2016). See also D. Bates, 'The Conqueror's Adolescence', *Anglo-Norman Studies* 25 (2003), 1–18.

4. Hugh of Flavigny, *Chronicon*, s.a. 1047, ed. G. H. Pertz, Monumenta Germaniae Historica: Scriptores 8 (Hanover, 1845); William of Jumièges, *Gesta Normannorum ducum*, VII.3(6). In general: Bates, *William*, 53–4; and, on the Truce: G. Koziol, *The Peace of God* (Leeds: Arc Medieval Press, 2018), 89–127.

5. van Houts, 'Origins of Herleva'.

6. *ASC* D 1052 (= 1051), with P. Stafford, *After Alfred: Anglo-Saxon Chronicles and Chroniclers, 900–1150* (Oxford: Oxford University Press, 2020), 222–7, 233–67. See further Garnett, *Conquered England*, 2007), 7–9, 40–4; Bates, *William*, 108–22.

7. Bates, *William*, 129–33.

8. Ibid., 144–5. See further J. Gillingham, 'William the Bastard at War', *Studies in Medieval History Presented to R. Allen Brown*, ed. C. Harper-Bill, C. Holdsworth and J. L. Nelson (Woodbridge: Boydell Press, 1989), 141–58, at 151–3.

9. Cf. G. Garnett, ' "Ducal" Succession in Early Normandy', in *Law and Government in Medieval England and Normandy: Essays in Honour of Sir James Holt*, ed. G. Garnett and J. Hudson (Cambridge: Cambridge University Press, 1994), 90–110.

10. Eadmer, *Historia novorum in Anglia*, 5–7, with Baxter, 'Edward the Confessor', in *Edward the Confessor*, ed. Mortimer, 107–8; M. Morris, *The Norman Conquest* (London: Hutchinson, 2012), 116–19.

11. A. Gautier, 'Harold, Harald, Guillaume et les autres: prétentions et prétendants à la succession d'Édouard le Confesseur (1042–1066)', *Annales de Normandie* 69 (2019), 29–56.

12. A. Gautier, 'Comment Harold prêta serment: circonstances et interprétations d'un rituel politique', *Cahiers de civilisation médiévale* 55 (2012), 33–57.

13. However, see A. Williams, 'The Art of Memory: The Posthumous Reputation of King Harold II Godwineson', *Anglo-Norman Studies* 42 (2020) 29–43, at 30–1, now raising the possibility of a later coronation.

14. Bates, *William*, 219–22. Note the recent arguments of D. Armstrong, 'The Norman Conquest of England, the Papacy, and the Papal Banner', *Haskins Society Journal* 32 (2021), 47–72, which considerably complicate the matter.

15. *Les Actes de Guillaume le Conquérant et de la reine Mathilde pour les abbayes caennaises*, ed. L. Musset (Caen: Société des antiquaires de Normandie, 1967), no. 2 (= *Recueil des actes des ducs*, ed. Fauroux, no. 231), with C. Letouzey-Réty, 'Les Abbesses de la Trinité de Caen, la reine Mathilde et l'Angleterre', *Annales de Normandie* 69 (2019), 57–69. See also Bates, *William*, 226–8.

16. E. M. C. van Houts, 'The Ship List of William the Conqueror', *Anglo-Norman Studies* 10 (1988), 159–183.

17. See most recently J. Gillingham, '1066 and Warfare: The Context and Place (Senlac) of the Battle of Hastings', in *1066 in Perspective*, ed. D. Bates (Leeds: Royal Armouries, 2018), 109–22, at 114–15.

18. William of Malmesbury, *Gesta regum Anglorum*, III.262.

19. William of Poitiers, *Gesta Giullelmi*, II.6, with Morris, *Norman Conquest*, 166–8.

20. *ASC* E 1066, TNA, E 31/1/3 (Little Domesday), fol. 14r.

21. B. S. Bachrach, 'Some Observations on the Military Administration of the Norman Conquest', *Anglo-Norman Studies* 8 (1986), 1–25.

22. M. Strickland, 'Military Technology and Conquest: The Anomaly of Anglo-Saxon England', *Anglo-Norman Studies* 18 (1997), 353–82, and 'La Chevalerie des Normands? La conquête et la conduite de la guerre dans le monde normand', in *911–2011: penser les mondes normands médiévaux*, ed. D. Bates and P. Bauduin (Caen: Presses Universitaires de Caen, 2016), 293–308.

23. *Carmen de Hastingae proelio*, ll. 533–50, ed. C. Morton and H. Muntz (Oxford: Oxford University Press, 1972).

24. Amatus, *Ystoire de li Normant*, I.3, ed. M. Guéret-Laferté (Paris: Champion, 2011). On Harold's death, see M. K. Lawson, *The Battle of Hastings* (3rd edn, published online, 2016: https://archive. org/details/LawsonBattleofHastings3rdedn), 181–6, 203–13; Bates, *William*, 241–2. On Amatus: G. A. Loud, 'Introduction', in *Amatus of Montecassino: The History of the Normans*, trans. P. N. Dunbar with G. A. Loud (Woodbridge: Boydell Press, 2004), 1–42.

Chapter 6: Court Propaganda: The Case for Conquest, 1066–84

1. William of Malmesbury, *Gesta regum Anglorum*, III.247; John of Worcester, *Chronicon*, s.a. 1066, ed. R. R. Darlington and P. McGurk (Oxford: Oxford University Press, 1995–8).

2. *ASC* D 1066. On the post-Hastings campaign: P. Dalton, 'After Hastings: William the Conqueror's Invasion Campaign, 15 October–25 December 1066', *Viator* 48 (2017), 139–78.

3. John of Worcester, *Chronicon*, s.a. 1066. John's source is a copy of the *Chronicle* similar to the D version, itself drawn up in Ealdred's circles. The silence of the latter may reflect new sensibilities after William's accession in late 1066, when the archbishop – who went on to anoint William too – had every reason to downplay his earlier involvement in Harold's regime.

4. Garnett, *Conquered England*, 33–44. See also Bates, *William*, 221–3.

5. William of Poitiers, *Gesta Guillelmi*, I.14.

6. Ibid. I.41.

7. *Councils and Synods With Other Documents Relating to the English Church, 871–1204*, ed. D. Whitelock, M. Brett and C. N. L. Brooke (Oxford: Oxford University Press, 1981), ii, 581–4, with Garnett, *Conquered England*, 5–9. See also S. Hamilton, *The Practice of Penance, 900–1050* (Woodbridge: Boydell Press, 2001), 194–6.

8. *Regesta regum Anglo-Normannorum: The Acta of William I (1066–87)*, ed. D. Bates (Oxford: Clarendon Press, 1998), no. 180.

9. *Anglo-Saxon Writs*, ed. F. E. Harmer (Manchester: Manchester University Press, 1952), no. 71. It is significant that this was in favour of Giso of Wells: S. Keynes, 'Giso, Bishop of Wells (1061–88)', *Anglo-Norman Studies* 19 (1997), 203–71; G. Garnett, *The Norman Conquest: A Very Short Introduction* (Oxford: Oxford University Press, 2009), 50–2. More generally: Garnett, *Conquered England*, 9–18.

10. C. Lewis, 'Audacity and Ambition in Early Norman England and the Big Stuff of the Conquest', *Anglo-Norman Studies* 40 (2018), 25–51, at 37–8, 49–51.

11. TNA E 31/2/2 (Great Domesday Book), fol. 100v.

12. See most recently S. Baxter, 'The Domesday Controversy: A Review and a New Interpretation', *Haskins Society Journal* 29 (2018), 225–93, and 'How and Why was Domesday Made?', *English Historical Review* 135 (2020), 1085–131.

13. TNA E 31/2/2 (Great Domesday Book), fol. 38r.

Chapter 7: The Bayeux Tapestry: Embroidered History, 1066–97

1. C. Hicks, *The Bayeux Tapestry: The Life Story of a Masterpiece* (London: Chatto & Windus, 2006). On the Tapestry, the best recent guides are P. Bouet and F. Neveux, *La Tapisserie de Bayeux: révélation et mystères d'une broderie du Moyen Âge* (Rennes: Ouest-France, 2013); L. Provero, *Dalla guerra alla pace: L'Arazzo di Bayeux e la conquista normanna dell'Inghilterra (secolo XI)* (Florence: Firenze University Press, 2020); D. Musgrove and M. Lewis, *The Story of the Bayeux Tapestry: Unravelling the Norman Conquest* (London: Thames & Hudson, 2021).

2. R. Gameson, 'The Origins, Art, and Message of the Bayeux Tapestry', in *The Study of the Bayeux Tapestry*, ed. R. Gameson (Woodbridge: Boydell Press, 1997), 157–211, at 161–74; C. Hart, 'The Bayeux Tapestry and Schools of Illumination at Canterbury', *Anglo-Norman Studies* 22 (2000), 117–67.

3. C. Norton, 'Viewing the Bayeux Tapestry, Now and Then', *Journal of the British Archaeological Association* 172 (2019), 52–89. See further, C. Norton, 'The Helmet and the Crown: The Bayeux Tapestry, Bishop Odo and William the Conqueror', *Anglo-Norman Studies* 43 (2021), 123–49.

4. N. Brooks with H. E. Walker, 'The Authority and Interpretation of the Bayeux Tapestry', *Anglo-Norman Studies* 1 (1979), 1–34, 191–9; S. Lewis, *The Rhetoric of Power in the Bayeux Tapestry* (Cambridge: Cambridge University Press, 1999), 116–31; H. M. Thomas, 'Turold, Wadard and Vitalis: Why are They on the Bayeux Tapestry?', *Anglo-Norman Studies* 28 (2016), 181–97. Among the (vast) further literature, especially valuable perspectives are to be found in D. J. Bernstein, *The Mystery of the Bayeux Tapestry* (London: Weidenfeld & Nicolson, 1986); H. E. J. Cowdrey, 'Towards an Interpretation of the Bayeux Tapestry', *Anglo-Norman Studies* 10 (1988), 49–65; Gameson, 'Origins, Art and Message'; L. Ashe, *Fiction and History in England, 1066–1200* (Cambridge: Cambridge University Press, 2007), 35–49; Bouet and Neveux, *Tapisserie de Bayeux*; Musgrove and Lewis, *Story of the Bayeux Tapestry*.

5. Gameson, 'Origins, Art and Message', 172–4.

6. Cowdrey, 'Towards an Interpretation'.

7. Baudri of Bourgueil (Baldricus Burgulianus), *Carmina*, l. 463, Editiones Heidelbergenses 19, ed. K. Hilbert (Heidelberg: Universitatsverlag Winter, 1979).

8. Cf. N. Marafioti, *The King's Body: Burial and Succession in Late Anglo-Saxon England* (Toronto: University of Toronto Press, 2014), 232–9.

9. Orderic Vitalis, *Historia ecclesiastica*, VII.15.

10. *Recueil des actes des ducs*, ed. Fauroux, nos 227 (Odo), 229 (Odo and Robert), 230 (Robert), 231 (Odo).

11. van Houts, 'Ship List'. See also C. W. Hollister, 'The Greater Domesday Tenants-in-Chief', in *Domesday Studies*, ed. J. C. Holt (Woodbridge: Boydell Press, 1987), 219–48, at 221–2, 243.

12. C. M. Nakashian, *Warrior Churchmen of Medieval England, 1000–1250: Theory and Reality* (Woodbridge: Boydell Press, 2016),

125–57; D. M. G. Gerrard, *The Church at War: The Military Activities of Bishops, Abbots and other Clergy in England, c.900–1200* (London: Routledge, 2017), 35–40.

13. William of Poitiers, *Gesta Guillelmi*, II.14, 37. See further D. R. Bates, 'The Character and Career of Odo, Bishop of Bayeux (1049/50–1097)', *Speculum* 50 (1975), 1–20.

14. Orderic Vitalis, *Historia ecclesiastica*, VII.8; William of Malmesbury, *Gesta regum Anglorum*, III.277; Guibert of Nogent, *Dei gesta per Francos*, VII.15, ed. R. B. C. Huygens, Corpus Christianorum: Continuatio Medievalis 127A (Turnhout: Brepols, 1996). See Bates, *William*, 441–5.

Chapter 8: The Fate of the English: Conquest to Colonisation, 1066–84

1. J. Gillingham, *The English in the Twelfth Century: Imperialism, National Identity and Political Values* (Woodbridge: Boydell Press, 2000), 209–31; M. Strickland, *War and Chivalry: The Conduct and Perception of War in England and Normandy, 1066–1217* (Cambridge: Cambridge University Press, 1996).

2. William of Poitiers, *Gesta Guillelmi*, II.32.

3. H. J. Tanner, 'The Expansion of the Power and Influence of the Counts of Boulogne under Eustace II', *Anglo-Norman Studies* 14 (1992), 251–86, esp. 272–4. Cf. R. Fleming, *Kings and Lords in Conquest England* (Cambridge: Cambridge University Press, 1991), 217–26.

4. R. Higham, 'William the Conqueror's Siege of Exeter in 1068', *Transactions of the Devonshire Association*, 146 (2014), 93–132.

5. Exeter, D.C. 2528, *Regesta*, ed. Bates, no. 138. See further, T. Gale, J. Langdon and N. Leishman, 'Piety and Political Accommodation in Norman England: The Case of the South-West', *Haskins Society Journal* 18 (2007), 110–31. A similar set of charters, also strongly echoing the Confessor's, was issued shortly after the siege in 1068: *Regesta*, ed. Bates, nos 181, 286, with S. Keynes, 'Regenbald the Chancellor (*sic*)', *Anglo-Norman Studies* 10 (1988), 185–222, at 218–20.

6. On Eadnoth and his family: A. Williams, *The English and the Norman Conquest* (Woodbridge: Boydell Press, 1995), 119–22.

7. Morris, *Norman Conquest*, 217–18.

8. Orderic Vitalis, *Historia Ecclesiastica*, IV.214–18. Edgar's movements are difficult to reconstruct. He does not attest the charters William issued at his Pentecost court (in which both Edwin and Morcar appear), on which grounds it is often suggested that he'd sought out refuge at the court of Malcolm: *Regesta*, ed. Bates, nos 181, 286, with N. Hooper, 'Edgar the Ætheling: Anglo-Saxon Prince, Rebel and Crusader', *Anglo-Saxon England* 14 (1985), 197–214, at 204. However, Edgar had never attested the Confessor's charters, so it is unclear why he should suddenly attest those of the Conqueror.

9. *ASC* D 1069; Orderic Vitalis, *Historia ecclesiastica*, IV.228. See further N. Arnold, 'The Defeat of the Sons of Harold in 1069', *Transactions of the Devonshire Association* 145 (2013), 33–56.

10. William of Malmesbury, *Gesta Pontificum*, III.99.

11. Bates, *William*, 313–21. Cf. D. M. Palliser, 'Domesday Book and the "Harrying of the North"', *Northern History* 29 (1993), 1–23.

12. Bates, *William*, 297, 350–1. See further, Williams, *English and the Norman Conquest*; H. M. Thomas, 'The Significance and Fate of the Native English Landholders of 1086', *English Historical Review* 118 (2003), 303–34.

13. Garnett, *Norman Conquest*, 73–89; Fleming, *Kings and Lords*, 215–31; S. Baxter and C. P. Lewis, 'Domesday Book and the Transformation of English Landed Society, 1066–86', *Anglo-Saxon England* 46 (2017), 343–403.

14. *The Chronicle of Walter of Guisborough*, ed. H. Rothwell (London: Offices of the Royal Historical Society, 1957), 216, with M. Clanchy, *From Memory to Written Record: England, 1066–1307* (Chichester: Wiley-Blackwell, 3rd edn, 2012), 41–5. More generally: N. Vincent, 'More Tales of the Conquest', in *Normandy and its Neighbours*, ed. Crouch and Thompson, 271–301, at 290–9.

Chapter 9: Church and State in Conquered England: Romancing the Stone, 1066–87

1. F. Barlow, *The English Church 1000–1066: A History of the Later Anglo-Saxon Church* (London: Longman, 1979). See also M. F. Giandrea, *Episcopal Culture in Late Anglo-Saxon England* (Woodbridge: Boydell Press, 2007).

2. H. E. J. Cowdrey, *Lanfranc: Scholar, Monk, and Archbishop* (Oxford: Oxford University Press, 2002), 29–45.

3. Cf. Alexander's letter to William: *PL*, cxlvi, col. 1413, with H. E. J. Cowdrey, 'Lanfranc, the Papacy and Canterbury' (1993), repr. in and cited from H. E. J. Cowdrey, *Popes and Church Reform in the 11th Century* (Aldershot: Routledge, 2000), no. X, 449–56.

4. For the relevant sources (with discussion): *Councils and Synods*, ed. Whitelock, Brett and Brooke, ii, 563–81.

5. H. Vollrath, *Die Synoden Englands bis 1066* (Paderborn: Ferdinand Schöningh, 1986), 193–290. See also C. Cubitt, 'Bishops and Councils in Late Saxon England: The Intersection of Secular and Ecclesiastical Law', in *Recht und Gericht in Kirche und Welt um 900*, ed. W. Hartmann (Munich: Oldenbourg, 2007), 151–67.

6. Cowdrey, *Lanfranc*, 1–28.

7. Garnett, *Conquered England*, 33–44.

8. *The Letters of Lanfranc, Archbishop of Canterbury*, ed. H. Clover and M. Gibson (Oxford: Oxford University Press, 1979), no. 1.

9. *Acta Lanfranci*, ed. J. Bately, *The Anglo-Saxon Chronicle: MS A* (Cambridge: D. S. Brewer, 1986), 84.

10. The essential guide remains Fernie, *Architecture of Norman England*, 89–193. See also Garnett, *Norman Conquest*, 91–114; R. Gem, *Studies in English Pre-Romanesque and Romanesque Architecture* (London: Pindar Press, 2003).

11. Fernie, *Architecture*, 98–102.

12. Raoul Glaber, *Historiarum libri quinque*, III.13, ed. and trans. J. France, *Rodulfus Glaber Opera* (Oxford: Oxford University Press, 1989). See J. Howe, *Before the Gregorian Reform: The Latin Church at the Turn of the First Millennium* (Ithaca, NY: Cornell University Press, 2016), 86–111.

13. Fernie, *Architecture*, 121. See further, Lewis, 'Audacity and Ambition', 28–30; E. Fernie, '1066 and Ecclesiastical Architecture', in *1066 in Perspective*, ed. Bates, 187–203, at 194–7; R. Plant, 'Ecclesiastical Architecture, *c.*1050 to *c.*1200', in *A Companion to the Anglo-Norman World*, ed. C. Harper-Bill and E. van Houts (Woodbridge: Boydell Press, 2003), 215–53, at 229–30.

14. Garnett, *Norman Conquest*, 103–4. See also Fernie, *Architecture*, 292, 294.

15. Fernie, *Architecture*, 131–40. See also M. Thurlby, 'The Roles of the Patron and the Master Mason in the First Design of the Romanesque Cathedral of Durham', in *Anglo-Norman Durham: 1093–1193*, ed. D. Rollason, M. Harvey and M. Prestwich (Woodbridge: Boydell Press, 1994), 161–84.

16. J. Bilson, 'Durham Cathedral, the Chronology of its Vaults', *Archaeological Journal* 2nd ser. 29 (1922), 101–60, at 101.

17. O. H. Creighton, '1066 and the Landscape', in *1066 in Perspective*, ed. Bates, 213–37, at 219–23.

18. *ASC* E 1086.

19. Cf. M. G. Shapland, *Anglo-Saxon Towers of Lordship* (Oxford: Oxford University Press, 2019); D. Roffe, 'Castle Construction, Conquest and Compensation', *Anglo-Norman Studies*, 41 (2019), 175–92.

20. R. Eales, 'Royal Power and Castles in Norman England', in *Medieval Knighthood* 3 (1990), 49–78, at 54–7.

Chapter 10: Settling the South: Ironarm in Italy, *c.*1030–45

1. William of Malmesbury, *Gesta regum Anglorum*, III.262.

2. G. A. Loud, *The Age of Robert Guiscard: Southern Italy and the Norman Conquest* (London: Longman, 2000), 81–91.

3. F. Panarelli, 'Goffredo Malaterra', *Dizionario biografico degli Italiani*, 57 (2001), 541–5. Cf. K. B. Wolf, *Making History: The Normans and Their Historians in Eleventh-Century Italy* (Philadelphia, PA: University of Philadelphia Press, 1995), 143–71.

4. Geoffrey of Malaterra, *De rebus gestis Rogerii Calabriae et Siciliae*

comitis et Roberti Guiscardi ducis fratris eius, I.5–6, ed. E. Pontieri (Bologna: N. Zanichelli, 2nd edn, 1927–8).

5. Amatus of Montecassino, *Ystoire de li Normant*, I.16–21.

6. William of Apulia, *Gesta Roberti Wiscardi*, I, ll. 11–57, ed. M. Mathieu (Palermo: Istituto Siciliano di Studi Bizantini e Neoellenici, 1961).

7. Adémar of Chabannes, *Chronicon*, III.55, ed. P. Bourgain with R. Landes and G. Pon, Corpus Christianorum: Continuatio Medievalis 129 (Turnhout; Brepols, 1999); Raoul Glaber, *Historiae*, III.3–4.

8. H. Hoffmann, 'Die Anfänge der Normannen in Süditalien', *Quellen und Forschungen aus italienischen Archiven und Bibliotheken*, 49 (1969), 95–144; Loud, *Age of Robert Guiscard*, 61–6. Cf. J. France, 'The Occasion of the Coming of the Normans to Southern Italy', *Journal of Medieval History* 17 (1991), 185–205.

9. G. A. Loud, 'Southern Italy in the Tenth Century', in *The New Cambridge Medieval History*, ii, *c.900–1024*, ed. T. Reuter (Cambridge: Cambridge University Press, 1999), 624–45, at 636–41.

10. P. Frankopan, *The First Crusade: The Call from the East* (London: Bodley Head, 2012), 57–70; A. Kaldellis, *Streams of Gold, Rivers of Blood: The Rise and Fall of Byzantium, 955 A.D. to the First Crusade* (Oxford: Oxford University Press, 2017), 231–79.

11. Geoffrey of Malaterra, *De rebus gestis*, I.7.

Chapter 11: Robert Guiscard:
A Cunning Count, c.1040–85

1. William of Malmesbury, *Gesta regum Anglorum*, III.262. (The translation is my own, adapted from that of Thomson and Winterbottom.)

2. Amatus, *Ystoire de li Normant*, III.9.

3. Ibid., IV.18. Cf. Geoffrey of Malaterra, *De rebus gestis*, I.16–17. For discussion: G. A. Loud, 'Anna Komnena and her Sources for the Normans of Southern Italy' (1991), repr. in G. A. Loud, *Conquerors and Churchmen in Norman Italy* (Aldershot: Routledge,

1999), no. XIII, 54–6; H. Taviani-Carozzi, *La Terreur du monde: Robert Guiscard et la conquête normande en Italie, mythe et histoire* (Paris: Fayard, 1996), 184–92.

4. Amatus, *Ystoire de li Normant*, III.11.

5. Malaterra, *De rebus gestis*, I.13; William of Apulia, *Gesta Roberti Wiscardi*, II, ll. 78–80. Cf. Amatus, *Ystoire de li Normant*, III.15–19.

6. William of Apulia, *Gesta Roberti Wiscardi*, II, ll. 82–266; Amatus, *Ystoire de li Normant*, III.39–41, with C. Guzzo, 'La battaglia di Civitate: un rilettura', *Archivio normanno-svevo* 5 (2017), 69–83.

7. For this and the following: Loud, *Age of Robert Guiscard*, 119–30.

8. P. Skinner, ' "Halt! Be Men!": Sikelgaita of Salerno, Gender and the Norman Conquest of Southern Italy', *Gender and History* 12 (2000), 622–41.

9. C. Hervé-Cummereuc, 'La Calabre dans l'état normand d'Italie du sud (XIe–XIIe siècles)', *Annales de Normandie* 45 (1995), 2–25. See also Taviani-Carozzi, *Terreur du mond*, 255–9.

10. G. M. Cantarella, 'Liaisons dangereuses: il papato e i Normanni', in *Il papato e i Normanni: temporale e spirituale in età normanna*, ed. E. D'Angelo (Florence: SISMEL edizioni del Galluzzo, 2011), 45–58.

11. On German involvement: G. A. Loud, 'German Emperors and Southern Italy during the Tenth and Eleventh Centuries', in *"Quei maledetti Normanni": studi offerti a Errico Cuozzo per i suoi settant'anni da Colleghi, Allievi, Amici*, ed. J.-M. Martin and R. Alaggio (Naples: Centro Europea di Studi Normanni, 2016), 583–605.

12. H. E. J. Cowdrey, *The Age of Abbot Desiderius: Montecassino, the Papacy, and the Normans in the Eleventh and Early Twelfth Centuries* (Oxford: Clarendon Press, 1983), 107–76.

13. *Le Liber censuum de l'église romaine*, ed. P. Fabre and L. Duchesne (Paris: Bibliothèque des écoles françaises d'Athènes et de Rome, 1889–1952), i, 421–2. Cf. William of Apulia, *Gesta Roberti Wiscardi*, II, ll. 400–5.

14. William of Apulia, *Gesta Roberti Wiscardi*, III, ll. 132–8. See C. D. Stanton, *Norman Naval Operations in the Mediterranean* (Woodbridge: Boydell Press, 2011), esp. 40–4, and 'The Norman

Kingdom of Sicily: Projecting Power by Sea', in *Warfare in the Norman Mediterranean*, ed. G. Theotokis (Woodbridge: Boydell Press, 2020), 177–94.

15. Taviani-Carozzi, *Terreur du mond*, 373–8; Loud, *Age of Robert Guiscard*, 163–5; J. C. Birk, *Norman Kings of Sicily and the Rise of the Anti-Islamic Critique: Baptized Sultans* (London: Palgrave Macmillan, 2016), 33–138; M. King, 'Holy War in the Central Mediterranean: The Case of the Zirids and the Normans', in *The Normans in the Mediterranean*, ed. E. A. Winkler and L. Fitzgerald (Turnhout: Brepols, 2021), 229–47. Cf. P. E. Chevedden, '"A Crusade from the Start": The Norman Conquest of Islamic Sicily, 1060–91', *Al-Masāq* 22 (2010), 191–225.

16. Taviani-Carozzi, *Terreur du mond*, 349–88; Loud, *Age of Robert Guiscard*, 165–85; Metcalfe, *Muslims*, 99–108.

17. Geoffey of Malaterra, *De rebus gestis*, III.31, 36.

Chapter 12: Under a Byzantine Banner: Into Asia Minor, 1038–77

1. A. Kaldellis, *Romanland: Ethnicity and Empire in Byzantium* (Cambridge, MA: Harvard University Press, 2019); P. Sarris, *Byzantium: A Very Short Introduction* (Oxford: Oxford University Press, 2015), esp. 19–40, 94–113.

2. Kaldellis, *Streams of Gold*, 21–228.

3. A. D. Beihammer, *Byzantium and the Emergence of Muslim-Turkish Anatolia, ca. 1040–1130* (Abingdon: Routledge, 2017), esp. 49–168. See also S. Vryonis, *Decline of Medieval Hellenism in Asia Minor and the Process of Islamization from the Eleventh Through the Fifteenth Century* (Berkeley, CA: University of California Press, 1971), 69–142.

4. Kaldellis, *Streams of Gold*, 171–3; J. Shepard, 'Byzantium's Last Sicilian Expedition: Scylitzes' Testimony', *Rivista di studi bizantini e neoellenici* n.s. 14–16 (1977–9), 145–59.

5. John Skylitzes, *Synopsis Historiarum*, XXIII.4, ed. J. Thurn (Berlin: De Gruyter, 1973); Anna Komnena, *Alexias*, I.5, ed. D. R. Reinsch and A. Kambylis (Berlin: De Gruyter, 2001);

Skylitzes Continuatus, VI.21, ed. and trans. E. McGeer, *Byzantium in the Time of Troubles: The Continuation of the Chronicle of John Skylitzes (1057–1079)* (Leiden: Brill, 2020). See also J. Shepard, 'The Uses of Franks in Eleventh-Century Byzantium', *Anglo-Norman Studies* 15 (1993), 275–305, at 283–4.

6. G. Theotokis, 'Rus, Varangian and Frankish Mercenaries in the Service of the Byzantine Emperors (9th-11th C.)', *Byzantina Symmeikta* 22 (2012), 126–56, at 142. See also Shepard, 'Uses of Franks', 285–7.

7. Michael Psellos, *Chronographia*, VII.24, ed. S. Impellizzeri (Milan: Fondazione Lorenzo Valla, 1984); Anna Komnena, *Alexias*, V.6.

8. William of Apulia, *Gesta Roberti Wiscardi*, II. ll. 46–74; William of Poitiers, *Gest Guillelmi*, I.59.

9. Skylitzes, *Synopsis Historiarum*, XXIII.4. On Hervé's career: J.-C. Cheynet, 'Le Rôle des Occidentaux dans l'armée byzantine avant la Première Croisade', in *Byzanz und das Abendland im 10. und 11. Jahrhundert*, ed. E. Konstantinou (Cologne: Böhlau, 1997), 111–28, at 119–21.

10. W. Seibt, 'Übernahm der französische Normanne Hervé (Erbebios Phrangopolos) nach der Katastrophe von Manzikert das Kommando über) die verbliebene Ostarmee?', *Studies in Byzantine Sigillography* 10 (2006), 89–96. Matthew of Edessa (Matt'ēos Uṙhayec'i records the alternative tradition that he was drowned on the orders of Constantine IX Doukas: T. L. Andrews, *Matt'ēos Uṙhayec'i and His Chronicle: History as Apocalypse in a Crossroads of Cultures* (Leiden: Brill, 2016), 93–4.

11. Amatus, *Ystoire de li Normant*, I.5–8. On the 'commander of the cavalry of Rome': J. F. O'Callaghan, *Reconquest and Crusade in Medieval Spain* (Philadelphia, PA: University of Pennsylvania Press, 2004), 26 (with n. 13).

12. Michael Attaleiates, *Historia*, ch. 18, ed. I. Pérez Martín and trans. A. Kaldellis and D. Krallis (Cambridge, MA: Harvard University Press, 2012). See also Kaldellis, *Streams of Gold*, 243.

13. Attaleiates, *Historia*, ch. 21. Cf. Psellos, *Chronographia*, VII.39. For discussion: Shepard, 'Uses of Franks', 297–8.

14. For the size of imperial forces (and, in particular, *tagmata*):

J. F. Haldon, *Warfare, State and Society in the Byzantine World, 565–1204* (London: Routledge, 1999), 103–4.

15. Amatus, *Ystoire de li Normant*, I.9.

16. Our main sources for the rebellion are Attaleiates, *Historia*, ch. 23; and Nikephoros Bryennios, *Historiarum libri quattuor*, II.4, 14–24, ed. P. Gautier (Brussels: Byzantion, 1975). See further Kaldellis, *Streams of Gold*, 256–61; Beihammer, *Emergence of Muslim-Turkish Anatolia*, 208–13.

17. L. Neville, *Heroes and Romans in Twelfth-Century Byzantium: The Material for History of Nikephoros Bryennios* (Cambridge: Cambridge University Press, 2012), 46–59.

Chapter 13: Bohemond and the Balkans: 'A Marvel to Behold', 1081–5

1. Anna Komnena, *Alexias*, XIII.10.

2. Amatus, *Ystoire de li Normant*, VII.7–8, 20, with Taviani-Carozzi, *Terreur du monde*, 317–21.

3. H. Bibicou, 'Une Page d'histoire diplomatique de Byzanze au XIe siècle: Michel VII Doukas, Robert Guiscard et la pension de dignitaires', *Byzantion* 29/30 (1959–60), 43–74. See also Amatus, *Ystoire de li Normant*, VII.26.

4. Anna Komnena, *Alexias*, XIII.10.

5. On Bohemond: L. Russo, *Boemondo: figlio del Guiscardo e principe di Antiochia* (Avellino: Sellino, 2008); G. Theotokis, *Bohemond of Taranto: Crusader and Conqueror* (Barnsley: Pen & Sword, 2021).

6. Y.-M. Bercé, *Le Roi cache: sauveurs et imposteurs: mythes politiques populaires dans l'Europe modern* (Paris: Fayard, 1990); R. Bartlett, *Blood Royal: Dynastic Politics in Medieval Europe* (Cambridge: Cambridge University Press, 2020), 360–78.

7. G. Theotokis, *The Norman Campaigns in the Balkans, 1081–1108* (Woodbridge: Boydell Press, 2014), 137–84. See further, Loud, *Age of Robert Guiscard*, 213–23; Taviani-Carozzi, *Terreur du monde*, 424–49, 468–85; Russo, *Boemondo*, 20–8; Theotokis, *Bohemond*, 19–61.

8. Anna Komnena, *Alexias*, III.9.

9. William of Apulia, *Gesta Roberti Wiscardi*, IV, ll. 270–505; Geoffrey of Malaterra, *De rebus gestis*, III.26–8.

10. William of Apulia, *Gesta Roberti Wiscardi*, IV, ll. 506–26; Geoffrey of Malaterra, *De rebus gestis*, III.33–4. On Byzantine fears in this connection: A. Kolia-Dermitrazi, 'The Norman Factor in the Gradual Alienation of East and West', in *The Fourth Crusade Revisited*, ed. P. Piatti (Vatican City: Liberia editrice vaticana, 2008), 32–53, at 41–2.

11. In addition to the works already cited: M Angold, *The Byzantine Empire, 1025–1204*, (London: Longman, 2nd edn, 1997), 129–31; P. Stephenson, *Byzantium's Balkan Frontier: A Political Study of the Northern Balkans, 900–1204* (Cambridge: Cambridge University Press, 2000), 165–72.

12. William of Apulia, *Gesta Roberti Wiscardi*, V, ll. 143–228. See also Anna Komnena, *Alexias*, VI.5–6.

Chapter 14: The First Crusade: Eastern Promises, 1096–1108

1. Good overviews can be found in J. France, *Victory in the East: A Military History of the First Crusade* (Cambridge: Cambridge University Press, 1994); T. Asbridge, *The First Crusade: A New History* (Oxford: Oxford University Press, 2004); C. Tyerman, *God's War: A History of the Crusades* (London: Allen Lane, 2006), 27–164. Refreshing new perspectives are offered by J. Rubenstein, *Armies of Heaven: The First Crusade and the Quest for Apocalypse* (New York: Basic Books, 2011); Frankopan, *Call from the East*; M. Wittow, 'Pirenne, Muhammad, and Bohemond: Before Orientalism', in *Crusading Europe: Essays in Honour of Christopher Tyerman*, ed. G. E. M. Lippiatt and J. L. Bird (Turnhout: Brepols, 2019), 17–49; Kaldellis, *Streams of Gold*, 280–301.

2. L. Kjaer, 'Conquests, Family Traditions and the First Crusade', *Journal of Medieval History* 45 (2019), 553–79. See also Kaldellis, *Streams of Gold*, 283–7.

3. Tyerman, *God's War*, 110–11.

4. Frankopan, *Call from the East*, 57–70. On Gregory VII's plans:

H. E. J. Cowdrey, 'Pope Gregory VII's "Crusading" Plans of 1074' (1982), repr. in H. E. J Cowdrey, *Popes, Monks and Crusaders* (London: Hambledon Continuum, 1984), no. X; and on the deeper causes of crusade in Europe: C. Erdmann, *The Origin of the Idea of Crusade*, trans. M. W. Baldwin and W. Goffart (Princeton: NJ: Princeton University Press, 1977); M. Bull, *Knightly Piety and the Lay Response to the First Crusade: The Limousin and Gascony c. 970–c. 1130* (Oxford: Clarendon Press, 1993); Tyerman, *God's War*, 27–57.

5. Frankopan, *Call from the East*, 71–86; Kaldellis, *Streams of Gold*, 287–9.

6. H. E. J. Cowdrey, 'Pope Urban II's Preaching of the First Crusade' (1970), repr. in Cowdrey, *Popes, Monks and Crusaders*, no. XVI.

7. J. Flori, *Pierre l'Ermite et la première croisade* (Paris: Fayard, 1999); R. Chazan, *In the Year 1096: The First Crusade and the Jews* (Philadelphia, PA: Jewish Publication Society, 1996). See also R. Chazan, '"Let Not a Remnant or a Residue Escape": Millenarian Enthusiasm in the First Crusade', *Speculum* 84 (2009), 289–313.

8. *Gesta Francorum et aliorum Hierosolimitanorum*, I.4, ed. R. Hill (Oxford: Oxford University Press, 1962); Geoffrey of Malaterra, *De rebus gestis*, IV.24; *Codice diplomatico barese*, v.1, *Le pergamene di S. Nicola di Bari (1075–1194)*, ed. F. Nitti di Vito (Bari: Commissione provinciale di archaeologia e storia patri, 1902), no. 22, with Russo, *Boemondo*, 59–62. For doubts: France, *Victory in the East*, 82; Tyerman, *God's War*, 76–7; Frankopan, *Call from the East*, 109–10. See also L. Russo, 'Norman Participation in the First Crusade: A Re-examination', in *Warfare in the Norman Mediterranean*, ed. G. Theotokis (Woodbridge: Boydell Press, 2020), 195–209; A. V. Murray, 'The Enemy Within: Bohemond, Byzantium and the Subversion of the First Crusade', in *Crusading and Pilgrimage in the Norman World*, ed. K. Hurlock and P. Oldfield (Woodbridge: Boydell Press, 2015), 32–47, at 35–7, who (like Russo) is willing to trust the anonymous here.

9. Albert of Aachen, *Historia Ierosolimitana*, II.14, ed. and trans. S. B. Edgington (Oxford: Oxford University Press, 2007); Anna Komnena, *Alexias*, X.9, with Kaldellis, *Streams of Gold*, 291–2.

10. J. Shepard, 'When Greek meets Greek: Alexius Comnenus and Bohemond in 1097–98', *Byzantine and Modern Greek Studies* 12 (1988), 185–277. See also J. H. Pryor, 'The Oaths of the Leaders of the First Crusade to Emperor Alexius I Comnenus: Fealty, Homage – πίστις, δουλεία', *Parergon* 2 (1984), 111–41.

11. Anna Komnena, *Alexias*, XI.3.

12. S. B. Edgington, *Baldwin I of Jerusalem, 1100–1118* (London: Routledge, 2019), 38–58. Cf. Frankopan, *Call from the East*, 150–3.

13. Frankopan, *Call from the East*, 157–72; Murray, 'Enemy Within', 41–7.

14. For the battle: France, *Victory in the East*, 260–96; on the relic: J. Riley-Smith, *The First Crusade and the Idea of Crusading* (London: Athlone Press, 1986), 95–8; T. Asbridge, 'The Holy Lance of Antioch: Power, Devotion and Memory on the First Crusade', *Reading Medieval Studies* 33 (2007), 3–36; and on the impact of victory: Rubenstein, *Armies of Heaven*, 205–27; A. D. Buck, '"Weighed by Such a Great Calamity, They were Cleansed for their Sins": Remembering the Siege and Capture of Antioch', in *Remembering the Crusades in Medieval Texts and Songs*, ed. A. D. Buck and T. W. Smith (Cardiff: University of Wales Press, 2019), 1–16.

15. T. S. Asbridge, *The Creation of the Principality of Antioch, 1098–1130* (Woodbridge: Boydell Press, 2000), 129–54, 163–80; A. V. Murray, 'The Nobility of the Principality of Antioch, 1098–1187: Names, Origins and Identity', in *Normans and the 'Norman Edge'*, ed. Stringer and Jotischky, 162–90; A. D. Buck, *The Principality of Antioch and its Frontiers in the Twelfth Century* (Woodbridge: Boydell Press, 2017), 62–85.

16. A. V. Murray, 'Norman Settlement in the Latin Kingdom of Jerusalem, 1099–1131', *Archivio normanno-svevo* 1 (2008), 61–86.

17. G. A. Loud, 'Norman Italy and the Holy Land' (1992), repr. in Loud, *Conquerors and Churchmen*, no. XIV; L. Russo, 'Bad Crusaders? The Normans of Southern Italy and the Crusading Movement in the Twelfth Century', *Anglo-Norman Studies* 38 (2016), 169–80; P. Z. Hailstone, *Recalcitrant Crusaders? The Relationship Between Southern Italy and Sicily, Crusading and the Crusader States, c.1060–1198* (Abingdon: Routledge, 2020).

18. N. Paul, *To Follow in Their Footsteps: The Crusades and Family Memory in the High Middle Ages* (Ithaca, NY: Cornell University Press, 2012).

19. William of Tyre, *Chronicon*, XI.29, ed. R. B. C. Huygens (Turnhout: Brepols, 1986), with Murray, 'Norman Settlement', 75–80. See also Edgington, *Baldwin I*, 182–5.

20. See further Buck, *Principality of Antioch*, 69–77, 88–101.

21. L. Russo, 'Il viaggio di Boemondo d'Altavilla in Francia (1106): un riesame', *Archivio storico italiano* 163 (2005), 3–42; J. Rubenstein, *Nebuchadnezzar's Dream: The Crusades, Apocalyptic Prophecy, and the End of History* (Oxford: Oxford University Press, 2019), 7–20.

22. B. Whalen, 'God's Will or Not? Bohemond's Campaign Against the Byzantine Empire (1105–1108)', in *Crusades: Medieval Worlds in Conflict*, ed. T. F. Madden et al. (Farnham: Ashgate, 2010), 111–26. See also Russo, *Boemondo*, 177–95; Theotokis, *Norman Campaigns*, 200–14; J. Harris, *Byzantium and the Crusades* (London: Bloomsbury, 2nd edn, 2014), 80–5.

Chapter 15: A Bridge Too Far?
North Africa, 1142–59

1. *Biblioteca Arabo-Sicula*, ed. and trans. (into Italian) M. Amari (Turin, 1880), i, 450–2; Geoffrey of Malaterra, *De rebus gestis*, IV.3. Sadly the only English translation is partial, starting with the years of the First Crusade: *The Chronicle of Ibn al-Athīr for the Crusading Period*, trans. D. S. Richards (Farnham: Ashgate, 2006–8). On the campaign: H. E. J. Cowdrey, 'The Mahdia Campaign of 1087' (1977), repr. in Cowdrey, *Popes, Monks and Crusaders*, no. XII.

2. F. Micheau, 'Le *Kitāb al-kāmil fī l-tāʾrīkh* d'Ibn al-Athīr: entre chronique et histoire', *Studia Islamica* 104/5 (2007), 81–101.

3. D. Abulafia, *The Great Sea: A Human History of the Mediterranean* (London: Allen Lane, 2011), 241–369. See also M. McCormick, *Origins of the European Economy: Communications and Commerce AD 300–900* (Cambridge: Cambridge University Press, 2001).

4. D. Abulafia, 'The Norman Kingdom of Africa and Norman Expeditions to Majorca and the Muslim Mediterranean', *Anglo-*

Norman Studies 7 (1985), 26–49, at 26–30. See further, D. Abulafia, 'The Crown and the Economy under Roger II and His Successors', *Dumbarton Oaks Papers* 37 (1983), 1–14, esp. 3–5; C. Dalli, 'Bridging Europe and Africa: Norman Sicily's Other Kingdom', in *Bridging the Gaps: Sources, Methodology and Approaches to Religion in History*, ed. J. Carvalho (Pisa: Pisa University Press, 2008), 77–94, at 80–4.

5. J. Johns, *Arabic Administration in Norman Sicily: The Royal Dīwān* (Cambridge: Cambridge University Press, 2002), 80–90, 215–18, 282–3; B. A. Catlos, 'Who was Philip of Mahdia and Why Did He Have to Die? Confessional Identity and Political Power in the Twelfth-Century Mediterranean', *Mediterranean Chronicle* 1 (2011), 73–103; Birk, *Norman Kings of Sicily*, 139–71. More generally: C. D. Stanton, 'Roger de Hauteville, Amir of Sicily', *Mediterranean Historical Review* 25 (2010), 113–32.

6. Stanton, *Norman Naval Operations*, 61–2, 65–6, 75.

7. H. Houben, *Roger II of Sicily: A Ruler between East and West*, trans. G. A. Loud and D. Milburn (Cambridge: Cambridge University Press, 2002), 8–50.

8. Ibid., 60–75.

9. *Annales Erphesfurtenses*, s.a. 1135, ed. O. Holder-Egger, *Monumenta Erphesfurtensia saec. XII. XIII. XIV.* (Hanover: Hahn, 1899).

10. Metcalfe, *Muslims*, 160–80. See also M. King, 'The Norman Kingdom of Africa and the Medieval Mediterranean' (PhD thesis, University of Minnesota, 2018), 102–35.

11. Ibn al-Athīr, *Chronicle*, s.a. 544 (=A.D. 1149–50), trans. D. S. Richards, ii, 32.

12. J. Johns, '*Malik Infrīqiya*: The Norman Kingdom of Africa and the Fāṭimids', *Libyan Studies* 18 (1987), 89–101. See also M. King, 'The Norman Kings of Africa?', *Haskins Society Journal* 28 (2016), 143–66.

13. Metcalfe, *Muslims*, 172–8; King, 'Norman Kingdom', 135–45.

14. Hugo Falcandus, *Liber de regno Sicilie*, ed. G. B. Siragusa (Rome, 1897), 27–8. See further, G. A. Loud, 'William the Bad or William the Unlucky? Kingship in Sicily 1154–1166', *Haskins Society Journal* 8 (1996), 99–114.

15. Hugo Falcandus, *Liber de regno Sicilie*, 6.

16. D. Abulafia, 'The End of Muslim Sicily', in *Muslims under Latin*

Rule, ed. J. Powell (Princeton, NJ: Princeton University Press, 1990), 103–33. See also Metcalfe, *Muslims*, 181–92; Birk, *Norman Kings*, 265–324.

Chapter 16: Northern Wales: A Wolf in Wolf's Clothing, 1068–98

1. *Vita Giffini filii Conani*, chs 10–13, ed. and trans. P. Russell (Cardiff, 2005).
2. M. Lieberman, *The March of Wales, 1067–1300: A Borderland of Medieval Britain* (Cardiff: University of Wales Press, 2008). See also R. R. Davies, *The Age of Conquest: Wales 1063–1415* (Oxford: Oxford University Press, 1987), 24–110; M. Lieberman, 'The Medieval "Marches" of Normandy and Wales', *English Historical Review* 125 (2010), 1357–81.
3. T. M. Charles-Edwards, *Wales and the Britons 350–1064* (Oxford: Oxford University Press, 2013), 552–69; B. Guy, 'The Pattern of English Policy Towards Wales in the Tenth and Eleventh Centuries', *Offa's Dyke Journal* 4 (forthcoming, 2022).
4. K. L. Maund, 'The Welsh Family Alliances of Earl Ælfgar of Mercia and his Family in the mid-Eleventh Century', *Anglo-Norman Studies* 11 (1989), 181–90. See further K. L. Maund, *Ireland, Wales, and England in the Eleventh Century* (Woodbridge: Boydell Press, 1991), 120–55; Baxter, *Earls of Mercia*, 42, 46–7, 58–9, 86–7; C. P. Lewis, 'The Shape of the Norman Principality of Gwynedd', in *Normans and the 'Norman Edge'*, ed. Stringer and Jotischky, 100–28; R. Thomas, 'The View from Wales: Anglo-Welsh Relations in the Time of England's Conquests', in *Conquests in Eleventh-Century England: 1016, 1066*, ed. L. Ashe and E. J. Ward (Woodbridge: Boydell Press, 2020), 287–306.
5. Cf. D. Stephenson, *Medieval Wales c. 1050–1332: Centuries of Ambiguity* (Cardiff: University of Wales Press, 2019), 48.
6. Davies, *Age of Conquest*, 88–92; Lieberman, *March of Wales*, 18–20.
7. C. P. Lewis, 'Hugh d'Avranches (*d.* 1101)', in *Oxford Dictionary of National Biography*, iii, 1–3.

8. C. P. Lewis, 'The Formation of the Honor of Chester', *Journal of the Chester Archaeological Society* 71 (1991), 37–68. See also C. P. Lewis, 'The Early Earls of Norman England', *Anglo-Norman Studies* 13 (1990), 207–22, esp. 219.

9. TNA E 31/2/2 (Great Domesday Book), fol. 269r. See Lewis, 'Principality of Gwynedd'.

10. See J. R. Davies, 'Aspects of Church Reform in Wales, *c*.1093–*c*.1223', *Anglo-Norman Studies* 30 (2008), 85–99.

11. *Brut y Tywysogion or the Chronicle of Princes: Peniarth MS 20 Version*, *s.a.* 1090 (=1093), ed. and trans. T. Jones (Cardiff: University of Wales Press, 1941–52); John of Worcester, *Chronicon*, *s.a.* 1093.

12. *Gruffudd ap Cynan: A Collaborative Biography*, ed. K. L. Maund (Woodbridge: Boydell Press, 1997). See also Maund, *Ireland, Wales, and England*, 82–90, 141–55; Thomas, 'View from Wales', 297–305.

13. Orderic Vitalis, *Historia ecclesiastica*, VI.2.

14. Ibid., VIII.3.

15. Matthew Paris, *Chronica majora*, *s.a.* 1250, ed. H. R. Luard, (London, 1872–80).

16. R. R. Davies, 'Kings, Lords and Liberties in the March of Wales, 1066–1272', *Transactions of the Royal Historical Society*, 5th ser., 29 (1979), 41–61. See further Davies, *Age of Conquest*, 82–107, 271–88; Stephenson, *Medieval Wales*, 10–12, 63–83; Lieberman, *March of Wales*.

17. *Cartae et alia munimenta quae ad dominium de Glamorganicia pertinent*, ed. G. T. Clark (Cardiff: University of Wales Press, 1910), ii, 554.

18. H. Fulton, 'Negotiating Welshness: Multilingualism in Wales Before and After 1066', in *Conceptualizing Multilingualism in England, c.800–c.1250*, ed. E. M. Tyler (Turnhout: Brepols, 2012), 145–70.

Chapter 17: Southern Wales: Making a Mark, 1068–98

1. D. Crouch, 'The Slow Death of Kingship in Glamorgan, 1067–1158', *Morgannwg* 29 (1985), 20–41; A. G. Williams, 'Norman Lordship in South-East Wales during the Reign of William I', *Welsh History Review* 16 (1993), 445–66. See also Bates, *William the Conqueror*, 430–2.
2. K. L. Maund, 'Bernard de Neufmarché (*d.* 1121×5?)', in *Oxford Dictionary of National Biography*, xl, 459. See also Maund, *Ireland, Wales, and England*, 148–50.
3. Lieberman, *Medieval March of Wales*, 107–12.
4. On which, see Stephenson, *Medieval Wales*, 35–62, 85–120.
5. Gillingham, *English in the Twelfth Century*, 19–39; R. [R.] Davies, *The Matter of Britain and the Matter of England* (Oxford: Clarendon Press, 1996). See further Davies, *First English Empire*, 32–53; H. Pryce, 'British or Welsh? National Identity in Twelfth-Century Wales', *English Historical Review* 116 (2001), 775–801.
6. H. Pryce, 'Welsh Rulers and European Change, *c.*1100–1282', in *Power and Identity in the Middle Ages: Essays in Memory of Rees Davies*, ed. H. Pryce and J. Watts (Oxford: Oxford University Press, 2007), 37–51. See also C. Insley, 'Kings, Lords, Charters, and the Political Culture of Twelfth-Century Wales', *Anglo-Norman Studies* 30 (2008), 133–53.

Chapter 18: Iberia: 'The Race of the Normans Declines No Labour', 1147–8

1. S. Lay, *The Reconquest Kings of Portugal: Political and Cultural Reorientation on the Medieval Frontier* (Basingstoke: Palgrave Macmillan, 2009), 71–102. See further J. Mattoso, *D. Afonso Henriques* (Lisbon: Temas & Debates, 2006); K. V. Jensen, *Crusading at the Edges of Europe: Denmark and Portugal c.1000–c.1250* (London: Routledge, 2017), 130–53.
2. *De expugnatione Lyxbonensi*, ed. and trans. C. W. David (New York, NY: Columbia University Press, 1936), with C. R. Cheney, 'The Authorship of the *De expugnatione Lyxbonensi*',

Speculum 7 (1932), 395–7. See also H. Livermore, 'The "Conquest of Lisbon" and its Author', *Portuguese Studies* 6 (1990), 1–16, with the caveats raised by C. West, 'All in the Same Boat? East Anglia, the North Sea World and the 1147 Expedition to Lisbon', in *East Anglia and its North Sea World in the Middle Ages*, ed. D. Bates and R. Liddiard (Woodbridge: Boydell Press, 2013), 287–300, at 290–1.

3. J. Phillips, *The Second Crusade: Extending the Frontiers of Christendom* (New Haven, CT: Yale University Press, 2007), 61–98. See further, Rubenstein, *Nebuchadnezzar's Dream*, 101–22.

4. *De expugnatione Lyxbonensi*, ed. David, 56.

5. Ibid., 58–68. For the details of the visit to Compostela: S. B. Edgington, 'The Lisbon Letter of the Second Crusade', *Historical Research* 69 (1996), 328–39, at 337.

6. *De expugnatione Lyxbonensi*, ed. David, 68–84. See further, A. Forey, 'The Siege of Lisbon and the Second Crusade', *Portuguese Studies* 20 (2004), 1–13.

7. L. Villegas-Aristizábal, 'Revisiting the Anglo-Norman Crusaders' Failed Attempt to Conquer Lisbon *c.*1142', *Portuguese Studies* 29 (2013), 7–20.

8. *De expugnatione Lyxbonensi*, ed. David, 106–10. I have adapted my translations from those given by David. See further B. Pohl, 'Keeping it in the Family: Re-Reading Anglo-Norman Historiography in the Face of Cultural Memory, Tradition and Heritage', in *Norman Tradition and Transcultural Heritage: Exchange of Cultures in the 'Norman' Peripheries of Medieval Europe*, ed. S. Burkhardt and T. Foerster (Farnham: Ashgate, 2013), 219–51.

9. G. Constable, 'The Second Crusade as Seen by Contemporaries', *Traditio* 9 (1953), 213–79, esp. 221–9.

10. *Les Annales de Saint-Pierre de Gand et de Saint-Amand*, ed. P. Grierson (Brussels: Palais des Académies, 1937), 111–12. See G. Constable, 'A Note on the Route of the Anglo-Flemish Crusaders of 1147', *Speculum* 28 (1953), 525–6.

11. Caffaro, *Ystoria captionis Almerie et Turtuose*, ed. L. T. Belgrano, Fonti per la storia d'Italia (Rome, 1890), 79–89; *Chronica regia Colonensis, s.a.* 1148, ed. G. Waitz, Monumenta Germaniae

Historica: Scriptores rerum Germanicarum in usum scholarum 18 (Hanover, 2nd edn, 1880).

12. A. Virgili, '*Angli cum multis aliis alienigenis*: Crusade Settlers in Tortosa (Second Half of the Twelfth Century)', *Journal of Medieval History* 35 (2009), 297–312. See further, L. Villegas-Aristizábal, 'Anglo-Norman Intervention in the Conquest and Settlement of Tortosa, 1148–1180', *Crusades* 8 (2009), 63–129.

13. Adémar of Chabannes, *Chronicon*, III.55; *Chronique de Saint-Pierre-le-Vif de Sens*, ed. R.-H. Bautier and M Gilles (Paris: Éditions du Centre national de la recherche scientifique, 1979), 112–14. See further, L. Musset, 'Aux Origines d'une classe dirigeante: les Tosny, grands barons normands du Xe au XIIIe siècle', *Francia* 5 (1977), 45–80, at 52–6; M. Aurell, *Les Noces du comte: mariage et pouvoir en Catalogne (785–1213)* (Paris: Publications de la Sorbonne, 1995), 56–8; L. Villegas-Aristizábal, 'Roger of Tosny's Adventures in the County of Barcelona', *Nottingham Medieval Studies* 52 (2008), 5–16.

14. L. Villegas-Aristizábal, 'The Changing Priorities in the Norman Incursions into the Iberian Peninsula's Muslim-Christian Frontiers, *c.*1018–*c.*1191', in *Normans in the Mediterranean*, ed. Winkler and Fitzgerald, 81–119.

15. L. H. Nelson, 'Rotrou of Perche and the Aragonese Reconquest', *Traditio* 26 (1970), 113–33; L. Villegas-Aristizábal, 'Norman and Anglo-Norman Participation in the Iberian Reconquista *c.*1018–*c.*1248' (PhD thesis, University of Nottingham, 2007), 112–33.

16. L. J. McCrank, 'Norman Crusaders in the Catalan Reconquest: Robert Burdet and the Principality of Tarragona, 1129–55', *Journal of Medieval History* 7 (1981), 67–82.

Chapter 19: Scotland:
Honoured Guests, 1072–1153

1. *PL*, cxcv, cols 711–38. For the problems with this edition: D. Broun, 'Attitudes of *Gall* to *Gaedhel* in Scotland before John of Fordun', in *Mìorun Mòr nan Gall, 'The Great Ill-Will of the*

Lowlander'? Lowland Perceptions of the Highlands, ed. D. Broun and M. MacGregor (Glasgow: University of Glasgow, 2007), 49–82, at 69 n. 60.

2. G. Molyneaux, *The Formation of the English Kingdom in the Tenth Century* (Oxford: Oxford University Press, 2015), esp. 15–47.

3. R. Fletcher, *Bloodfeud: Murder and Revenge in Anglo-Saxon England* (London: Allen Lane, 2002), 31–57; *Charters of Northern Houses*, ed. D. Woodman, Anglo-Saxon Charters 16 (Oxford: Oxford University Press/British Academy, 2012), 9–16.

4. *Monasticon Anglicanum*, ed. W. Dugdale et al. (London: Longman, Hurst, Rees, Orme and Brown, 1817–30), iii, 313. That the text is a forgery is noted by David X. Carpenter in the forthcoming critical edition of the charters of William II and Henry I (undertaken with Richard Sharpe).

5. A. Woolf, *From Pictland to Alba, 789–1070* (Edinburgh: Edinburgh University Press, 2007), esp. 312–50; D. Broun, *Scottish Independence and the Idea of Britain: From the Picts to Alexander III* (Edinburgh: Edinburgh University Press, 2007), 71–97; T. M. Charles-Edwards, 'Picts and Scots', *Innes Review* 59 (2008), 168–88. On Strathclyde: F. Edmonds, 'The Expansion of the Kingdom of Strathclyde', *Early Medieval Europe* 23 (2015), 43–66.

6. N. McGuigan, *Máel Coluim III 'Canmore': An Eleventh-Century Scottish King* (Edinburgh: John Donald, 2021), 167–207; D. Broun, 'Southern Scotland as Part of the Scottish Kingdom: The Evidence of the Earliest Charters', in *The Battle of Carham: A Thousand Years On*, ed. N. McGuigan and A. Woolf (Edinburgh: John Donald, 2018), 33–49.

7. M. Strickland, 'Securing the North: Invasion and the Strategy of Defence in Twelfth-Century Anglo-Scottish Warfare', *Anglo-Norman Studies* 12 (1990), 177–98.

8. McGuigan, *Máel Coluim III.*

9. Broun, *Scottish Independence*, 101–3; Bates, *William the Conqueror*, 360–2, 425–7.

10. R. Oram, *Domination and Lordship: Scotland, 1070–1230* (Edinburgh: Edinburgh University Press, 2011), 56–7. On Henry I's illegitimate offspring: K. Thompson, 'Affairs of State: The Illegitimate Children of Henry I', *Journal of Medieval History* 29 (2003), 129–51.

11. A. Taylor, *The Shape of the State in Medieval Scotland, 1124–1290* (Oxford: Oxford University Press, 2016).

12. *PL*, cxcv, cols 711–38, with Broun, 'Attitudes of *Gall* to *Gaedhel*', at 69–71.

13. William of Malmesbury, *Gesta regum Anglorum*, V.400, with B. Weiler, 'William of Malmesbury on Kingship', *History* 95 (2005), 3–22, at 9–10. See further, Weiler, 'William of Malmesbury, King Henry I, and the *Gesta regum Anglorum*', *Anglo-Norman Studies* 31 (2009), 157–76.

14. Symeon of Durham, *Historia regum Anglorum*, ed. T. Arnold, *Symeonis monachi omnia opera*, ii (London: Longman, 1885), 191–2.

15. John of Hexham, *Historia*, ch. 4, ed. T. Arnold, *Symeonis monachi omnia opera*, ii (London: Longman, 1885); Richard of Hexham, *De gestis regis Stephani*, s.a. 1138, ed. R. Howlett, *Chronicles of the Reigns of Stephen, Henry I, and Richard I*, iii (London: Longman, 1886); Aelred of Rievaulx, *Relatio de standardo*, ed. Howlett, *Chronicles of the Reigns*, iii, 181–99; John of Worcester, *Chronicon*, s.a. 1138.

16. *Jordan Fantosme's Chronicle*, ll. 1,175–8, ed. R. C. Johnston (Oxford: Oxford University Press, 1981); William of Newburgh, *Historia regum Anglicarum*, II.23, ed. and trans. P. G. Walsh and M. J. Kennedy (Warminster: Aris & Phillips, 1998–2007). See further, Bartlett, *Making of Europe*, 78–82; Gillingham, *English in the Twelfth Century*, 14–15, 41–58, 101–3; Strickland, *War and Chivalry*, 291–329, 337–40.

17. G. W. S. Barrow, *The Anglo-Norman Era in Scottish History* (Oxford: Oxford University Press, 1980); A. Grant, 'At the Northern Edge: Alba and the Normans', in *Norman Expansion: Connections, Continuities and Contrasts*, ed. K. J. Stringer and A. Jotischky (Farnham: Ashgate, 2013), 49–85; J. A. Green, 'The Normans in the North', in *Normans and the 'Norman Edge'*, ed. Stringer and Jotischky, 53–75.

18. Broun, 'Attitudes of *Gall* to *Gaedhel*'.

19. Davies, *Domination and Conquest*, 50–1. See further, B. Weiler, 'Knighting, Homage, and the Meaning of Ritual: The Kings of England and Their Neighbors in the Thirteenth Century', *Viator* 37 (2006), 275–300.

20. P. Dalton, *Conquest, Anarchy and Lordship: Yorkshire, 1066–1154* (Cambridge: Cambridge University Press, 1994), 88, 92–4, 96.

21. *Regesta Regum Anglo-Normannorum*, ii, *1100–1135*, ed. C. Johnson and H. A. Cronne (Oxford: Clarendon Press, 1956), no. 648. See further, J. A. Green, 'David I and Henry I', *Scottish Historical Review* 75 (1996), 1–19.

22. *The Charters of David I: The Written Acts of David I, King of Scots, 1124–53, and of his Son, Henry, Earl of Northumberland, 1139–52*, ed. G. W. S. Barrow (Woodbridge; Boydell Press, 1999), no. 16, with Oram, *Domination and Lordship*, 65–6; Broun, 'Southern Scotland', 42–5; R. Sharpe, 'People and Languages in Eleventh- and Twelfth-Century Britain and Ireland: Reading the Charter Evidence', in *The Reality Behind Charter Diplomacy in Anglo-Norman Britain*, ed. D. Broun (Glasgow: University of Glasgow, 2011), 1–119, at 71–8.

23. Barrow, *Anglo-Norman Era*, 61–90. See also R. M. Blakely, *The Brus Family in England and Scotland, 1100–1295* (Woodbridge: Boydell Press, 2005), 8–27.

Chapter 20: The Power Behind the Throne: Scotland Under Ada de Warenne, 1153–78

1. William of Newburgh, *Historia rerum Anglicarum*, I.25.

2. V. Chandler, 'Ada de Warenne, Queen Mother of Scotland (*c.*1123–1178)', *Scottish Historical Review* 60 (1981), 119–39; J. A. Nelson, 'Queens and Queenship in Scotland, *circa* 1067–1286' (unpublished. PhD thesis, King's College London, 2007), 91–125. Cf. D. Crouch, *The Beaumont Twins: The Roots and Branches of Power in the Twelfth Century* (Cambridge: Cambridge University Press, 1986), 29–51; E. van Houts, 'The Warenne View of the Past, 1066–1203', *Anglo-Norman Studies* 26 (2004), 103–22.

3. Barrow, *Anglo-Norman Era*, 61–117; K. J. Stringer, 'Aspects of the Norman Diaspora in Northern England and Southern Scotland', in *Normans and the 'Norman Edge'*, ed. Stringer and Jotischky, 9–47.

4. Cf. J. Bannerman, 'The King's Poet and the Inauguration of Alexander III', *Scottish Historical Review* 68 (1989), 120–49, esp. 124–7, 132–3.

5. E. J. Ward, 'Child Kingship in England, Scotland, France, and Germany, *c.*1050–*c.*1250' (unpublished PhD thesis, University of Cambridge, 2017), 31–3, 161–4. See further, Bartlett, *Blood Royal*, 114–23.

6. *A Scottish Chronicle Known as the Chronicle of Holyrood*, ed. M. O. Anderson and A. O. Anderson (Edinburgh: Scottish History Society, 1938), 124–5, with Oram, *Domination and Lordship*, 109–14.

7. C. J. Neville, 'The Beginnings of Royal Pardon in Scotland', *Journal of Medieval History* 42 (2016), 559–87.

8. BL Cotton Charter, xviii, 45 (*Charters of David I*, ed. Barrow, no. 16). For a reproduction: G. W. S. Barrow, *Scotland and its Neighbours in the Middle Ages* (London: Hambledon Continuum, 1992), pl. 1a. On address clauses: R. Sharpe, 'Address and Delivery in Anglo-Norman Royal Charters', in *Charters and Charter Scholarship in Britain and Ireland*, ed. M.-T. Flanagan and J. A. Green (Basingstoke: Palgrave Macmillan, 2005), 32–52.

9. D. Broun, 'The Writing of Charters in Scotland and Ireland in the Twelfth Century', in *Charters and the Use of the Written Word in Medieval Society*, ed. K. J. Heidecker (Turnhout: Brepols, 2000), 113–31; 'The Adoptions of Brieves in Scotland', in *Charters and Charter Scholarship*, ed. Flanagan and Green, 164–83. Cf. H. Pryce, 'Culture, Power and the Charters of Welsh Rulers', in *Charters and Charter Scholarship*, ed. Flanagan and Green, 184–202; Insley, 'Kings, Lords, Charters'.

10. D. Baker, '"A Nursery of Saints": St Margaret of Scotland Reconsidered', *Studies in Church History: Subsidia* 1 (1978), 119–141; G. W. S. Barrow, 'Scottish Rulers and the Religious Orders, 1070–1153', *Transactions of the Royal Historical Society,* 5th ser., 3 (1953), 77–100. See also Broun, 'Writing of Charters'.

11. Taylor, *Shape of the State*.

12. *Charters of David I*, ed. Barrow, no. 16; *Regesta regum Scottorum*, ii, *The Acts of William I, 1165–214*, ed. G. W. S. Barrow with W. W. Scott (Edinburgh: Edinburgh University Press, 1971), no. 80. See

Taylor, *Shape of the State*, 50–1, 177–84; S. Reynolds, 'Fiefs and Vassals in Scotland: A View from Outside' (2003), repr. in S. Reynolds, *The Middle Ages without Feudalism: Essays in Criticism and Comparison on the Medieval West* (Farnham: Ashgate, 2012), no. iv; H. MacQueen, 'Tears of Legal Historian: Scottish Feudalism and the *ius commune*', *Juridical Review*, n.s. (2003), 1–28.

13. Davies, *First English Empire*, 170.

Chapter 21: Strongbow in Leinster: Stealing a March, 1167–71

1. Gerald of Wales, *Topographia Hibernie*, ed. J. J. O'Meara, *Proceedings of the Royal Irish Academy* 52 (1948–50), 113–78, at 176–7. On Gerald's ambitions: Bartlett, *Gerald of Wales*, 54–62.

2. *ASC* 1086 E (= 1087), ed. S. Irvine, *The Anglo-Saxon Chronicle: MS E* (Cambridge: Cambridge University Press, 2004). See further Davies, *First English Empire*, 4–30.

3. Gerald of Wales, *Itinerarium Kambrie*, II.1, ed. J. S. Brewer, *Giraldi Cambrensis: Opera*, 8 vols. (London, 1861–91); William of Malmesbury, *Gesta regum Anglorum*, V.409.

4. Charles-Edwards, *Wales and the Britons*, 583–98; Broun, *Scottish Independence*, 124–57; D. Ó Corráin, *The Irish Church, its Reform and the English Invasion* (Dublin, 2017), 5–42.

5. Ó Corráin, *Irish Church*, 58–64; Cowdrey, *Lanfranc*, 144–7; M. T. Flanagan, *Irish Society, Anglo-Norman Settlers, Angevin Kingship: Interactions in Ireland in the Late Twelfth Century* (Oxford: Oxford University Press, 1989), 7–55; M. Philpott, 'Some Interactions between the English and Irish Churches', *Anglo-Norman Studies* 20 (1998), 187–204; M. Brett, 'Canterbury's Perspective on Church Reform in Ireland, 1070–1115', in *Ireland and Europe in the Twelfth Century: Reform and Renewal*, ed. D. Bracken and D. Ó Riain-Raedel (Dublin: Four Courts Press, 2006), 13–35.

6. *The Letters of Lanfranc, Archbishop of Canterbury*, ed. H. Clover and M. Gibson (Oxford: Oxford University Press, 1979), nos 9–10. On his background and training, see Brett, 'Canterbury's

Perspective', 33–5, with the response in E. Boyle, 'The Twelfth-Century English Transmission of a Poem on the Threefold Division of the Mind, Attributed to Patrick of Dublin (d. 1084)', in *'A Fantastic and Abstruse Latinity?' Hiberno-Continental Cultural and Literary Interactions in the Middle Ages*, ed. W. R. Keller and D. Schlüter (Münster: Nodus Publikationen, 2017), 102–16, at 104–6.

7. Robert of Torigny, *Chronica, s.a.* 1155, ed. T. N. Bisson, *The Chronography of Robert of Torigni* (Oxford: Oxford University Press, 2020); *Sigeberti Gemblacensis chronographiae auctarium Affligemense, s.a.* 1156, ed. P. Gorissen (Brussels: Palais des Académies, 1952), with C. Veach, 'Henry II and the Ideological Foundations of Angevin Rule in Ireland', *Irish Historical Studies* 42 (2018), 1–25, at 5–6.

8. A. Duggan, 'The Making of a Myth: Giraldus Cambrensis, *Laudabiliter*, and Henry II's Lordship of Ireland', *Studies in Medieval and Renaissance History*, 3rd ser., 4 (2007), 107–70.

9. *The Letters and Charters of Henry II*, ed. N. Vincent (Oxford: Oxford University Press, 2020), no. 1468. While the document itself is suspect (probably a forgery produced by Gerald of Wales), Henry's grant of permission to recruit in Bristol is perfectly plausible (and is mentioned in other sources).

10. Cf. Oskanen, *Flanders and the Anglo-Norman World*, 179–218.

11. *Letters and Charters*, ed. Vincent, nos 691, 1071, 1986, 2006, 2653, with Flanagan, *Irish Society*, 112–17, 121–3; N. Vincent, 'Did Henry II Have a Policy Towards the Earls?', in *War, Government and Aristocracy in the British Isles, c.1150–1500*, ed. C. Given-Wilson et al. (Woodbridge: Boydell Press, 2008), 1–25 at 9.

12. I. Warntjes, 'Regnal Succession in Early Medieval Ireland', *Journal of Medieval History* 30 (2004), 377–410.

13. M. T. Flanagan, 'Negotiating Across Legal and Cultural Borders: Aífe, Daughter of Diarmait Mac Murchada, King of Leinster, and Marriage, Motherhood and Widowhood in Twelfth-Century Ireland and England', *Peritia* 30 (2019), 71–95. See also Flanagan, *Irish Society*, 112–36.

14. C. Downham, *Medieval Ireland* (Cambridge: Cambridge University Press, 2017), 81–113, 238–78.

Chapter 22: Hugh de Lacy:
Lord of Meath, 1171–7

1. Gerald of Wales, *Expugnatio Hibernica*, chs 13–15, ed. and trans. A. B. Scott and F. X. Martin (Dublin: Royal Irish Academy, 1978).

2. Ibid., ch. 28. Note, *Letters and Charters*, ed. Vincent, no. 1882, providing possible confirmation of Gerald on this point.

3. *Letters and Charters of Henry II*, ed. Vincent, no. 786. See also ibid., nos 244, 1011, 1076, 1133, 1434, with discussion in Flanagan, *Irish Society*, 114, 121–3.

4. For different (largely complementary) perspectives: Gerald of Wales, *Expugnatio Hibernica*, chs 30–2; *La Geste des Engleis en Yreland*, ll. 2,577–756, ed. E. Mullaly (Dublin: Four Courts Press, 2002), 119–23. See Flanagan, *Irish Society*, 167–228.

5. S. Duffy, 'Ireland's Hastings: The Anglo-Norman Conquest of Dublin', *Anglo-Norman Studies* 20 (1998), 69–85.

6. P. Gleeson, 'Making Provincial Kingship in Early Ireland: Cashel and the Creation of Munster', in *Power and Place in Europe in the Early Middle Ages*, ed. J. Carroll, A. Reynolds and B. Yorke (Oxford: Oxford University Press, 2019), 346–68.

7. D. P. McCarthy, *The Irish Annals: Their Genesis, Evolution and History* (Dublin: Four Courts Press, 2008), 188–96; N. Evans, *The Present and the Past in Medieval Irish Chronicles* (Woodbridge: Boydell Press, 2010), 45–66.

8. M. T. Flanagan, 'Henry II, the Council of Cashel and the Irish Bishops', *Peritia* 10 (1996), 184–211.

9. Ó Corráin, *Irish Church*, 104–15. See also M. T. Flanagan, *The Transformation of the Irish Church in the Twelfth and Thirteenth Centuries* (Woodbridge: Boydell Press, 2010).

10. Veach, 'Henry II'. See also N. Vincent, 'Angevin Ireland', in *The Cambridge History of Ireland*, i, *600–1550*, ed. B. Smith (Cambridge: Cambridge University Press, 2018), 185–221, at 209–11.

11. Ó Corráin, *Irish Church*, 108–9.

12. N. Vincent, 'Regional Variations in the Charters of King Henry II (1154–89)', in *Charters and Charter Scholarship in Britain and*

Ireland, ed. Flanagan and Green, 70–106, at 74–5. Particularly noteworthy is that the formula does not appear in Henry II's grant of Dublin to the men of Bristol: *Letters and Charters*, ed. Vincent, no. 313.

13. *Letters and Charters*, ed. Vincent, no. 1440.
14. C. Veach, *Lordship in Four Realms: The Lacy Family, 1166–1241* (Manchester: Manchester University Press, 2014), 33.
15. *Expugnatio Hibernica*, ch. 41; *Mac Cartaig's Book, s.a.* 1173, ed. S. Ó hInnse, *Miscellaneous Irish Annals (A.D. 1114–1437)* (Dublin: Dublin Institute for Advanced Studies, 1947).
16. Veach, *Lordship in Four Realms*, 31–2.
17. Gerald of Wales, *Expugnatio Hibernica*, chs 13–15, with Gillingham, *English in the Twelfth Century*, 41–2; M. Saunton, *The Historians of Angevin England* (Oxford: Oxford University Press, 2017), 96–100; C. Veach, 'Aristocratic Violence and the English Invasion of Ireland', in *The English Invasion of Ireland*, ed. S. Duffy and P. Crooks (forthcoming). On Gerald and his family: H. Pryce, 'Giraldus and the Geraldines', in *The Geraldines and Medieval Ireland: The Making of a Myth*, ed. P. Crooks and S. Duffy (Dublin: Four Courts Press, 2016), 53–68; C. Veach, 'The Geraldines and the Conquest of Ireland', in ibid., 69–92, at 69–77.
18. Saunton, *Historians of Angevin England*, 353–61.
19. Veach, 'Henry II', 17–21.
20. H. M. Thomas, *The English and the Normans: Ethnic Hostility, Assimilation, and Identity 1066–c.1220* (Oxford: Oxford University Press, 2003). See also Sharpe, 'Peoples and Languages', 19–21.
21. Gillingham, *English in the Twelfth Century*, 145–60.
22. Veach, *Lordship in Four Realms*, 47–73.
23. S. Church, *King John: England, Magna Carta and the Making of a Tyrant* (London: Macmillan, 2015), 9–32.
24. C. Veach, 'King John and Royal Control in Ireland: Why William de Briouze had to be Destroyed', *English Historical Review* 129 (2014), 1051–78.

Chapter 23: The End of Empire?
John and Normandy, 1204

1. *Annales de Margam*, *s.a.* 1202, ed. H. R. Luard, *Annales Monastici*, i, Rolls Series (1864), 1–40, with M. Morris, *King John: Treachery, Tyranny and the Road to Magna Carta* (London: Hutchinson, 2015), 153.

2. Morris, *King John*, 7–13, 39–45. See also M. Powicke, *The Loss of Normandy, 1189–1204: Studies in the History of the Angevin Empire* (Manchester: Manchester University Press, 2nd edn, 1960), 253–6.

3. D. Power, 'La Chute de la Normandie ducale (1202–4): un réexamen', in *La Guerre en Normandie (XIᵉ–XVᵉ siècle)*, ed. A. Curry and V. Gazeau (Caen: Presses universitaires de Caen, 2020), 37–62.

4. N. Vincent, *John: An Evil King?* (London: Allen Lane, 2020), 100–1.

5. T. K. Moore, 'The Loss of Normandy and the Invention of *Terre Normannorum*, 1204', *English Historical Review* 125 (2010), 1071–109; D. Crouch, *William Marshal* (London: Routledge, 3rd edn, 2016), 109–16.

6. J. A. Green, 'Unity and Disunity in the Anglo-Norman State', *Historical Research* 62 (1989), 115–34, esp. 130–3; D. Crouch, 'Normans and Anglo-Normans: A Divided Aristocracy?', in *England and Normandy in the Middle Ages*, ed. D. Bates and A. Curry (London: Hambledon Continuum, 1994), 51–67.

7. N. Vincent, *Peter des Roches: An Alien in English Politics, 1205–1238* (Cambridge: Cambridge University Press, 1996), esp. 34–41.

8. Church, *King John*, 140–3; Morris, *King John*, 96–9.

9. G. Duby, *The Legend of Bouvines: War, Religion and Culture in the Middle Ages*, trans. C. Tihanyi (Oxford: Polity Press, 1990); J. France, 'The Battle of Bouvines 27 July 1214', in *The Medieval Way of War: Studies in Medieval Military History in Honor of Bernard S. Bachrach*, ed. G. I. Halfond (Farnham: Ashgate, 2015), 251–71.

10. J. C. Holt, *The Northerners: A Study in the Reign of King John* (Oxford: Clarendon Press, rev. edn, 1992), 100.

11. D. Carpenter, *Magna Carta* (London: Penguin, 2015).

12. N. C. Vincent, 'English Liberties, Magna Carta (1215) and the Spanish Connection', in *1212–1214, el trieno que hizo a Europa* (Pamplona: Institución Príncipe de Viana D.L, 2011), 243–62.

13. Carpenter, *Magna Carta*, 235–44. See also Veach, 'King John'.

14. Davies, *First English Empire*, 20–30, 74–88, 142–71. See also C. Veach, 'The Angevin Empire in the British Isles', in *The Angevin Empire: New Interpretations*, ed. S. D. Church and M. Strickland (forthcoming).

Chapter 24: 'Wonder of the World': Emperor Frederick II, 1198–1250

1. Frederick's Sicilian identity comes through strongly in D. Abulafia, *Frederick II: A Medieval Emperor* (London: Allen Lane, 1988); and O. B. Rader, *Friedrich II: Ein Sizilianer auf dem Kaiserthron: Eine Biographie* (Munich: C. H. Beck, 2010).

2. Peter of Eboli, *Liber ad honorem Augusti*, II.43, ll. 1,377–8, ed. M. Strähl, *Petrus de Ebulo: Liber ad honorem Augusti sive de rebus Siculis. Codex 120 II der Burgerbibliothek Bern* (Sigmaringen: Jan Thorbecke, 1994); *Annales Casinenses, s.a.* 1195, ed. G. H. Pertz, Monumenta Germaniae Historica: Scriptores 19 (Hanover, 1866); *Iohannis Codagnelli Annales Placentini, s.a.* 1211, 1212, 1226, ed. O. Holder-Egger (Hanover: Impensis Bibliopolii Hahniani, 1901), with W. Stürner, *Friedrich II. 1194–1250* (Darmstadt: Wissenschaftliche Buchgesellschaft, rev. edn, 2009), i, 41–9; Abulafia, *Frederick II*, 90. Cf. Rader, *Friedrich II.*, 50.

3. P. Csendes, *Heinrich VI.* (Darmstadt: Wissenschaftliche Buchgesellschaft, 1993), 144–58; T. Foerster, '*Romanorum et regni Sicilie imperator*. Zum Anspruch Kaiser Heinrichs VI. auf das normannische Königreich Sizilien', *Archiv für Diplomatik* 54 (2008), 37–46.

4. T. Kölzer, 'Constanza d'Altavilla', in *Dizionario Biografico degli Italiani*, xxx (Rome: Istituto della Enciclopedia italiana, 1984), 346–56.

5. G. Baaken, 'Die Verhandlungen zwischen Kaiser Heinrich VI.

und Papst Coelestin III. in den Jahren 1195–1197', *Deutsches Archiv* 27 (1971), 457–513; B. Bolton, 'Celestine III and the Defence of the Patrimony', in *Pope Celestine III (1191–1198): Diplomat and Pastor,* ed. J. Doran and D. J. Smith (Aldershot: Ashgate, 2008), 317–53.

6. DD Ks 43, 44, in *Die Urkunden der Kaiserin Konstanze,* ed. T. Közler, Monumenta Germaniae Historica: Diplomata regum et imperatorum Germaniae 11.3 (Hanover: Hahnsche Buchhandlung, 1990).

7. B. Wiedemann, 'Papal Authority and Power during the Minority of Emperor Frederick II', in *Authority and Power in the Medieval Church, c.1000–c.1500,* ed. T. W. Smith (Turnhout: Brepols, 2020), 67–77.

8. Stürner, *Friedrich II.,* i, 85–105.

9. Rader, *Friederich II.*

10. B. Schneidmüller, *Die Welfen: Herrschaft und Erinnerung (819–1252)* (Stuttgart: Urban-Taschenbücher, 2000), 263–7.

11. T. Broekmann, *Rigor iustitiae: Herrschaft, Recht und Terror im normannisch-staufischen Süden (1050–1250),* (Darmstadt: Wissenschaftliche Buchgesellschaft, 2005); T. Foerster, 'Imperial Tradition and Norman Heritage: Cultures of Violence and Cruelty', in *Norman Tradition,* ed. Burkhardt and Foerster, 161–88.

12. Broekmann, *Rigor iustitiae,* 260–368; B. Weiler, *Kingship, Rebellion and Political Culture: England and Germany, c.1215–c.1250* (Basingstoke: Palgrave Macmillan, 2007), esp. 3–10, 39–75.

13. Broekmann, *Rigor iustitiae,* 25–259. See also Strickland, 'La Chevalerie des Normands?'; Foerster, 'Imperial Tradition'.

14. E. Kantorowicz, *Kaiser Friedrich der Zweite* (Berlin: Bondi, 1927–31), with M. Ruehl, '"In This Time without Emperors": The Politics of Ernst Kantorowicz's Kaiser Friedrich der Zweite Reconsidered', *Journal of the Warburg and Courtauld Institutes* 63 (2000), 187–242; R. E. Lerner, *Ernst Kantorowicz: A Life* (Princeton, NJ: Princeton University Press, 2017), esp. 68–116.

Afterlives of the Normans:
A Europe Transformed

1. S. Sønnesyn, 'The Rise of the Normans as Ethnopoiesis', in *Norman Tradition*, ed. Burkhardt and Foerster, 203–18.
2. Van Houts, 'Exogamy'.
3. R. H. C. Davis, *The Normans and Their Myth* (London: Thames & Hudson, 1976).
4. G. A. Loud, 'The "Gens Normanorum" – Myth or Reality?', *Anglo-Norman Studies* 4 (1982), 104–16, 204–6; A. Plassmann, *Origo gentis. Identitäts- und Legitimitätsstiftung in früh- und hochmittelalterlichen Herkunftserzählungen* (Berlin: De Gruyter, 2006). See also M. Bennett, 'Norman Conquests: Nature, Nurture, Normanitas', in *Normans in the Mediterranean*, ed. Winkler and Fitzgerald, 43–65.
5. Bartlett, *Making of Europe*. See also D. C. Douglas, *The Norman Achievement 1050–1100* (Berkeley, CA: University of California Press, 1969), and *The Norman Fate 1100–1154* (Berkeley, CA: University of California Press, 1976).

Index

Individuals of the Norman period are indexed by forename since the usage of surnames was not fully established during this period.